CASPIAN SEA

ASSYRIA

Carchemish

Khorsabad
Nineveh
Mosul
Nimrud

MESOPOTAMIA

TIGRIS R.

PERSIA
(IRAN)

Dura

EUPHRATES R.

Behistun
Rock

Baghdad

BABYLONIA

Babylon

Nippur

SUMER

Susa

Ur

Persepolis

PERSIAN GULF

The Ancient
NEAR EAST

THE TREASURES OF TIME

FIRSTHAND
ACCOUNTS BY
FAMOUS
ARCHAEOLOGISTS
OF THEIR WORK
IN THE
NEAR EAST

The Treasures of Time

SELECTED, EDITED, AND INTRODUCED BY

LEO DEUEL

THE WORLD PUBLISHING COMPANY

CLEVELAND AND NEW YORK

PUBLISHED BY The World Publishing Company
2231 WEST 110TH STREET, CLEVELAND 2, OHIO

PUBLISHED SIMULTANEOUSLY IN CANADA BY
NELSON, FOSTER & SCOTT LTD.

Library of Congress Catalog Card Number: 61-12019

FIRST EDITION

CONTENTS

CONTENTS

MESOPOTAMIA

SYRIA AND PALESTINE

CONTENTS

ANATOLIA, CRETE, AND GREECE

ILLUSTRATIONS

(following page 192)

The sarcophagus from the tomb of Seti I

The Serapeum near Memphis

The mummy of Ramses II

A tablet found at Tell el-Amarna

The step pyramid at Medûm

A papyrus containing the Sayings of Jesus

The antechamber of Tutankhamen's tomb

The gigantic head at Nimrud

The cliff at Behistun

A tablet containing an Assyrian account of the Deluge

A Sumerian headdress and ornaments found at Ur

The Ur-Nammu law code

The first alphabetical tablet found at Ras Shamra

Glueck's excavation of Ezion-Geber

ILLUSTRATIONS

Pottery jars in which Dead Sea Scrolls were found

A Dead Sea Scroll

The monastery at Khirbet Qumran

Caves in which Dead Sea Scrolls were found

Schliemann's excavation at Troy

The royal archives at Boghazköy

Hogarth's excavation at Ephesus

The Palace of Minos

A clay tablet written in Linear Script B

"The treasures of time lie high, in Urnes, Coynes, and Monuments, scarce below the roots of some vegetables. Time hath endlesse rarities, and shows of all varieties; which reveals old things in heaven, makes new discoveries in earth, and even earth itself a discovery."

—Sir Thomas Browne, *Hydriotaphia*

FOREWORD

Archaeology is steadily advancing by going backward in time to uncover and illuminate mankind's history and prehistory beyond traditional, literary testimonies or such religiously inspired assertions as that of seventeenth-century fundamentalists, who insisted that man was created on October 23, 4004 B.C. Few chapters in the study of humanity have changed so drastically our habits of thought; few have stirred so much the awe, the pride, the curiosity, and the imagination of scholars and public alike as the dramatic achievements of archaeology during the past hundred-odd years.

Archaeology's spectacular triumphs have been told frequently with emphasis on the suspense and high adventure manifested in the discoveries of new sites and of old, sometimes long-forgotten tombs, palaces, and cities. Popular books have reviewed the march of archaeology by retelling episodes in terms of the picturesque personalities who contributed to its growth. Often this type of literature has paraphrased the writings of the pioneers themselves, many of them vigorous and sensitive writers. Unfortunately, quite a few of these original reports and memoirs have long been out of print or are buried in journals or special collections, and are no longer readily available.

This volume attempts to trace the reconquest of lost peoples and civilizations as seen through the eyes of the men principally responsible for the great discoveries and excavations. Only narratives which record actual participation in explorations are included. In each case, the author selected is identified with the chief pioneering work. Ideally, such a documentary history of archaeology might aim at a fairly comprehensive coverage of the field. But the subject is so vast and such a wealth of material is available that this would be impossible within the compass of a single book. Here the range of archaeology can only be indicated by representative selections that highlight some of the major milestones. The pieces chosen describe investigations that have revolutionized conceptions of the human past and helped to push back the frontiers of history. Together, these pieces form a first-hand record of the evolution of archaeological inquiry from its crude beginnings to its present sophistication.

In the annals of archaeology—at least in those of the recovery of civilizations that existed before our own, with which this book is exclusively concerned—Egypt and Mesopotamia deserve priority not only for their pre-eminence in the evolution of archaeological studies but also for their vitality. For in Egypt, Mesopotamia, and the adjacent areas of the eastern Mediterranean, traditions, skills, and values were evolved which are the very roots of Western civilization. The light of the Occident was received from southwestern Asia and the Nile Valley. Europe herself is of Oriental lineage; the science, philosophy, and literature of Hellas flourished first in Asia Minor. The ancient Near East, then, which has been gradually uncovered by archaeological spadework, is our matrix.

The classical age of Greece and Rome has been disregarded because archaeology has played only a comparatively minor role in enlarging or modifying our knowledge of it. For the same reason, so has all of Europe, apart from Crete and Mycenaea, whose culture was probably the first synthesis of the Near-Eastern heritage with more or less indigenous "European" elements. The Indus Valley and Shang China, momentous new frontiers of archaeological recovery of early civilizations, are also excluded because they did not contribute directly to Western culture. Besides, since they apparently emerged later than Sumer and protodynastic Egypt, they probably owed their main impulse to the western Orient, where settled agricultural life and urban communities began.

Drama has not been left out of the picture. These lively and authentic accounts of digging up the past are true adventure stories. Archaeology is both a science and an art. It is shaped by imagination as much as by scientific discipline and sound reasoning. In some of the practitioners one or the other element may predominate; in several the two elements are wonderfully blended. To ignore the romance of archaeology, the thrilling moments of discovery, even its somewhat shady origins in and affinities with treasure-hunting and tomb-robbing, would be like staging *Hamlet* without the Prince of Denmark. At the same time, there is much more to archaeology than just lucky windfalls. It involves scholarship as well as toil with a pickax. Popular, romanticized surveys are apt to stress gaudy treasures, gigantic structures, gorgeous graves. Graves, indeed, in all excavations, are obviously the most reliable troves of artifacts. Yet increasingly the emphasis tends to be on minutiae with little aesthetic appeal or material value—on bones, tablets, scrolls, and potsherds. Since Petrie in the 1880s, it has been clear that excavators had other tasks than supplying exotic curiosities to museums, those "ghastly charnel-houses of murdered evidence." In archaeology, as that other nineteenth-century pioneer, General Pitt-Rivers, has stated, "the value of relics, viewed as evidence, may be said to be in inverse ratio to their intrinsic value."

Nor does archaeology necessarily even entail actual digging. There have always been armchair archaeologists like Champollion, who soil their fingers with ink instead of dirt. Some of the nineteenth century's most notable and engrossing archaeological efforts—in which abandoned sites were tracked down, surveyed, and recorded—were accomplished with little or no digging at all. Today, significant archaeological findings are made by physicists in their laboratories, as well as by airmen, divers, botanists, dendrochronologists, and philologists. What counts is observation that stimulates interpretation of the available data and relates the data to already established historical knowledge.

While the following pieces were selected for their documentary, historic, or methodological interest, adventure and literary quality were not overlooked. In several instances, the writing is of a high order. Henry Austen Layard, for instance, has been hailed as one of the finest travel writers in the language. Indeed, it seems that the lures and thrills of archaeology have, like love or flying, turned quite a few men into inspired authors. Others may have had neither inclination nor occasion to put down their experience in a polished version. Yet the importance of their work and its place in the design of this anthology warranted inclusion.

The elusive, not fully explicable appeal of archaeology can perhaps only be recaptured by firsthand accounts of its practitioners. Besides the fascination of unlocking secrets, finding buried treasure, and achieving an extension in time, there may also be a feeling of kinship with long-gone generations and people, a kind of ancestor worship. And there is the morbid attraction of decayed buildings and deserted cities—the Gothic *Ruinenschmerz* on which Rose Macaulay has written a delightful book and which W. S. Gilbert called "a fascination frantic in a ruin that's romantic."

The pleasures of archaeology also have an ironical side since preservation of the records of vanished civilizations, which make possible a reconstruction of the past, has often been the result of tragedy. The horrible sacrificial murders in the royal graves of Ur have been a boon to archaeologists. The firing of Mycenaean cities by barbarian invaders baked the Linear B clay tablets which would otherwise have been pulverized. Shipwrecks in the Mediterranean saved great treasures of Greek art. Mount Vesuvius' tantrums, which strangled and sealed Pompeii and Herculaneum, prompted Goethe to say, "Many a calamity happened in this world, but never one that has caused so much entertainment to posterity as this one."

Egypt

1. GIOVANNI BELZONI

In Egyptian archaeology the appearance of Giovanni Belzoni along the banks of the Nile was almost as significant as that of another adventurer of quasi-Italian origin, Napoleon Bonaparte. In 1798, when Napoleon embarked on his ill-conceived and nearly disastrous Egyptian campaign, he was accompanied by a great many savants, who made an extensive investigation of Egyptian antiquities which was eventually recorded in magnificent publications. European scholars were enraptured. Most precious of all, a Napoleonic soldier found the Rosetta Stone which furnished Champollion with a key to unlock the Egyptian scripts. Thus the first systematic study of Egyptology was promoted by military conquest.

Not that five thousand years of Egyptian history had been completely forgotten. Unlike the buried cities of Mesopotamia, grandiose, highly visible Egyptian monuments had kept their fame since the visit of Herodotus in the fifth century B.C. In Hellenistic and Roman days, the temple of Karnak and the pyramids of Gizeh near Memphis were major tourist attractions. Throughout the Middle Ages and early modern times, enterprising Moslem and Western travelers submitted to the lure of these ancient structures. Among these travelers were Johannes Helffrich, a German who left a highly imaginative account of the great Sphinx in the sixteenth century, and Richard Pococke, a perceptive Englishman, whose memoirs had a great deal to do with making a visit to the pyramids fashionable.

Pococke, in 1743, was also the first modern to describe the celebrated Valley of the Kings, which, according to recent accounts, contains sixty-two rock-hewn burial chambers. Like his successors, he found the place infested with bandits. Following Pococke and as an aftermath of the Napoleonic venture, there was an invasion of antiquaries, artists, and treasure seekers—some of them a combination of all three. Outright robbers and dealers joined in what became a bonanza, inflated by the greed of museums and private collectors for mummies, sarcophagi, papyri, statues, furniture, jewlery, scarabs, and other exotic items, even obelisks. Of these treasure seekers Belzoni was simply the most colorful and successful.

Archaeologists of a later day usually classify him with tomb robbers, although they almost invariably succumb to that eccentric man's innocent enthusiasm for all things Egyptian and to the charm of his writing. These archaeologists' sensibilities are lacerated by Belzoni's account of a visit to a necropolis near Thebes, where with "every step I took I crushed a mummy in some part or other. . . . I sank altogether among the broken mummies with a crash of bones, rags and wooden cases, which raised such a dust as kept me motionless for a quarter of an hour, waiting till it subsided again. . . . I could not avoid being covered with bones, legs, arms and heads rolling from above." Yet, Belzoni was by no means callously destructive or predatory. He is among the most sensitive narrators of the entire Egyptological literature, and he tells us that upon entering a tomb he was so overcome by its contents that for weeks he wandered about like a man in a trance. Considering how shamelessly the Egyptian treasures were looted at the time by such people as his countryman Drovetti, whose agents waylaid Belzoni with a gun, and Belzoni's ertswhile employer, the British consul-general Henry Salt—not to speak of the local fellahin—Belzoni cuts a fairly good figure in an age that had simply no inkling of scientific techniques in excavation and whose principal goal was to supply the increasing demands of the European market. In any case, some of the best Western museum collections were built up by Belzoni and his contemporaries. It has even been claimed that, despite his battering-ram method of opening tombs, Belzoni foreshadowed a sound scientific approach. Howard Carter, who, a century later, also discovered royal tombs, reminds us that Belzoni's were the first large-scale excavations in the Valley, and feels that "we must give Belzoni credit for the manner in which they were carried out. There are," Carter has said, "episodes which give the modern excavator rather a shock . . . but on the whole the work was extraordinarily good."

Born in Padua in 1778, Giovanni Battista Belzoni was a physical giant of six feet seven. He came to England in 1803 and there earned a precarious livelihood as a circus strong man. In the meantime, he dabbled in engineering and constructed a hydraulic machine that he hoped to persuade Mohammed Ali, the upstart ruler of Egypt, to adopt for regulation and irrigation schemes for the Nile. Stranded in Egypt, Belzoni soon drifted into other projects, and visited ancient sites as far upstream as Elephantine and Philae. Commissioned by Henry Salt, he proved his technical skill by transporting the giant bust of Ramses II, usually called the Young Memnon, from Thebes to Alexandria for shipment to the British Museum. An obelisk which he carried away from Upper Egypt slipped into the Nile, but Belzoni managed to fish it out. He rightly established a ruined site on the Red Sea as the ancient Greco-Roman seaport of Berenice. After collecting museum pieces and excavating up and down the Nile, he turned, in 1817, to the Valley of the Kings. Here he opened several tombs. By far the most important and one of the most elaborate in the entire valley, often referred to as "Belzoni's Tomb," is that of Seti I, a pharaoh of the late fourteenth century B.C. Nineteenth Dynasty, and father of Ramses II. The tomb had been known in Greek antiquity and had been looted by tomb robbers, probably soon after its sealing, but was otherwise wonderfully intact. Belzoni spent more than twelve months investigating it, sketching, and making wax imprints. It was a labor of love and inspired him to perhaps the most attractive passages in his *Narrative*. A highlight of his discoveries in the tomb of Seti I was an empty alabaster sarcophagus. After Belzoni had exhibited it in a specially constructed Egyptian hall in London, the sarcophagus was sold to Sir John Soane for £2,000; it is now in the Soane Museum in London. For almost a century and a half, Belzoni's investigation of Seti's tomb seemed to have been exhaustive. Then, in 1960, excavators discovered additional stone stairs and a corridor which may prove to lead to a secret chamber.

When he had published the first edition of his *Narrative of the Operations and Recent Discoveries within the Pyramids, Temples,*

Tombs, and Excavations in Egypt and Nubia, Belzoni left in 1823 for equatorial Africa. There, while on his way to Timbuktu, he died of a tropical disease as had his friend the Anglo-Swiss explorer John Burckhardt.

Exploring the Valley of the Kings

GIOVANNI BELZONI

ON THE 16TH [OF OCTOBER, 1817] I recommenced my excavations in the valley of Beban el Malook, and pointed out the fortunate spot, which has paid me for all the trouble I took in my researches. I may call this a fortunate day, one of the best perhaps of my life; I do not mean to say, that fortune has made me rich, for I do not consider all rich men fortunate; but she has given me that satisfaction, that extreme pleasure, which wealth cannot purchase; the pleasure of discovering what has been long sought in vain, and of presenting the world with a new and perfect monument of Egyptian antiquity, which can be recorded as superior to any other in point of grandeur, style, and preservation, appearing as if just finished on the day we entered it; and what I found in it will show its great superiority to all others. . . . I caused the earth to be opened at the foot of a steep hill, and under a torrent, which, when it rains in the desert, pours a great quantity of water over the very spot I have caused to be dug. No one could imagine, that the ancient Egyptians would make the entrance into such an immense and superb excavation just under a torrent of water; but I had strong reason to suppose, that there was a tomb in that place, from indications I had observed in my pursuit. The Fellahs who were accustomed to dig were all of opinion, that there was nothing in that spot, as the

From Belzoni's *Narrative of the Operations and Recent Discoveries within the Pyramids, Temples, Tombs, and Excavations in Egypt and Nubia* (1820). In this selection Belzoni's own spelling has been preserved, although modern usage is followed in the editor's introductory material. This practice is observed throughout the book.

situation of this tomb differed from that of any other. I continued
the work, however, and the next day, the 17th, in the evening,
we perceived the part of the rock that was cut, and formed the
entrance. On the 18th, early in the morning, the task was resumed, and about noon the workmen reached the entrance,
which was eighteen feet below the surface of the ground. The
appearance indicated, that the tomb was of the first rate: but
I did not expect to find such a one as it really proved to be. The
Fellahs advanced till they saw that it was probably a large tomb,
when they protested they could go no farther, the tomb was so
much choked up with large stones, which they could not get out
of the passage. I descended, examined the place, pointed out to
them where they might dig, and in an hour there was room
enough for me to enter through a passage that the earth had
left under the ceiling of the first corridor, which is thirty-six feet
two inches long, and eight feet eight inches wide, and when
cleared of the ruins, eight feet nine inches high. I perceived immediately by the painting on the ceiling, and by the hieroglyphics
in basso relievo, which were to be seen where the earth did not
reach, that this was the entrance into a large and magnificent
tomb. At the end of this corridor I came to a staircase twenty-
three feet long, and of the same breadth as the corridor. The
door at the bottom is twelve feet high. At the foot of the staircase I entered another corridor, thirty-seven feet three inches
long, and of the same width and height as the other, each side
sculptured with hieroglyphics in basso relievo, and painted. The
ceiling also is finely painted, and in pretty good preservation.
The more I saw, the more I was eager to see, such being the
nature of man: but I was checked in my anxiety at this time, for
at the end of this passage I reached a large pit, which intercepted
my progress. This pit is thirty feet deep, and fourteen feet by
twelve feet three inches wide. The upper part is adorned with
figures, from the wall of the passage up to the ceiling. The passages from the entrance all the way to this pit have an inclination downward of an angle of eighteen degrees. On the opposite
side of the pit facing the entrance I perceived a small aperture
two feet wide and two feet six inches high, and at the bottom of
the wall a quantity of rubbish. A rope fastened to a piece of

wood, that was laid across the passage against the projections which form a kind of door, appears to have been used by the ancients for descending into the pit; and from the small aperture on the opposite side hung another, which reached the bottom, no doubt for the purpose of ascending. We could clearly perceive, that the water which entered the passages from the torrents of rain ran into this pit, and the wood and rope fastened to it crumbled to dust on touching them. At the bottom of the pit were several pieces of wood, placed against the side of it, so as to assist the person who was to ascend by the rope into the aperture. I saw the impossibility of proceeding at the moment. Mr. Beechey, who that day came from Luxor, entered the tomb, but was also disappointed of advancing any farther.

The next day, the 19th, by means of a long beam we succeeded in sending a man up into the aperture, and having contrived to make a bridge of two beams, we crossed the pit. The little aperture we found to be an opening forced through a wall, that had entirely closed the entrance, which was as large as the corridor. The Egyptians had closely shut it up, plastered the wall over, and painted it like the rest of the sides of the pit, so that but for the aperture, it would have been impossible to suppose, that there was any farther proceeding; and any one would conclude, that the tomb ended with the pit. The rope in the inside of the wall did not fall to dust, but remained pretty strong, the water not having reached it at all; and the wood to which it was attached was in good preservation. It was owing to this method of keeping the damp out of the inner parts of the tomb that these apartments are so well preserved. I observed some cavities at the bottom of the well, but found nothing in them, nor any communication from the bottom to any other place; therefore we could not doubt their being made to receive the waters from the rain, which happens occasionally in this mountain. The valley is so much raised by the rubbish, which the water carries down from the upper parts that the entrance into these tombs has become much lower than the torrents; in consequence, the water finds its way into the tombs, some of which are entirely choked up with earth.

When we had passed through the little aperture, we found

ourselves in a beautiful hall, twenty-seven feet six inches by twenty-seven feet ten inches, in which were four pillars three feet square. . . . At the end of this room, which I call the entrance-hall, and opposite the aperture, is a large door, from which three steps lead down into a chamber with two pillars. This is twenty-eight feet two inches by twenty-five feet six inches. The pillars are three feet ten inches square. I gave it the name of the drawing room; for it is covered with figures, which, though only outlined, are so fine and perfect, that one would think they had been drawn only the day before. Returning into the entrance-hall, there is on the left of the aperture a large staircase, which descended into a corridor. It is thirteen feet four inches long, seven and a half wide, and has eighteen steps. At the bottom we entered a beautiful corridor, thirty-six feet six inches by six feet eleven inches. We perceived that the paintings became more perfect as we advanced farther into the interior. They retained their gloss, or a kind of varnish over the colours, which had a beautiful effect. The figures are painted on a white ground. At the end of this corridor we descended ten steps, which I call the small stairs, into another, seventeen feet two inches by ten feet five inches. From this we entered a small chamber, twenty feet four inches by thirteen feet eight inches, to which I gave the name of the Room of Beauties; for it is adorned with the most beautiful figures in basso relievo, like all the rest, and painted. When standing in the centre of this chamber, the traveller is surrounded by an assembly of Egyptian gods and goddesses. Proceeding farther, we entered a large hall, twenty-seven feet nine inches by twenty-six feet ten inches. In this hall are two rows of square pillars, three on each side of the entrance, forming a line with the corridors. At each side of this hall is a small chamber: that on the right is ten feet five inches by eight feet eight inches; that on the left, ten feet five inches by eight feet nine inches and a half. This hall I termed the Hall of Pillars; the little room on the right, Isis' Room, as in it a large cow is painted . . . that on the left, the Room of Mysteries, from the mysterious figures it exhibits. At the end of this hall we entered a large saloon, with an arched roof or ceiling, which is separated from the Hall of Pillars only by a step; so that the two may be reckoned one. The saloon is thirty-one feet ten inches by twenty-seven feet. On the right of the saloon is a small chamber without any thing in it, roughly cut, as if unfinished, and without painting: on the left we entered a chamber with two square pillars, twenty-five feet eight inches by twenty-two feet ten inches. This I called the Sideboard Room, as it has a projection of three feet in form of a sideboard all round, which was perhaps intended to contain the articles necessary for the funeral ceremony. The pillars are three feet four inches square, and the whole beautifully painted as the rest. At the same end of the room, and facing the Hall of Pillars, we entered by a large door into another chamber with four pillars, one of which is fallen down. This chamber is forty-three feet four inches by seventeen feet six inches; the pillars three feet seven inches square. It is covered with white plaster, where the rock did not cut smoothly, but there is no painting on it. I named it the Bull's or Apis' Room, as we found the carcass of a bull in it, embalmed with asphaltum; and also, scattered in various places, an immense quantity of small wooden figures of mummies six or eight inches long, and covered with asphaltum to preserve them. There were some other figures of fine earth baked, coloured blue, and strongly varnished. On each side of the two little rooms were some wooden statues standing erect, four feet high, with a circular hollow inside, as if to contain a roll of papyrus, which I have no doubt they did. We found likewise fragments of other statues of wood and of composition.

But the description of what we found in the centre of the saloon, and which I have reserved till this place, merits the most particular attention, not having its equal in the world, and being such as we had no idea could exist. It is a sarcophagus of the finest oriental alabaster; nine feet five inches long, and three feet seven inches wide. Its thickness is only two inches; and it is transparent when a light is placed in the inside of it. It is minutely sculptured within and without with several hundred figures, which do not exceed two inches in height, and represent, as I suppose, the whole of the funeral procession and ceremonies relating to the deceased, united with several emblems. I cannot give an adequate idea of this beautiful and invaluable piece of antiquity, and can only say, that nothing has been brought into Europe from Egypt that can be compared with it. The cover was not there: it had been taken out, and broken into several pieces, which we found in digging before the first entrance. The sarcophagus was over a staircase in the centre of the saloon, which communicated with a subterraneous passage, leading downwards, three hundred feet in length. At the end of this passage we found a great quantity of bats' dung, which choked up the way, so that we could go no farther without digging. It was nearly filled up too by the falling in of the upper part. One hundred feet from the entrance is a staircase in good preservation; but the rock below changes its substance, from a beautiful solid calcareous stone, becoming a kind of black rotten slate, which crumbles into dust only by touching. This subterraneous passage proceeds in a southwest direction through the mountain. I measured the distance from the entrance, and also the rocks above, and found that the passage reaches nearly halfway through the mountain to the upper part of the valley. I have reason to suppose, that this passage was used to come into the tomb by another entrance; but this could not be after the death of the person who was buried there, for at the bottom of the stairs just under the sarcophagus a wall was built, which entirely closed the communication between the tomb and the subterraneous passage. Some large blocks of stone were placed under the sarcophagus horizontally, level with the pavement of the saloon, that no one might perceive any stairs or subterranean passage was there. The door-way of the sideboard room had been walled up, and forced open, as we found the stones with which it was shut, and the mortar in the jambs. The staircase of the entrance-hall had been walled up also at the bottom, and the space filled with rubbish, and the floor covered with large blocks of stone, so as to deceive any one who should force the fallen wall near the pit, and make him suppose, that the tomb ended with the entrance-hall and the drawing room. I am inclined to believe, that whoever forced these passages must have had some spies with them, who were well acquainted with the tomb throughout. The tomb faces the northeast, and the direction of the whole runs straight southwest. . . .

The Arabs made such reports of this discovery, that it came to the ears of Hamed Aga of Kenneh; and it was reported to him, that great treasure was found in it. On hearing this, he immediately set off with some of his soldiers to Thebes, generally a journey of two days, but such was his speed in travelling, that he arrived in the valley of Beban el Malook in thirty-six hours by land. Before his arrival some Arabs brought us intelligence, that they saw from the tops of the mountains a great many Turks on horseback entering the valley, and coming toward us. I could not conceive who they could be, as no Turks ever came near this place. Half an hour after they gave us the signal of their approach, by firing several guns. I thought an armed force was sent to storm the tombs and rocks, as no other object could bring the Turks there; at last, when this mighty power reached us, I found it to be the well-known Hamed Aga of Kenneh, for some time commander of the eastern side of Thebes, and his followers. Accordingly I was at a loss to conceive what he wanted there, as we were on the west, and under another ruler; but I suppose, in case of a treasure being discovered, the first that hears of it seizes it as a matter of privilege. He smiled, and saluted me very cordially; indeed more so than usual, I presume for the sake of the treasure I had discovered, of which he was in great expectation. I caused as many lights to be brought as we could muster, and we descended into the tomb. What was on the walls of this extraordinary place did not attract his attention in the least; all the striking figures and lively paintings were lost to him; his views were directed to the treasure alone; and his numerous followers were like hounds, searching in every hole and corner. Nothing, however, being found to satisfy their master or themselves, after a long and minute survey, the Aga at last ordered the soldiers to retire, and said to me, "Pray where have you put the treasure?" "What treasure?" "The treasure you found in this place." I could not help smiling at his question, which confirmed him in his supposition. I told him that we had found no treasure there. At this he laughed, and still continued to entreat that I would show it to him. "I have been told," he added, "by a person to whom I can give credit, that you have found in this place a large golden cock, filled with diamonds and pearls. I must see it. Where is it?"

I could scarcely keep myself from laughing, while I assured him that nothing of the kind had been found there. Seeming quite disappointed, he seated himself before the sarcophagus, and I was afraid he would take it into his head, that this was the treasure, and break it to pieces, to see whether it contained any gold; for their notions of treasure are confined to gold and jewels. At last he gave up the idea of the riches to be expected, and rose to go out of the tomb. I asked him what he thought of the beautiful figures painted all around. He just gave a glance at them, quite unconcerned, and said, "This would be a good place for a harem, as the women would have something to look at." At length, though only half persuaded there was no treasure, he set off with an appearance of much vexation.

2. AUGUSTE MARIETTE

The era of conscientious excavation in Egypt was inaugurated by Auguste Mariette, the nemesis of freebooting diggers, tomb-robbers, and unprincipled traders in antiquities. He has been called the father and founder of Egyptian archaeology. With him proper supervision of archaeological work began. Mariette was appointed the first director of the Service of Antiquities in 1858. In this capacity he was instrumental in organizing the Egyptian National Museum at Bulaq, which was later transferred to Cairo. Mariette, who renewed the Napoleonic tradition of French leadership in Egyptological research, was the first of a line of illustrious French scientists to preside, until 1952, over Egypt's archaeological affairs. (When concluding the Anglo-French Entente in 1904, a clause in the joint declaration of the two powers provided that the post of director-general of the Egyptian Antiquities Department, together with the direction of the Cairo Museum, should be held by a Frenchman.) It is said that he owed his appointment to the insistence of the builder of the Suez Canal, Ferdinand de Lesseps, and to the Khedive's desire to placate Napoleon III. As Mariette's successor Gaston Maspero stated it, Said Pasha, badly needing French subsidies, "came to the conclusion that he would be more acceptable to the Emperor if he made some show of taking pity on the Pharaohs."

The Khedive Said Pasha, who had little interest in ancient Egyptian civilization and considered Mariette's painfully accumulated treasures as little more than a kind of glorified piggy bank in his financial distress, proved difficult to handle. But Mariette held his own. In 1859, when a provincial governor seized a treasure of gold and gems found by Mariette in order to present it to Said himself, Mariette boarded the sycophantic governor's boat and, according to Maspero, "as persuasion did not succeed, he passed to action; he threatened to throw one man into the water, to blow out another's brains, to send a third to the galleys, and to hang a fourth; and following his words with blows, he obtained, on giving a receipt for it, delivery of the box containing the treasure." Thereupon he rushed to Said, who, with the magnanimity of oriental caprice, treated the whole matter as a joke and, apart from a few minor items, refrained from claiming the treasure. He promised instead that a building worthy of Mariette's Egyptian collection should be erected at Bulaq. On another occasion, when the gems sent for the Egyptian exhibit at the 1867 Paris Exposition caught the fancy of Empress Eugénie, the Khedive agreed to let her have them only if Mariette consented, saying that "there is one more powerful than myself at Bulaq . . . [it is] to him that you must address your request." The dedicated Frenchman refused his empress's entreaties.

It is to the glory of Mariette that he realized before almost anyone else that a country's artifacts, antiquities, and any kind of cultural testimony are not articles for export. No matter how unappreciative the rulers or native population may have been of these treasures, Mariette devoted himself with single-minded stubbornness to this principle. He died dreaming of the great museum he aspired to build in Egypt.

More than thirty major excavations are to his credit. He worked at Karnak, Thebes, and Tanis of Biblical fame in the Delta; he cleared the temples at Edfu and Abu Simbel in the far south; and he discovered the valley temple of the second Gizeh pyramid. In a shaft within that temple, Mariette excavated what is probably one of the world's supreme masterpieces, the diorite statue of the Fourth-Dynasty Pharaoh Chephren. Yet, most celebrated of all his findings was the Serapeum at Saqqara.

The accidental notice of a sphinx in the garden of an Alexandrian villa changed Mariette's entire career and turned him to archaeology. He had been sent to Egypt in 1850 by the Louvre to search for Coptic manuscripts. But his attention was soon diverted. Boldly announcing his discovery of the Serapeum, he advised his Paris employers of his changed interests and of the need for further financial aid. After devoting four years to the project, he returned to the Louvre as assistant conservator of Egyptian monuments. Then, in 1858, he settled permanently in

Egypt. The Serapeum with its subterranean galleries remains one of the chief tourist attractions of the country.

The Cemetery of the Sacred Bulls

AUGUSTE MARIETTE

THE SERAPEUM is one of the edifices of Memphis rendered famous by a frequently quoted passage of Strabo, and by the constant mention made of it on the Greek papyri. It had long been sought for, and we had the good fortune to discover it in 1851.

Strabo, in his description of Memphis, expresses himself thus:

> One finds also (at Memphis) a temple of Serapis in a spot so sandy that the wind causes the sand to accumulate in heaps, under which we could see many sphinxes, some of them almost entirely buried, others only partially covered; from which we may conjecture that the route leading to this temple might be attended with danger if one were surprised by a sudden gust of wind.

If Strabo had not written this passage, in all probability the Serapeum would to this day lie buried under the sands of the necropolis at Sakkarah. In 1850 I had been commissioned by the French Government to visit the Coptic convents of Egypt, and to make an inventory of such manuscripts in Oriental languages as I should find there. I noticed at Alexandria, in M. Zizinia's garden, several sphinxes. Presently I saw more of these same sphinxes at Cairo, in Clot-Bey's garden. M. Fernandez had also a certain number of such sphinxes at Geezeh. Evidently there must be somewhere an avenue of sphinxes which was being pillaged. One day, attracted to Sakkarah by my Egyptological studies, I perceived the head of one of these same sphinxes obtruding itself from the sand. This one had never been touched, and was cer-

From Mariette's *The Monuments of Upper Egypt* (1877).

tainly in its original position. Close by lay a libation-table, on which was engraved in hieroglyphs an inscription to Osiris-Apis. The passage in Strabo suddenly occurred to my mind. The avenue which lay at my feet must be the one which led up to that Serapeum so long and so vainly sought for. But I had been sent to Egypt to make an inventory of manuscripts, not to seek for temples. My mind, however, was soon made up. Regardless of all risks, without saying a word, and almost furtively, I gathered together a few workmen, and the excavation began. The first attempts were hard indeed, but, before very long, lions and peacocks and the Grecian statues of the dromos, together with the monumental tablets or stelae of the temple of Nectanebo, were drawn out of the sand, and I was able to announce my success to the French Government, informing them, at the same time, that the funds placed at my disposal for the researches after the manuscripts were exhausted, and that a further grant was indispensable. Thus was begun the discovery of the Serapeum.

The work lasted four years. The Serapeum is a temple built without any regular plan, where all was conjecture, and where the ground had to be examined closely, inch by inch. In certain places the sand is, so to speak, fluid, and presents as much difficulty in excavating as if it were water which ever seeks its own level. Besides all this, difficulties arose between the French and the Egyptian Governments, which obliged me several times to discharge all my workmen. It was owing to these circumstances (to say nothing of other trials) that the work proved so long, and that I was compelled to spend four years in the desert—four years, however, I can never regret.

Apis, the living image of Osiris revisiting the earth, was a bull who, while he lived, had his temple at Memphis (Mitrahenny), and, when dead, had his tomb at Sakkarah. The palace which the bull inhabited in his lifetime was called the *Apieum;* the *Serapeum* was the name given to his tomb.

As far as we can judge by the remains found during our researches, the Serapeum resembled in appearance the other Egyptian temples, even those which were not funereal in their character. An avenue of sphinxes led up to it, and two pylons stood before it, and it was surrounded by the usual enclosure.

But what distinguished it from all other temples was that out of one of its chambers opened an inclined passage leading directly into the rock on which the temple was built, and giving access to vast subterranean vaults which were the *Tomb of Apis*.

The Serapeum, properly so called, no longer exists, and where it stood there is now nothing to be seen but a vast plain of sand mingled with fragments of stones scattered about in indescribable confusion. But the most beautiful and interesting part of the subterranean vault can still be visited.

The Tomb of Apis consists of three distinct parts which have no direct communication with one another.

The first and most ancient part carries us back as far as the XVIIIth dynasty and Amenophis III. It served as the burial-place of the sacred bulls up to the end of the XXth dynasty. Here the tombs are separate. Every dead Apis had his own sepulchral chamber hewn here and there, as it were at random, out of the rock. These chambers are now hidden under the sand, and were never possessed of any very great interest.

The second part comprises the tombs of Apis from the time of Sheshonk I (XXIInd dynasty) to that of Tahraka (the last king of the XXVth dynasty). In this part a new system was adopted. Instead of isolated tombs, a long subterranean gallery was made, on each side of which mortuary chambers were excavated, to be used whenever an Apis expired at Memphis. This gallery is also inaccessible now, the roof having in some places fallen in, and the remainder not being sufficiently secure to allow of its being visited by travellers.

In approaching the entrance to the tomb of Apis by the ordinary path, one sees to the right, *i.e.*, toward the North, a somewhat larger circular hole. Here are to be found the vaults which preceded those we are about to visit. This hole was caused by the falling in of a portion of the stonework. In blowing up the débris with gunpowder, we discovered, not an Apis, but a human mummy. A gold mask covered its face, and jewels of every description were arranged on its breast. All the inscriptions were in the name of Rameses's favourite son, who was for a long time governor of Memphis. It may therefore be reasonably supposed that it was here this prince was buried.

The third part is that which is now so well known. Its history begins with Psammetichus I (XXVIth dynasty), and ends with the later Ptolemies. The same system of a common vault has been followed here as in the second part, only on a much grander scale. These galleries cover an extent of about 350 metres, or 1,150 English feet; and from one end to the other the great gallery measures 195 metres, or about 640 English feet. Moreover, granite sarcophagi have been used here. Their number throughout the whole extent of the galleries is 24. Of these only three bear any inscription, and they contain the names of Amasis (XXVIth dynasty), Cambyses and Khebasch (XXVIIth dynasty). A fourth, with cartouches without any name, most probably belongs to one of the last Ptolemies. As to their dimensions, they measure on an average 7 feet 8 inches in breadth, by 13 feet in length, and 11 feet in height; so that, allowing for the vacuum, these monoliths must weigh, one with the other, not less than 65 tons each.

Such are the three parts of the Tomb of Apis.

It is well known that the exploration of this tomb has furnished science with unhoped-for results. For what the traveller now sees of it is merely its skeleton. But the fact is that, although it had been rifled by the early Christians, the tomb, when first discovered, still possessed nearly all that it had ever contained that was not gold or other precious matter. There existed a custom which had especially contributed to enrich the tomb with valuable documents. On certain days in the year, or on the occasion of the death and funeral rites of an Apis, the inhabitants of Memphis came to pay a visit to the god in his burial-place. In memory of this act of piety they left a stela, *i.e.* a square-shaped stone, rounded at the top, which was let into one of the walls of the tomb, having been previously inscribed with an homage to the god in the name of his visitor and his family. Now these documents, to the number of about five hundred, were found, for the most part, in their original position . . . and as many of them were dated according to the fashion of the time, that is with the year, month and day of the reigning king, a comparison of these inscribed tablets must necessarily prove of the greatest importance, especially in fixing chronology.

3. GASTON MASPERO

According to one archaeologist, tomb robbery is "the world's second oldest profession," and the text of several papyri record its prevalence and persistence more than a millennium before the birth of Christ. With a few rare exceptions, none of the splendid mausoleums managed to protect the bodies of the rulers and high dignitaries buried in them from the greed of their surviving compatriots. Indeed, the very prominence and magnificence of the pyramids jeopardized the chances of the buried pharaohs. Nor were the robbers thwarted by the removal of the remains of Eighteenth-Dynasty pharaohs to hidden and secretly sealed rock graves in the Valley of the Kings. Tomb robbing continued unabated, probably aided by information from the very officials who had taken part in the burials.

The physical preservation of the deceased was of course basic to Egyptian religious beliefs and hence of their elaborate funerary practices. These tenets are symbolized in the legend of the savior-god Osiris, whose resurrection was secured by the gathering of the scattered pieces of his mutilated body by his faithful wife Isis. Strangely, it was the fate of the dead pharaohs—who, like all Egyptians in later days, identified themselves with the god—to emulate the martyrdom of Osiris. And just as the body of the beloved god was recovered, so the mummies of many of the prominent Egyptian kings were found, long after they were believed to have been destroyed. In the story of Egyptian archaeology, the discovery altogether of thirty-odd royal mummies, among them some of the most famous names in Egyptian history, is indeed one of the most thrilling episodes.

In 1881 next to nothing was known about the fate of the pharaohs' mummies. But from evidence gathered gradually, the strange migrations of the royal mummies can now be pieced together. Apparently to escape the robbers, the bodies were repeatedly shifted and reburied. In order to safeguard them better, they were then collected within a few caves. The most important of these mass burials was in the shaft at Deir el-Bahari outside the Valley of the Kings. There the mummies were left undisturbed and forgotten until a few articles bearing royal insignia appeared on the market in the late 1870s. Some mummies were among the offerings, though their sale was illegal. It was reported that "the head and hands and feet were wrenched off and sold on the sly, while the torso was kicked about the ruined temples until jackals came and carried it away." Thus an American visitor purchased a head and hand from one of the notorious tomb robbers to whom the ravaging of the royal crypt was eventually traced. Another affluent American was offered the "complete" body of Ramses II, but incredulously turned down the proposition.

When the robbers were finally tracked down and the bodies of some of the most famous pharaohs of the Eighteenth, Nineteenth, and Twentieth Dynasties were recovered, the world was almost as fascinated by the find in the remote Deir el-Bahari cliff as fifty years later by the discovery of Tutankhamen's tomb. The man largely responsible for the 1881 archaeological coup was Gaston Maspero, Mariette's successor as director of Egyptian antiquities. With the aid of Emile Brugsch, Maspero supervised this fabulous discovery in the first year of his tenure.

Maspero was the outstanding French archaeological administrator in Egypt. After he had returned to Paris as professor of Egyptology, he was persuaded in 1899 to resume his old post in Egypt as director of antiquities. Under Maspero the Egyptian National Museum was enormously expanded. It was moved in 1902 to Cairo and the collections were meticulously catalogued. Apart from his great, though now outdated, guide to the Cairo Museum, Maspero wrote several outstanding books on ancient Egypt and the Near East, which, in translation, were also widely popular with the English-speaking public. Before the recovery of the royal mummies, Maspero had been able to announce to Mariette that, despite the latter's skepticism, the Fifth-Dynasty pyramids of Saqqara had yielded lengthy inscriptions in archaic third-millennium B.C. hieroglyphs, the now renowned Old Kingdom Pyramid Texts. Maspero died in Paris in 1916, two years after resigning his Cairo directorship.

A Windfall of Royal Mummies

GASTON MASPERO

FOR SOME YEARS it had been known that the Arabs of el-Qurna had dug out one or two royal tombs, whose location they refused to reveal. In the spring of 1876 an English general named Campbell had shown me the hieratic ritual of the High Priest Pinotem, purchased at Thebes for four hundred pounds. In 1877 Monsieur de Saulcy, on behalf of a friend in Syria, sent me photographs of a long papyrus that had belonged to Queen Notemit, mother of Hrihor (the end of it is now in the Louvre and the beginning in England). Monsieur Mariette had also arranged to purchase from Suez two other papyri, written in the name of a Queen Tiuhathor Henttaui. About the same time the funerary statuettes of King Pinotem appeared on the market, some of them delicate in workmanship, others coarse. In short, the fact of a discovery became so certain that as early as 1878, I could state of a tablet belonging to Rogers-Bey that "it came from a tomb in the neighborhood of the as yet unknown tombs of Hrihor's family"; its actual source is the hiding place at Deir el-Bahari, where we found the mummy for which it had been written.

To search for the site of these royal vaults was, then, if not the first, at least one of the primary objects of the journey that I made in Upper Egypt during March and April 1881. I did not plan to take borings or to start excavations in the Theban necropolis; the problem was of a different nature. What had to be done was to extract from the fellahs the secret that they had so faith-

From Maspero's "Rapport sur la trouvaille de Deir-el-Bahari," *Institut Egyptien Bulletin,* Ser. 2, No. 2 (1881). Translated from the French by Willard R. Trask.

fully kept until then. I had but one fact to proceed on: the leading merchants of antiquities were a certain Abd-er-Rassul Ahmed, of El-Sheik Abd-el-Qurna, and a certain Mustapha Aga Ayad, vice-consul of England and Belgium at Luxor. To go after the latter was not easy: protected as he was by diplomatic immunity, he could not be prosecuted by the excavations administration. On April 4th I sent the chief of police at Luxor an order to arrest Abd-er-Rassul Ahmed, and I telegraphed to His Excellency Daud Pasha, Mudir [governor] of Qena, as well as to the Ministry of Public Works, asking to be authorized to conduct an immediate inquiry into his actions. Questioned on shipboard first by Monsieur Emile Brugsch and then by Monsieur de Rochemonteix, who was kind enough to put his experienced help at my disposal, he denied everything with which I charged him according to the almost unanimous testimony of European travelers—the discovery of the tomb, the sale of the papyri and the funerary statues, the breaking of the coffins. I accepted his proposal to have his house searched, less in the hope of finding anything compromising there than to give him an opportunity to think it over and come to terms with us. Gentleness, threats—nothing availed; and on April 6, the order to open the official investigation having arrived, I sent Abd-er-Rassul Ahmed and his brother Hussein Ahmed to Qena, where the Mudir was demanding their appearance for trial.

The investigation was energetically carried on but, on the whole, failed of its object. The interrogations and arguments, conducted by the magistrates of the mudiria [province] in the presence of our delegate, the official inspector of Dendera, Ali-Effendi Habib, resulted only in bringing out considerable testimony in favor of the accused. The notables and mayors of el-Qurna declared several times, on oath, that Abd-er-Rassul Ahmed was the most loyal and disinterested man in that part of the country, that he had never excavated and would never excavate, that he was incapable of diverting the most insignificant antique, still less of violating a royal tomb. The only interesting detail revealed by the investigation was the insistence with which Abd-er-Rassul Ahmed asserted that he was the servant of Mustapha Aga, vice consul of England, and that he lived in the latter's house. He thought that by making himself out to belong to the vice consul's household, he gained the advantage of diplomatic privileges and could claim some sort of protection from Belgium or England. Mustapha Aga had encouraged him in this mistaken belief, together with all his associates; he had convinced them that by sheltering themselves behind him they would thenceforth be safe from the agents of the native administration; and it was only by this trick that he had succeeded in getting the entire trade in antiquities in the Theban plain into his own hands.

So Abd-er-Rassul Ahmed was given provisional freedom, on the recognizance of two of his friends, Ahmed Serur and Ismaïl Sayid Nagib, and went home with the certificate of spotless honor conferred on him by the leading men of el-Qurna. But his arrest, the two months he had spent in prison, and the vigor with which the inquiry had been conducted by His Excellency Daud Pasha, had clearly shown that Mustapha Aga was unable to protect even his most faithful agents; then too, it was known that I planned to return to Thebes during the winter and that I was determined to reopen the matter myself, while the mudiria would also begin further investigations. Some timid accusations reached the Museum, we learned a few more details from abroad, and, even better, disagreement arose among Abd-er-Rassul and his four brothers: some of them thought the danger had passed forever and that the Museum directorate had been defeated; others considered that the wisest course would be to come to terms with the directors and reveal the secret to them. After a month of discussions and quarreling, the eldest of the brothers, Mohammed Ahmed Abd-er-Rassul, suddenly decided to speak up. He went secretly to Qena and informed the Mudir that he knew the site that had been fruitlessly sought for a number of years; the tomb contained not merely two or three mummies but about forty, and most of the coffins were marked with a small snake, like the one displayed on the headdresses of the Pharaohs. His Excellency Daud Pasha immediately referred the information to the Ministry of the Interior, which transmitted the dispatch to His Highness the Khedive. His Highness, to whom I had spoken of the matter on my return from Upper Egypt, at once recognized the importance of this unexpected declaration and decided to send one of the Museum staff to Thebes. I had just returned to Europe, but I had left Monsieur Emile Brugsch, assistant curator, the necessary powers to act in my stead. As soon as the order arrived he set out for Thebes, on Saturday July 1st, accompanied by a friend on whom he could rely and by Ahmed Effendi Kamal, Secretary-Interpreter to the Museum. On reaching Qena, he found a surprise awaiting him: Daud Pasha had searched the premises of the Abd-er-Rassul brothers and had seized several precious objects, among them three papyri of Queen Maekere, Queen Isimkheb, and Princess Neskhonsu. It was a promising beginning. To ensure the success of the delicate undertaking that was about to begin, His Excellency put at our agents' disposition his *wekil* and several other employees of the mudiria, whose zeal and experience proved to be of great service.

On Wednesday the 6th, Messrs. Emile Brugsch and Ahmed Effendi Kamal were led by Mohammed Ahmed Abd-er-Rassul directly to the spot where the funeral vault opened. The Egyptian engineer who had excavated it long ago had laid his plans in the most skillful manner possible—never was hiding place more effectively concealed. The chain of hills that here separates the Biban el-Muluk from the Theban plain forms a series of natural basins between the Asasif and the Valley of Queens. Of these basins, the best known hitherto was the one in which stands the monument of Deir el-Bahari. In the rock wall that divides Deir el-Bahari from the following basin, directly behind the hill of El-Sheikh 'Abd el-Qurna, and some sixty meters above the level of the cultivated ground, a vertical shaft was sunk eleven and a half meters deep by two meters wide. At the bottom, in its western wall, was cut the entrance to a corridor 1.4 meters wide by 80 centimeters high. After running for 7.4 meters, the corridor turns suddenly northward and continues for some 60 meters, but not remaining of the same dimensions throughout—in some places it reaches a width of 2 meters, at others it is only 1.3 meters wide. Toward the middle of it, five or six roughly hewn steps reveal a marked change in level, and, to the right, a sort of uncompleted niche shows that the architect had once considered changing the direction of the gallery yet again. It finally leads into a sort of irregular oblong chamber about 8 meters long.

The first thing Monsieur Emile Brugsch saw when he reached the bottom of the shaft was a white and yellow coffin bearing the name of Neskhonsu. It was in the corridor, some 60 centimeters from the entrance; a little farther on was a coffin whose shape suggested the style of the XVIIth Dynasty, then Queen Tiuhathor Henttaui, then Seti I. Beside the coffins and scattered over the ground were boxes with funerary statuettes, canopic jars, libation vessels of bronze, and, farther on, in the angle formed by the corridor where it turns northward, the funeral tent of Queen Isimkheb, folded and crumpled, like something of no value that a priest in a hurry to get out had carelessly thrown into a corner. All along the main corridor were the same profusion of objects and the same disorder; he was forced to crawl, never knowing upon what hand or foot might be set. The coffins and mummies, fleetingly glimpsed by the light of a candle, bore historic names, Amenophis I, Thutmose II, in the niche near the stairway, Ahmose I and his son Siamun, Soqnunrî, Queen Ahhotpu, Ahmose Nefertari, and others. The confusion reached its height in the chamber at the end, but no more than a glance sufficed to reveal that the style of the XXth Dynasty was predominant. Mohammed Ahmed Abd-er-Rassul's report, which at first seemed exaggerated, was actually far short of the truth. Where I had expected to find one or two obscure kinglets, the Arabs had disinterred a whole vault of Pharaohs. And what Pharaohs! perhaps the most illustrious in the history of Egypt, Thutmose III and Seti I, Ahmose the Liberator and Ramses II the Conqueror. Monsieur Emile Brugsch, coming so suddenly into such an assemblage, thought that he must be the victim of a dream, and like him, I still wonder if I am not dreaming when I see and touch what were the bodies of so many famous personages of whom we never expected to know more than the names.

Two hours sufficed for this first examination, then the work of removal began. Three hundred Arabs were quickly got together by the Mudir's officials and set to work. The Museum's boat, hastily summoned, had not yet come; but one of the pilots was present, Rais Mohammed, a reliable man. He went to the bottom of the shaft and undertook to bring out its contents. Messrs. Emile Brugsch and Ahmed Effendi Kamal received the objects as they emerged from underground, transported them to the foot of the hill, and placed them side by side, never relaxing their vigilance for an instant. Forty-eight hours of energetic work were enough to bring up everything; but the task was only half finished. The convoy had to be conducted across the Theban plain and beyond the river to Luxor; several of the coffins, lifted only with the greatest effort by twelve or sixteen men, took seven or eight hours to travel from the mountain to the river bank, and it is easy to imagine what such a journey was like in the dust and heat of July.

Finally, on the evening of the 11th, mummies and coffins were all at Luxor, carefully wrapped in mats and cloth. Three days later the Museum's steamboat arrived; no sooner was the load aboard than it started back to Bulaq with its cargo of kings. Strangely enough, from Luxor to Qift, on both banks of the Nile fellah women with their hair down followed the boat howling, while the men fired shots as they do at funerals. Mohammed Abd-er-Rassul was rewarded with five hundred pounds sterling, and I thought it proper to appoint him *reïs* of the excavations at Thebes. If he serves the Museum with the same skill that he used so long to its detriment, we may hope for more fine discoveries. . . .

4. WALLIS BUDGE

After royal mummies, hidden tombs, and the wonderful works of Egyptian art, accidental finding of a few clay tablets written in cuneiform, a non-Egyptian script, seems insignificant indeed. It is a token of the advances in the methods and attitudes of archaeologists since the days of Belzoni that diggings of no material or aesthetic value, from a rubbish heap at Tell el-Amarna, site of the heretic Akhenaten's short-lived capital about 190 miles above Memphis, have come to be hailed as perhaps the most important discovery of them all. For on the tablets were the diplomatic letters from the royal archives of Amenhotep III and his son Amenhotep IV, alias Akhenaten. This correspondence referred to a particularly confusing and crucial period in New Kingdom Egypt during the late fifteenth and early part of the fourteenth century B.C. Light was thrown not only on Egypt herself, but also on international affairs of those days, with startling sidelights on Syria-Palestine, the then virtually unknown kingdoms of the Mitanni and the Hittites, and possibly even on the Hebrews—a Habiru by the name of Joshua is mentioned—and the early Greeks. In fact, the tablets added so much to our knowledge of the period when Egypt under her apostate king was in decline, that historians now frequently call it the "Amarna Age."

When, in 1887, an Egyptian peasant woman dug in the refuse of Tell el-Amarna for a nitrous substance called *sebakh* that was used as fertilizer, she came across several hundred clay tablets with strange markings. Not knowing what they were, she sold them to a neighbor for two shillings. He in turn cleared ten pounds by offering them to dealers in antiquities. By now the cuneiform writing of the baked clay tablets was clearly established, but grave doubts were thrown on their genuineness. Why should Babylonian inscriptions crop up in ancient Egyptian sites? Several of the experts took a look. Monsieur E. Grébaut, who was then director of the Service of Antiquities, would not commit himself, and the illustrious Franco-German Assyriologist Oppert declared the tablets forgeries. Never had cuneiform tablets been found in Egypt. Then the English Orientalist Sir Wallis Budge, who had a thorough knowledge of cuneiform, appeared on the scene during one of his numerous missions for the British Museum. Budge identified the tablets as diplomatic documents of unique importance.

Here then were undoubtedly genuine communications written in the Babylonian lingua franca to the pharaohs by satellite rulers in Palestine and Syria. Others were sent by the Kassites at Babylon, the kings of Assyria and the Hittites. Lesser princes begged for Egyptian gold. The letters point up the critical situation prevailing in the eastern Mediterranean due to population pressures and raids from Asia Minor and the desert hinterland of the Fertile Crescent. The Hittites were apparently pushing into northern Syria and had overrun the Mitanni, while the Habiru, whom some scholars identify with the Hebrews of Exodus, were occupying the south. Rulers of vassal cities and Egyptian governors from such familiar places as Byblos, Ashkelon, Megiddo, and Jerusalem pleaded for Egyptian help against the invaders. Assurances of loyalty to the Egyptian crown, intermingled with accusations against rival cities and their leaders, depict the climate of a world in turmoil and disintegration. The pharaoh, apparently occupied with his religious reforms in his new capital, paid scant attention to Egypt's deteriorating power in the empire's Asiatic borderlands.

In the light of the Tell el-Amarna tablets a great deal of ancient history of the second millennium B.C. has had to be rewritten. Like the extensive archives of Mari, Boghazköy, and Ras Shamra that were found in our century, the Tell el-Amarna documents added enormously to our knowledge of ancient Near-Eastern affairs. Thenceforth several major excavations were launched at the site of Akhenaten's capital. Among the first to undertake a campaign was Flinders Petrie, followed later by such outstanding modern archaeologists as Leonard Woolley, Henri Frankfort, and J. D. S. Pendlebury. A pre-World War I German mission discovered the beautiful bust of Akhenaten's queen, Nefertiti, and carried it to Berlin.

Sir Ernest Alfred Thompson Wallis Budge, a Cornishman of humble origin who enjoyed the patronage of Gladstone and became keeper of Egyptian and Assyrian antiquities in the British Museum, conducted several archaeological excavations in Mesopotamia, Upper Egypt, and the Sudan. From 1886 on, he went to Egypt on sixteen official visits that yielded the museum a unique collection of Greek papyri and hieroglyphic texts, including such rediscovered works as Aristotle's *Constitution of Athens* and the odes of Bacchylides. Budge's ability in maintaining amiable relationships with dealers and native diggers served him and the museum in good stead, though it led him into rather unpleasant squabbles with fellow archaeologists and even into a libel suit. His methods of getting archaeological material out of the country of its discovery in disregard of the laws have been called by Seton Lloyd a "very blatant piece of sharp practice." Budge tried to justify his Mesopotamian acquisitions on the grounds of the Turkish government's inability to enforce its own laws and to acquire the objects for the Imperial Ottoman Museum.

Apart from these activities, Budge's own output was enormous. He did original research in Syriac, Coptic, and Ethiopian texts; was a facile, but not always meticulous, translator; and made his best contributions in the deciphering of Egyptian papyri written in hieratic. In addition, Budge wrote widely on archaeology for the general public.

The Tell el-Amarna Tablets

WALLIS BUDGE

Before I had been in Cairo many hours I found that everybody was talking about the discoveries which had been made in Upper Egypt, and the most extraordinary stories were afloat. Rumours of the "finds" had reached all the great cities of Europe, and there were representatives of several Continental Museums in Cairo, each doing his best, as was right, to secure the lion's share. The British officials with whom I came in contact thought, or said they thought, that whatever the objects might be which had been discovered, they ought to go to the Bûlâk Museum, and that any attempt made to obtain any part of them for the British Museum must be promptly crushed. The Egyptian officials of the Service of Antiquities behaved according to their well-known manner. No official of the Bûlâk Museum knew where the "finds" had been made, or what they consisted of, and M. Grébaut [Maspero's successor as Director of the Service of Antiquities] and his assistants went about the town with entreaties and threats to every native who was supposed to possess any information about them. Instead of recognizing the fact that, rightly or wrongly, the "finds" were at that moment in the hands of native dealers, and trying to make arrangements to secure them by purchase, they went about declaring that the Government intended to seize them, and to put in prison all those who were in any way mixed up in the matter. M. Grébaut was unwise enough to hint publicly that the tortures which were sanctioned at Ḳanâ might be revived, but the tortures and persecution of 1880 had taught the natives how little Government officials were to be trusted, and one and all refused to give him any information. Every move

From Budge's *By Nile and Tigris* (1920). Reprinted by permission of John Murray (Publishers) Ltd.

which he made was met by a counter move by the natives, and they were always successful.

Meanwhile very definite rumours about the "finds" in Upper Egypt drifted down the river to Cairo, and some members of the Government insisted that M. Grébaut should take active steps to secure some of the treasures which had been found, and they ordered him to make a journey to Upper Egypt, and find out for himself what was taking place there. They placed one of Isma'îl Pâshâ's old pleasure-steamers at his disposal, and ordered an adequate force of police to accompany him. Before he left for the South he called upon me at the Royal Hotel, and although he threatened me with arrest and legal prosecution afterwards, if I attempted to deal with the natives, I found him a very agreeable and enlightened man, and we had a pleasant conversation. He told me that his great ambition was to be regarded as a worthy successor of Maspero, and that there was one mark of public recognition which I could help him to obtain. The Trustees of the British Museum, he reminded me, had presented a set of their magnificent Egyptological publications to Maspero, which was a very distinguished mark of honour, and a public acknowledgment of his scholarly eminence, and he hoped that the Trustees would honour him in the same way. I told him that I thought he might do a great deal towards getting that honour by adopting a liberal policy in dealing with their representative in Egypt, and that in any case I would duly report the conversation to the Principal Librarian. That same evening I learned that he had told off some of his police to watch the hotel in which I was staying, and that he had ordered them, to report to him my goings out and comings in, and the names of all antiquity dealers who had speech with me.

I left Cairo that night for Asyût, and soon after leaving Bûlâk ad-Dakrûr station I was joined in the train by a Frenchman and a Maltese, who told me that they were "interested" in anticas, and that there were police in the train who had been ordered to watch both them and me. At Dêr Mawâs, the station for Ḥajjî Ḳandîl, or Tall al-'Amârnah, the Frenchman left the train, and set out to try to buy some of the tablets said to have been found at Tall al-'Amârnah, and as he left the station some of the police from the train followed him. At Asyût, the Maltese and myself embarked on the steamer, and the remainder of the police followed us. As the steamer tied up for the night at Akhmîm and Kanâ I had plenty of time at each place to examine the antiquities which the dealers had in their houses, and to bargain for those I wanted. At Akhmîm I found a very fine collection in the hands of a Frenchman who owned a flour-mill in Cairo, and he caused the police to be entertained at supper whilst he and I conducted our deal for Coptic manuscripts. He told me that it was he who had sold to Maspero all the Coptic papyri and manuscripts which the Louvre had acquired during the last few years, and then went on to say that if he had known that Maspero intended to dispose of these things he would not have let him have them at such a low price. Thus I learned at first hand that the Director of the Service of Antiquities had bought and disposed of antiquities, and exported them, which the British authorities in Cairo declared to be contrary to the law of the land.

As there was work for me to do in Aswân, I decided to make no stay in Luxor on my way up the river, but during the few hours which the steamer stopped there I learned from some of the dealers, and from my friend, the Rev. Chauncey Murch of the American Mission, some details of the "finds" which had been made. I took the opportunity of sending a couple of natives across the river to fetch me skulls for Professor Macalister, who wanted more and more specimens. During one of the visits which I made to Western Thebes the previous year I was taken into a huge cave at the back of the second row of hills towards the desert, which had been used by the ancient Egyptians as a cemetery. There I saw literally thousands of poorly-made mummies and "dried bodies," some leaning against the sloping sides of the cave, and others piled up in heaps of different sizes. I had no means of carrying away skulls when I first saw the cave, or I should certainly have made a selection then.

There was little to be had at Armant, but I saw at Jabalên, which marks the site of Crocodilopolis, a number of pots of unusual shape and make, and many flints. On arriving at Aswân I was met by Captain W. H. Drage (now Colonel Drage Pâshâ) and Doone Bey, who gave me much assistance in packing up

the remainder of the Kûfî grave-stones, which I had been obliged
to leave there earlier in the year. My friend, the Ma'amûr, produced a further supply of skulls from the pit in the hill across
the river, and I learned incidentally that the natives had nick-
named me "Abû ar-Ra'wûs," or "father of skulls." The general
condition of the town had changed astonishingly, for the British
soldiers had departed to the north, their camps and barracks
were deserted and as silent as the grave, and Aswân was just a
rather large sleepy Nile village. And the change across the river
was great. The paths which we had made with such difficulty
were blocked with sand, and the great stone stairway and the
ledge above it were filled with sand and stones which had slid
down from the top of the hill, and the tombs were practically
inaccessible.

Soon after my return to Luxor I set out with some natives one
evening for the place on the western bank where the "finds" of
papyri had been made. Here I found a rich store of fine and rare
objects, and among them the largest roll of papyrus I had ever
seen. The roll was tied round with a thick band of papyrus cord,
and was in a perfect state of preservation, and the clay seal
which kept together the ends of the cord was unbroken. The roll
lay in a rectangular niche in the north wall of the sarcophagus
chamber, among a few hard stone amulets. It seemed like sacrilege to break the seal and untie the cord, but when I had copied
the name on the seal, I did so, for otherwise it would have been
impossible to find out the contents of the papyrus. We unrolled a few feet of the papyrus an inch or so at a time, for it
was very brittle, and I was amazed at the beauty and freshness
of the colours of the human figures and animals, which, in the
dim light of the candles and the heated air of the tomb, seemed
to be alive. A glimpse of the Judgment Scene showed that the
roll was a large and complete Codex of the Per-em-hru, or "Book
of the Dead," and scores of lines repeated the name of the man
for whom this magnificent roll had been written and painted,
viz., "Ani, the real [as opposed to honorary] royal scribe, the
registrary of the offerings of all the Gods, overseer of the
granaries of the Lords of Abydos, and scribe of the offerings of
the Lords of Thebes." When the papyrus was unrolled in London

the inscribed portion of it was found to be 78 feet long, and at each end was a section of blank papyrus about 2 feet long. In another place, also lying in a niche in the wall, was another papyrus Codex of the Book of the Dead, which, though lacking the beautiful vignettes of the Papyrus of Ani, was obviously much older, and presumably of greater importance philologically. The name of the scribe for whom it was written was Nu, and the names of his kinsfolk suggested that he flourished under one of the early kings of the XVIIIth dynasty. In other places we found other papyri, among them the Papyrus of the priestess Anhai, in its original painted wooden case, which was in the form of the triune god of the resurrection, Ptaḥ-Seker-Àsàr, and a leather roll containing Chapters of the Book of the Dead, with beautifully painted vignettes, and various other objects of the highest interest and importance. I took possession of all these papyri, etc., and we returned to Luxor at daybreak. Having had some idea of the things which I was going to get, I had taken care to set a tinsmith to work at making cylindrical tin boxes, and when we returned from our all-night expedition I found them ready waiting for me. We then rolled each papyrus in layers of cotton, and placed it in its box, and tied the box up in *gumâsh*, or coarse linen cloth, and when all the papyri and other objects were packed up we deposited the boxes in a safe place. This done we all adjourned a little after sunrise to a house (since demolished) belonging to Muḥammad Muḥassib, which stood on the river front, and went up on the roof to enjoy the marvellous freshness of the early morning in Egypt, and to drink coffee.

Whilst we were seated there discussing the events of the past night, a little son of the house, called Mursî, came up on the roof, and, going up to his father, told him that some soldiers and police had come to the house, and were then below in the court-yard. We looked over the low wall of the roof, and we saw several of the police in the courtyard, and some soldiers posted outside as sentries. We went downstairs, and the officer in charge of the police told us that the Chief of the Police of Luxor had received orders during the night from M. Grébaut, the Director of the Service of Antiquities, to take possession of every house containing antiquities in Luxor, and to arrest their owners and

myself, if found holding communication with them. I asked to
see the warrants for the arrests, and he told me that M. Grébaut
would produce them later on in the day. I asked him where
M. Grébaut was, and he told me at Naḳâdah, a village about
twelve miles to the north of Luxor, and went on to say that
M. Grébaut had sent a runner from that place with instructions
to the Chief of the Police at Luxor to do what they were then
doing—that is, to take possession of the houses of all dealers and
to arrest us. He then told Muḥammad and myself that we were
arrested. At this moment the runner who had been sent by
Grébaut joined our assembly in the casual way that Orientals
have, and asked for *bakhshîsh*, thinking that he had done a
meritorious thing in coming to Luxor so quickly. We gave him
good *bakhshîsh*, and then began to question him. We learned that
M. Grébaut had failed to reach Luxor the day before because
the *ra'îs*, or captain of his steamer, had managed to run the
steamer on to a sandbank a little to the north of Naḳâdah, where
it remained for two days. It then came out that the captain had
made all arrangements to celebrate the marriage of his daughter,
and had invited many friends to witness the ceremony and assist
at the subsequent feast, which was to take place at Naḳâdah on
the very day on which M. Grébaut was timed to arrive at Luxor.
As the captain felt obliged to be present at his daughter's marriage, and the crew wanted to take part in the wedding festivities,
naturally none of the attempts which they made to re-float the
steamer were successful. Our informant, who knew quite well
that the dealers in Luxor were not pining for a visit from
M. Grébaut, further told us that he thought the steamer could
not arrive that day or the day after. According to him, M. Grébaut
determined to leave his steamer, and to ride to Luxor, and his
crew agreed that it was the best thing to do under the circumstances. But when he sent for a donkey it was found that there
was not a donkey in the whole village, and it transpired that as
soon as the villagers heard of his decision to ride to Luxor, they
drove their donkeys out into the fields and neighbouring villages,
so that they might not be hired for M. Grébaut's use.

The runner's information was of great use to us, for we saw
that we were not likely to be troubled by M. Grébaut that day,

and as we had much to do we wanted the whole day clear of interruptions. Meanwhile, we all needed breakfast, and Muhammad Muhassib had a very satisfying meal prepared, and invited the police and the soldiers to share it with us. This they gladly agreed to do, and as we ate we arranged with them that we were to be free to go about our business all day, and as I had no reason for going away from Luxor that day, I told the police officer that I would not leave the town until the steamer arrived from Aswân, when I should embark in her and proceed to Cairo. When we had finished our meal the police officer took possession of the house, and posted watchmen on the roof and a sentry at each corner of the building. He then went to the houses of the other dealers, and sealed them, and set guards over them.

In the course of the day a man arrived from Ḥajjî Ḳandîl, bringing with him some half-dozen of the clay tablets which had been found accidentally by a woman at Tall al-'Amârnah, and he asked me to look at them, and to tell him if they were *ḳadîm, i.e.,* "old" or *jadîd, i.e.,* "new"—that is to say, whether they were genuine or forgeries. The woman who found them thought they were bits of "old clay," and useless, and sold the whole "find" of over 300 tablets to a neighbour for 10 piastres (2s.)! The purchaser took them into the village of Ḥajjî Ḳandîl, and they changed hands for £E10. But those who bought them knew nothing about what they were buying, and when they had bought them they sent a man to Cairo with a few of them to show the dealers, both native and European. Some of the European dealers thought they were "old," and some thought they were "new," and they agreed together to declare the tablets forgeries so that they might buy them at their own price as "specimens of modern imitations." The dealers in Upper Egypt believed them to be genuine, and refused to sell, and, having heard that I had some knowledge of cuneiform, they sent to me the man mentioned above, and asked me to say whether they were forgeries or not; and they offered to pay me for my information. When I examined the tablets I found that the matter was not as simple as it looked. In shape and form, and colour and material, the tablets were unlike any I had ever seen in London or Paris, and the writing on all of them was of a most unusual character and puzzled me for hours. By degrees I came to the conclusion that the tablets were certainly not forgeries, and that they were neither royal annals nor historical inscriptions in the ordinary sense of the word, nor business or commercial documents. Whilst I was examining the half-dozen tablets brought to me, a second man from Ḥajjî Ḳandîl arrived with seventy-six more of the tablets, some of them quite large. On the largest and best written of the second lot of tablets I was able to make out the words "A-na Ni-ib-mu-a-ri-ya," *i.e.*, "To Nib-muariya," and on another the words "[A]-na Ni-im-mu-ri-ya shar mâtu Mi-iṣ-ri," *i.e.*, "to Nimmuriya, king of the land of Egypt." These two tablets were certainly letters addressed to a king of Egypt called "Nib-muariya," or "Nimmuriya." On another tablet I made out clearly the opening words "A-na Ni-ip-khu-ur-ri-ri-ya shar mâtu [Miṣri])," *i.e.*, "To Nibkhurririya, king of the land of [Egypt,"] and there was no doubt that this tablet was a letter addressed to another king of Egypt. The opening words of nearly all the tablets proved them to be letters or despatches, and I felt certain that the tablets were both genuine and of very great historical importance.

Up to the moment when I arrived at that conclusion neither of the men from Ḥajjî Ḳandîl had offered the tablets to me for purchase, and I suspected that they were simply waiting for my decision as to their genuineness to take them away and ask a very high price for them, a price beyond anything I had the power to give. Therefore, before telling the dealers my opinion about the tablets, I arranged with them to make no charge for my examination of them, and to be allowed to take possession of the eighty-two tablets forthwith. They asked me to fix the price which I was prepared to pay for the tablets, and I did so, and though they had to wait a whole year for their money they made no attempt to demand more than the sum which they agreed with me to accept.

I then tried to make arrangements with the men from Ḥajjî Ḳandîl to get the remainder of the tablets from Tall al-'Amârnah into my possession, but they told me that they belonged to dealers who were in treaty with an agent of the Berlin Museum in Cairo. Among the tablets was a very large one, about 20 inches long and broad in proportion. We now know that it contained a list of the dowry of a Mesopotamian princess who was going to marry a king of Egypt. The man who was taking this to Cairo hid it between his inner garments, and covered himself with his great cloak. As he stepped up into the railway coach this tablet slipped from his clothes and fell on the bed of the railway, and broke in pieces. Many natives in the train and on the platform witnessed the accident and talked freely about it, and thus the news of the discovery of the tablets reached the ears of the Director of Antiquities. He at once telegraphed to the Mudîr of Asyût, and ordered him to arrest and put in prison everyone who was found to be in possession of tablets, and, as we have seen, he himself set out for Upper Egypt to seize all the tablets he could find. Meanwhile, a gentleman in Cairo who had obtained four of the smaller tablets and paid £E100 for them, showed them to an English professor, who promptly wrote an article upon them, and published it in an English newspaper. He post-dated the tablets by nearly 900 years, and entirely misunderstood the nature of their contents. The only effect of his article was to increase the importance of the tablets in the eyes of the dealers, and, in consquence, to raise their prices, and to make the acquisition of the rest of the "find" more difficult for everyone.

5. FLINDERS PETRIE

Egyptian archaeology became respectable with Mariette; it came of age with Petrie. Mariette's techniques still included dynamite as an excavation agent and were in the eyes of later workers rather primitive, but he at least saw that even more primitive methods were abandoned. He did not have any concerted plan of excavation, paid little regard to preservation, failed to report his researches adequately in publications, and concentrated on conspicuous treasures that would swell his cherished museum collections. His methods were still a far cry from scientific archaeology. After Petrie had perfected his painstaking techniques, there was little excuse for anyone to continue such rough-and-ready procedures.

When Petrie started working in Egypt in 1881, a few months before the death of Mariette, he was quite outspoken in condemning the prevailing practices. Fully aware that he was breaking new ground in archaeology, he displayed the singlemindedness of a pioneer of genius, and had nothing but scorn for his colleagues' work. While engaged at the pyramids of Gizeh he was horrified to see how fragments of a temple near the Sphinx had been wrecked by explosives, instead of being carefully restored. Of Mariette's work, he wrote, "Nothing was done with any uniform plan, work is begun and left unfinished, no regard is paid to future requirements of exploration and no civilised or laboursaving appliances are used. It is sickening to see the rate at which everything is being destroyed, and the little regard paid to preservation." Measured by twentieth-century standards, which Petrie more than anybody else helped to set up, conditions in Egypt were appalling. We know of frescoes chopped up to ship the most colorful sections to museums. Anything that had no tangible price or was not apt to excite curiosity-seekers in museums was simply discarded. Excavators only searched for big, odd, and precious objects. Needless to say, no attention was paid to broken implements, particularly to the ubiquitous broken pottery invariably to be found at any ancient, once-inhabited site. Here Petrie effected a revolution. All details of such artifacts— their color, fabric, shape, decorations, and so forth—were to be looked upon as vital pieces of information. Out of these scattered bits of evidence—reinforced if possible by inscriptions and other "objects, positions and probabilities"—a reliable record of the past could be constructed. This entailed the heroically pedantic attention to minutiae that distinguished the new spirit of archaeology.

The gathering of vital testimony was developed into a fine art "of securing all the requisite information, of realising the importance of everything found and avoiding oversights, of proving and testing hypotheses constantly, as work goes on, of securing everything of interest" not only to the excavator himself but to other students. An artifact had to be identified within the site where it had been originally deposited in order to be a meaningful piece of cultural testimony. Systematic and reasonably exhaustive search was to be accompanied by meticulous, regular recording through illustrations and verbal descriptions. In that manner scientific accuracy, still virtually absent from the work of Mariette in Egypt and that of his contemporary Layard in Mesopotamia, was introduced into archaeology by Petrie. Yet, despite his exacting standards, Petrie never envisaged archaeology as simply collecting, classifying, and analyzing the remote and forever dead. Its task, he said, should be not so much to show the mummy as "to show the Egyptian when he was a mummy in expectation."

Apart from formulating the general principles of archaeological spadework, Petrie added novel techniques and specific methods. His most fruitful innovation, which is by now an essential tool for investigating prehistoric or chronologically uncertain sites, is sequence-dating. This revolutionary idea is based on Petrie's observation that local pottery undergoes changes of style that can be grouped in a sequence corresponding to successive physical levels of human occupation. Thus, trivial fragments gathered from varied sites in a culturally well-circumscribed region permit the construction of a chronologically relative time scale whose units are not years but ceramic types. "This system enables us to deal with material which is entirely undated otherwise; and the larger the quantity of it the more accurate are the results." Once historically datable material is found in conjunction with these artifacts, the relative time scale can be transformed into one that is absolute.

Henceforth, apparently insignificant potsherds came to be recognized as the most valuable archaeological aids. Petrie himself applied the method mainly to pre- and proto-dynastic Egypt and to Palestine. In the latter country, when excavating in 1890 at Tell el-Hesi, Petrie proceeded first to establish a continuous, though relative, scale by gathering vessels from the various layers. And then through the association of some of the pottery with Egyptian scarabs or other objects that were historically datable, the chain of development in Palestine could be assigned to an actual sequence of "historical" ages.

By such cross-dating of different civilizations by means of datable artifacts Petrie devised comparative archaeology. Petrie was the first to turn attention to the Cretan and Mycenaean ware that occurred in layers of the Middle and New Kingdom of Egypt. On the basis of these alien objects in Egypt soil, carefully recorded and dated, Petrie made it possible to give a chronological outline of the great Aegean civilizations that the discoveries of Schliemann and Evans brought to light.

It now seems strange to realize that Petrie's coming to Egypt owed little to sober, scientific impulses, but was stimulated by his father's enthusiasm for mystical theories about the Great Pyramid and the magical properties and prophecies held to be inherent in its numerical properties. However, the son's meticulous mathematical investigations on the spot soon cured him of any such fantasies. As he confessed later, "the ugly little fact killed the beautiful theory." At first he was little interested in excavation, but soon he was fully absorbed in studying the way in which the pyramids were constructed. As a result of his investigations, he published, in 1883, the *Pyramids and Temple of Gizeh,* long a standard work. Encouraged by his engineer father since his early youth, surveying and measuring had been a prime occupation of his. And through his parents' and his own precocious interests in languages, mathematics, and foreign civilizations, Petrie was excellently prepared for his career in Near-Eastern archaeology.

Petrie's archaeological contributions lack the glamour and excitement of some of the fabulous discoveries of his contemporaries. They are, nevertheless, of the first rank and hold their own with his methodological achievements. They extend over sixty years, and range over all periods of Egyptian history. His researches are largely responsible for establishing the historicity of the first two Egyptian dynasties and veritably put pre-dynastic Egypt on the map. Among his other accomplishments, he discovered the sixth-century B.C. Ionian trading colony Naucratis in the Delta; explored in the Fayum; made excavations pertaining to Hyksos, Coptic, and Roman Egypt; and opened a tomb at Lahun in which were some of the finest jewelry and other ornaments ever found in Egypt. In a single season in Palestine, he helped to reorient archaeology in the Holy Land. In addition to his field work and a vast amount of publication, Petrie served from 1893 as Edwards Professor of Egyptology at University College, London. By 1926, when Petrie left Egypt, he had accomplished most of his lifework. He thenceforth lived in Palestine, where he died in 1942.

Petrie's popular account of his work at Medûm reflects his lifelong interest in the principal monuments of Egyptian civilization, the pyramids. At Medûm he was able not only to apply his skill in measuring and mathematics, but also to find evidence of architectural developments and cultural beginnings. Ravaged more by seekers for building material than by time, the partly dismantled structure at Medûm revealed the stages of pyramidal evolution. It was originally planned as a mastaba-step pyramid and on it a more advanced pyramid, of which there is little left today, was subsequently imposed. Among the seventy-odd pyramids of Egypt, this structure built by Cheops' father Seneferu is the oldest true pyramid. Because of its age and successive enlargements and modifications it is also among the most interesting of the "Mountains of Pharaoh."

A "Missing Link" of the Pyramids

FLINDERS PETRIE

AFTER HAVING sampled the civilization of each of the great periods of Egyptian history, back to the twelfth dynasty . . . I longed more than ever to discover the beginning of things. For this Medum offered the best chance for reaching back. The presumption was that it belonged to the beginning of the fourth dynasty; and here we might perhaps find something still undeveloped, and be able to gauge our way in the unknown. Could we there see the incipient stages, or at least their traces? Could we learn how conventional forms and ideas had arisen? Could we find Egypt not yet full grown, still in its childhood?

I called together a selected lot of my old workers from Illahun, and we went over and made a camp at the cemetery of Medum; there we lived over four months, and I unravelled what could be traced on the questions that awaited us. Broadly, it may be said, that we learned more of our ignorance than our knowledge: the beginning seems as remote as ever, for nearly all the conventions are already perfected there; but many new questions have been opened, and we at least see more of the road, though the goal is still out of view.

The first question to settle was that of the age of the pyramid and cemetery. All the indications pointed to as early an age as we knew, but not before Seneferu, the first king of the fourth dynasty, and predecessor of Khufu. Yet the theory that the pyramids were built in chronological order, from north to south, had led some to suppose that this was of the twelfth dynasty.

The most promising means of ascertaining the age was to search for any remains of the pyramid temple on the chance of

From Petrie's *Ten Years' Digging in Egypt* (1893). Reprinted by permission of the Lutterworth Press.

inscriptions such as I had found of Khafra at Gizeh and of Usertesen II at Illahun. But where was the temple? No sign of such a building could be seen anywhere to the east of the pyramid, and some holes I sunk in the space within the pyramid enclosure showed nothing. I hesitated for some days, while other work was going on, looking at the great bank of rubbish against the side of the pyramid, rubbish accumulated by the destruction of its upper part. At last I determined on the large excavation needful, for I felt that we must solve the matter if possible. So, marking out a space which would have held two or three good-sized London houses, and knowing that we must go as deep as a tall house before we could get any result, I began a work of several weeks, with as many men as could be efficiently put into the area. At first it was easy enough, but soon we found large blocks, which we could scarcely move; and these slipped away and rolled down at the stages of our work, upsetting all our regular cutting. But they all had to be got out of the way, by lifting, rolling or breaking up. At last we had a hole that could be seen for miles off across the valley, and so deep that the sides looked perilously high on either hand when one stood in the bottom. The pavement was reached, and we found at one end of our great excavation a wall, and one side of a large stele just showing.

We needed then to lengthen the pit, and the falls from our fresh work soon buried all that we had found. A fresh trouble came with a strong gale, which blew away the sand, and let the loose stones come rattling down from the rubbish which formed the sides of our hole. One great fall came near burying us in the bottom of the work: and it was three weeks before I again saw the building. At last we uncovered the court-yard, and found two steles; and moreover instead of a mere court there appeared a doorway on the east side, and crawling in I found a chamber and passage still roofed over and quite perfect. We had, in fact, found an absolutely complete, though small, temple; not a stone was missing, nor a piece knocked off; the steles and the altar between them stood just as when they were set up; and the oldest dated building in the land has stood unimpaired amidst all the building and the destruction that has gone on in Egypt throughout history.

The question about the age was settled indirectly. The original construction had no ornament or inscriptions. But numerous mentions of Seneferu, both during the ages near his own, and of the eighteenth dynasty, showed plainly what the Egyptians knew about the builder.

The pyramid of Medum differs from nearly all the others. It is really the primitive tomb-building or mastaba, such as often is found with successive coats added around it in the cemetery here; but this was enlarged by seven coats of masonry, widening and heightening it, until a final coat over all covered the slope from top to bottom at one angle. It is thus the final stage of complication of the mastaba tomb, and the first type of the pyramid. Later kings saved the intermediate stages, and built pyramids all at one design, without any additions. This architectural feature is another proof of the early age of this pyramid. And it is remarkably akin to the pyramid of Khufu which follows it. Both have the same angle; and therefore the ratio of height to circuit, being that of a radius to its circle, holds good. The approximate ratio adopted was 7 to 44; the dimensions of the pyramid of Seneferu are 7 and 44 times a length of 25 cubits; those of Khufu are 7 and 44 times a length of 40 cubits. Hence the design of the size of the great pyramid of Gizeh was made by Khufu on the lines of the pyramid of Medum, which was built by his predecessor. Fragments of Seneferu's wooden coffin were found inside the pyramid; but the place had long since been plundered.

The tombs at Medum proved of great interest. One of the largest was built on a very irregular foundation; and below the ground level I found the walls by which the builders had guided their work. Outside of each corner a wall was built up to the ground level; the sloping profile of the side was drawn on it; and then the wall was founded and built in line between the profiles. But the most attractive matter was the study of the inscriptions on the tombs, which show us the earliest forms of the hieroglyphs yet known. To preserve and examine their record I made a full-sized copy of the whole, and then published that reduced by photo-lithography. The evidence is the most valuable that we can yet obtain, on the earliest traceable civilization of the Egyptians. We have no remains certainly dated older than these; and the

objects used as hieroglyphs here must have been already long
familiar for them to have been used for signs. They therefore
lead us back to the third dynasty, or even earlier times; and they
show us various objects which are as yet quite unknown to us
till much later ages.

We can thus estimate the architecture of the pre-pyramid
period. There were columns with spreading capitals and abaci,
set up in rows to support the roof. There were papyrus columns
with a curious bell-top on the flower, the source of the heavier
conventional form of later times; these were probably carved in
wood, and originated from a wooden tent pole. There were
octagonal fluted columns tapering to the top, and painted with
a black dado, a white ornamental band, and red above. There
was the cornice of uraeus serpents, which is so familiar in later
times. And the granaries were already built with sloping sides,
as seen on later tombs. In short, all the essentials of an advanced
architecture seem to have been quite familiar to the Egyptians;
and we must cease to argue from the simplicity of the religious
buildings which we know—such as the granite temples of Gizeh,
or the limestone temple of Medum—for deciding on the architecture of the fourth and third dynasties. We seem to be as far
from a real beginning as ever.

The animals drawn here show that the domestication of various
species was no uncommon thing; apes, monkeys, many kinds of
horned cattle, ibexes, &c., and various birds, all appear familiarly
in this age. And of the wild birds the eagle, owl, and wagtail are
admirably figured, far better than in later times. The Libyan race
was already a civilized ally of Egypt, using bows and arrows
much as we see them subsequently. The tools employed were of
the established types; the adze and the chisel of bronze; the sickle
of flint teeth set in wood; the axe of stone; the head of the bow
drill—all these are shown us. And the exactitude of the standards
of measure was a matter of careful concern; the cubit here does
not differ from the standard of later times more than the thickness of a bit of stout card. The draught-board was exactly the
same as that which is found down to Greek times.

Some matters, however, point to a stage which passed away
soon after. The sign for a seal is not a scarab, or a ring, but a

cylinder of jasper, set in gold ends, and turning on a pin attached
to a necklace of stone beads. Cylinders are often met with in
early times, but died out of use almost entirely by the eighteenth
dynasty. This points to a connection with Babylonia in early
times. The numerals are all derived from various lengths of rope;
pointing to an original reckoning on knotted ropes, as in many
other countries. And some suggestion of the original home of
Egyptian culture near the sea is made by the signs for water
being all black or dark blue-green. This is a colour that no one
living on the muddy Nile would ever associate with water; rather
should we suppose it to have originated from the clear waters of
the Red Sea.

Another glimpse of the prehistoric age in Egypt is afforded by
the burials at Medum. The later people always buried at full
length, and with some provision for the body, such as food, head-
rests, &c. Such burials are found among the nobles at Medum.
But most of the people there buried in a contracted form, nose
and knees, or at least with the thigh bent square with the body
and heels drawn up. And moreover, no food-vessels or other
objects are put in. Yet there was no mere indifference shown;
the bodies are in deep well tombs, often placed in large wooden
boxes, which must have been valuable in Egypt, and always
lying with the head to the north, facing the east. Here is clearly
a total difference in beliefs, and probably also in race. We know
that two races, the aquiline-nosed and the snouty, can be distinguished in early times; and it seems that the aborigines used
the contracted burial, and the dynastic race the extended burial,
which—with its customs—soon became the national mode.

Is it likely that the bulk of the people should have resisted
this change for some 800 years, and then have suddenly adopted
it in two or three generations? Does not this rapid adoption of
the upper-class custom, between the beginning of the fourth
dynasty and the immediately succeeding times, suggest that the
dynastic race did not enter Egypt till shortly before we find their
monuments? At least, the notion that the stages preceding the
known monuments should be sought outside of Egypt, and that
this is the explanation of the dearth of objects before the fourth

dynasty, is strengthened by the change of custom and belief which we then find.

The mutilations and diseases that come to light are remarkable. One man had lost his left leg below the knee; another had his hand cut off and put in the tomb; others seem to have had bones excised, and placed separately with the body. In one case acute and chronic inflammation and rheumatism of the back had united most of the vertebrae into a solid mass down the inner side. In another case there had been a rickety curvature of the spine. To find so many peculiarities in only about fifteen skeletons which I collected, is strange. These are all in the Royal College of Surgeons now, for study.

Medum has, then, led us some way further back than we had reached before in the history of Egyptian civilization; but it has shown how vastly our information must be increased before the problems are solved.

6. BERNARD GRENFELL

The little Egyptian village of Behnesa looks even less impressive than the sandy wastes of Tell el-Amarna. But it was the Oxyrhynchus of the Hellenistic era and once the capital of its nome or district. In a country so rich in still-prominent physical remains of its past splendor, Oxyrhynchus seemed the least likely to tempt the archaeologist's spade. What induced English scholars to start digging there toward the end of the nineteenth century was a recent interest in written documents, papyri, which could have been preserved only in so dry a climate as Egypt's. This interest led to the rise of a new branch of archaeology with a strong philological orientation, which soon became a science in its own right: papyrology.

In its most widely accepted sense papyrology is restricted to the recovery and study of texts in the ancient classical languages, particularly Greek texts that date approximately from the beginning of the Ptolemaic rule to the advent of the Arabs. While the bulk of these texts are written on papyrus, a few now also associated with papyrology may be inscribed on vellum, leather, bone, wood, or pottery; inscriptions on stone, however, are the subject of epigraphy. That papyrology deals almost exclusively with material of Egyptian origin is due to the simple fact that with very few exceptions, among which the Dead Sea Scrolls are conspicuous, ancient texts written on perishable material and of roughly the same period as their original composition are not apt to turn up anywhere else. This is the case even though papyrus, a writing material made from the fibers of an Egyptian reed, continued to be used in Europe until the early Middle Ages.

In modern times, the first Greek papyri to be discovered were found in 1753, when the villa of a minor Epicurean philosopher, Philodemos, was excavated at Herculaneum. The badly charred rolls were ingeniously unrolled by a Franciscan father, Antonio

Piaggio. Though of indifferent literary value, they aroused considerable attention in European learned circles when Winckelmann discussed them in his *Open Letters* in 1762. The first Greek papyri of Egyptian origin were discovered in the 1770s in the Fayum, the district southwest of Cairo that has ever since remained one of their principal sources. Of the fifty or so rolls found by natives in an earthenware pot, all but one were burned, allegedly for their aromatic properties. The sole survivor was acquired by Cardinal Stefano Borgia who in 1778 published the text, which related to Hellenistic administrative matters.

Largely because of the conventional objectives of archaeologists, hunting papyrus was left to the chance discoveries and ransacking of the fellahin. One shudders to think how much had been destroyed by the natives before they became aware of the demand for papyri. Once the odd European propensity for this "rubbish" came to be known, illicit diggers indulged in what Maspero had called "unbridled pillage" for papyrus, just as they had formerly turned their avarice on the mummies. Wallis Budge in his autobiography tells some gruesome stories on the subject. He, as agent of the British Museum, purchased from more or less surreptitious sources some of the most precious of all papyri, among them Aristotle's lost treatise on the *Constitution of Athens*. Earlier, in the middle of the nineteenth century, the first literary papyrus to appear was the XXIV book of the *Iliad,* soon followed by the last orations of Demosthenes' contemporary Hyperides. But, according to Frederic Kenyon, a former director of the British Museum, "up to the year 1877 all the known manuscripts on papyrus, literary or non-literary, amounted to a total of less than two hundred."

At about that time there was a great increase in discoveries of papyri as the natives began to dig in the ruins of the Fayum for the same nitrous fertilizing substance that had resulted in the discovery of the Tell el-Amarna tablets. And then, during the season of 1889–90, Flinders Petrie made an interesting find in the Ptolemaic cemetery of the Fayum town of Gurob. At first he had been disappointed in the objects he encountered, particularly in the coffins, which he described as "of the most marvellous rudeness; a few are good enough to be grotesque, but others are things of which a Pacific islander would be ashamed." Yet, these coffins, which reflected the dismal decadence to which Egyptian art had descended after three thousand years, had as their inner layer "comparatively fine cartonnages." In many instances these had been made of a kind of papier-mâché, of discarded papyri that had been moistened, pasted together, and pressed into the desired shape. Some of the papyri that had been put to such a strange use by the ancient undertakers, were still in a fairly good condition and contained fully legible material that was deciphered and edited by Oxford scholars in 1890–94. While most of these writings were legal and official documents, they also included a part of both the *Antiope* by Euripides and, in a copy that may have been written during Plato's lifetime, of the dialogue *Phaedo*.

Encouraged by Petrie's finds and by the response among scholars the world over, there was launched in 1895 the first scientifically planned and directed campaign for the specific purpose of excavating papyri. Both Petrie and David Hogarth were connected with the earlier exploits, but soon the principal work came to be carried out by two young Oxford scholars, Bernard P. Grenfell and Arthur S. Hunt, who conducted regular campaigns for a decade on behalf of the Egypt Exploration Fund. The two friends formed a most productive team and the "Dioscuri of Oxford" became throughout the world of learning a byword for proficient papyrological research. Their first dig in the northern Fayum met with great success, though less than the one they initiated outside the Fayum in 1897 at Oxyrhynchus. At the site of this city, known in antiquity for its substantial Greek population and later as a flourishing Christian center, Grenfell and Hunt's anticipations were borne out by the discovery of so many fascinating and precious documents that the sheer physical handling of them was "almost embarrassing." However, both men were equal to the scholarly tasks the literary and documentary windfall entailed. Their accurate deciphering, sound identifications, critical comments, and fine translations gained them great respect from other students, who also marveled at their prompt publication of much of the material. At Oxford in 1908 Grenfell was appointed professor of papyrology and Hunt was made a lecturer on the same subject. When the former's health gave way, Hunt succeeded him. Later Grenfell's health improved and they were able to resume their partnership.

The first campaign at Oxyrhynchus in 1897 produced several finds that have remained unsurpassed. The most famous of all is a document containing a collection of Sayings of Jesus that Grenfell and Hunt called "Logia," a somewhat controversial term because of its usage in early Christian literature. The problems raised by this and some Christian documents they encountered later—including further Sayings of Jesus (1903) and fragments of an unknown gospel—have divided theologians ever since. Some hold the "Logia" to have been a source, in addition to Mark, for the synoptic Gospels of Matthew and Luke, though the Sayings found at Oxyrhynchus are of unknown, non-canonical wording.

Other discoveries of the first dig at Oxyrhynchus almost equal the theological fragments in value. Among them are beautiful poetic passages ascribed to Alcman and Sappho. A longer poem, which is an appeal by the poetess to her estranged brother, is now generally recognized as genuine.

Additional excavations were carried out in the Fayum from 1898 to 1902. Some of these operations were sponsored by the University of California and had as their main objective the town of Tebunis. There a cemetery of crocodiles was found and it was noticed by chance that the reptilian mummies had been stuffed with papyri. These singular repositories yielded interesting official documents concerning Ptolemaic domestic regulations.

Such non-literary papyri lack the glamour of the literary and theological texts but are scarcely less important because of the vital economic, administrative, and social data they furnish. In Hunt's words, not being "designed for the public eye and posterity . . . [they] are as a class ephemeral and personal. Their value lies largely in the insight they afford into the business of common everyday life, from the official in his office down to the labourer in his fields. They draw aside the curtain, so to say, and show us the figures actually at work, off their guard, free of all artificiality and pose."

When Grenfell and Hunt returned to Oxyrhynchus in January 1906, the success of their further digging was immediate and so phenomenal that it soon brought a host of other expeditions, German, French, and Italian, to the area. Here "amid hundreds of smaller fragments there were a couple of cores of rolls, containing ten or twelve columns, other pieces containing five or six, and many more one or two columns." The greatest discoveries were classical texts of Greek masterpieces, such as two large fragments of Pindar's *Paeans,* the *Hypsipyle* of Euripides, a first-rate manuscript of Plato's *Symposium,* and the by now famous *Hellenica,* a historical work on ancient Greece by an unidentified Greek historian of the highest caliber.

By 1907 the "Oxford Dioscuri" had done their fieldwork. The editing and publishing of their vast material occupied them for the years to come. Despite their rapid pace of work, increasingly shouldered by Hunt during Grenfell's long breakdown, the job was not fully completed in their lifetimes, and there may very well be further surprises in what remains to be edited and published.

Manuscripts From the Sands of Egypt

BERNARD GRENFELL

I HAD FOR SOME TIME felt that one of the most promising sites in Egypt for finding Greek manuscripts was the city of Oxyrhynchus, the modern Behneseh, situated on the edge of the western desert 120 miles south of Cairo. Being the capital of the Nome, it must have been the abode of many rich persons who could afford to possess a library of literary texts. Though the ruins of the old town were known to be fairly extensive, and it was probable that most of them were of the Graeco-Roman period, neither town nor cemetery appeared to have been plundered for antiquities in recent times. Above all, Oxyrhynchus seemed to be a site

From Grenfell's "Oxyrhynchus and its Papyri," *Egyptian Exploration Fund, Archaeology Report* 1896-97.

where fragments of Christian literature might be expected of an earlier date than the fourth century, to which our oldest manuscripts of the New Testament belong; for the place was renowned in the fourth and fifth centuries on account of the number of its churches and monasteries, and the rapid spread of Christianity about Oxyrhynchus, as soon as the new religion was officially recognized, implied that it had already taken a strong hold during the preceding centuries of persecution.

The wished-for opportunity for digging at Oxyrhynchus offered itself last autumn, when leave was obtained for Professor Flinders Petrie and myself to excavate anywhere in the strip of desert, ninety miles long, between the Faiyûm and Minyeh. Behneseh was chosen for our headquarters, and work was begun there early in December by Professor Petrie, who, after making a preliminary survey of the site, and digging for a week, found that both the town and tombs belonged to the Roman period. So when I arrived on December 20th, accompanied by my colleague Mr. A. S. Hunt, Professor Petrie at once handed over the excavations at Behneseh to us, and himself left to explore the edge of the desert within the limits of the concession, ultimately settling down at the early Egyptian cemetery of Desbâsheh, forty miles to the north, with what success is related by himself elsewhere.

The ruins of Oxyrhynchus are eight miles west from Beni-Mazar, a railway-station on the Nile, and are just inside the desert, separated on the east from the Bahr Yusuf by a narrow strip of cultivation. At a point some fifteen miles to the north the Libyan hills recede far back into the desert, and, not returning until far above Behneseh, form a bay like the entrance to the Hammâmât Valley at Koptos, so that to the west of Oxyrhynchus there is a broad flat plain stretching for six miles up to a series of low basalt hills, through which runs the road to the small oasis of Bahrîyeh.

The area of the ancient town is 1¼ miles long, and in most parts ½ mile broad, its modern representative, Behneseh, still occupying a small fraction of it on the east side. Though now consisting only of a few squalid huts and four picturesque but dilapidated mosques, it was an important place until mediaeval times, and all the debris near the village, amounting to nearly half the whole site, is strewn with Arabic pottery. Its decline is doubtless due to its unprotected situation on the desert side of the Bahr Yusuf, which renders it exposed to frequent nocturnal raids by the Bedawîn, who have settled in large numbers along this part of the desert edge. One of these raids took place while we were there, and an unsuccessful attempt was made to get into our hut. Though an application addressed to Cairo resulted in measures being promptly taken to prevent our being troubled again, it is hardly surprising that the Behneseh *fellahin* are gradually migrating to the rising village of Sandafeh on the opposite bank of the Bahr Yusuf.

Behneseh has, however, still a claim to distinction in its Arabic cemetery, the largest in the district, and a place of peculiar sanctity, owing to the number of *shékhs* buried there, including a local saint of much repute, Dakrûri, whose tomb is a conspicuous object 1½ miles off in the desert plain to the west. Numbers of these domed tombs are scattered about, chiefly on eminences, in the central part of the site, many of them containing ancient columns taken from the town; and most of the Arabic mounds immediately to the west and south-west of the village have been used for purposes of burial.

My first impressions on examining the site were not very favourable. As has been said, about half of it was Arabic; and, with regard to the other half, a thousand years' use as a quarry for limestone and bricks had clearly reduced the buildings and houses to utter ruin. In many parts of the site which had not been used as a depository for rubbish, especially to the north-west, lines of limestone chips or banks of sand marked the positions of buildings of which the walls had been dug out; but of the walls themselves scarcely anything was left, except part of the town wall enclosing the north-west of the site, the buildings having been cleared away down to their foundations, or to within a few courses of them. It was obvious from the outset that the remains of the Roman city were not only much worse preserved than those of the Faiyûm towns which we had dug the year before, and in which most of the houses still had their walls partly standing, but that, if papyri were to be found, they must be looked for not in the shallow remains of houses, but in the rubbish mounds. These, of course, might cover buildings, but it was more probable that they would not; and there is a great difference between digging houses which after being deserted had simply fallen in and become covered with sand, and digging rubbish mounds. In the former there is always the chance of finding valuable things which have been left behind or concealed by the last occupants, such as a hoard of coins or a collection of papyrus rolls buried in a pot; while in rubbish mounds, since the objects found must have been thrown away deliberately, they were much less likely to be valuable, and were quite certain to be in much worse condition. The result of our excavations showed that I had been so far right in that the rubbish mounds were nothing but rubbish mounds; and the miscellaneous small *anticas* which we found are of little interest, while the number of papyri which are sufficiently well preserved to be of use was but trifling compared to the mass which is hopelessly fragmentary or defaced. Fortunately, however, the total find of papyri was so enormous that even the small residue of valuable ones forms a collection not only larger than any one site has hitherto produced, but probably equal to any existing collection of Greek papyri. . . .

We started work upon the town on January 11th by setting some seventy men and boys to dig trenches through a low mound on the outside of the site, a little to the north of the supposed temple. The choice proved a very fortunate one, for papyrus scraps at once began to come to light in considerable quantities, varied by uncial fragments and occasional complete or nearly complete official and private documents. Later in the week Mr. Hunt, in sorting the papyri found on the second day, noticed on a crumpled piece of papyrus, written on both sides in uncial characters, the Greek word ΚΑΡΦΟC ("mote"), which at once suggested to him the verse in the Gospels about the mote and the beam. A further examination showed that the passage in the papyrus really was the conclusion of the verse in question, but that the rest of the writing differed considerably from the Gospels, and was, in fact, a leaf out of a book containing a collection of Christ's sayings, some of which were new. The following day Mr. Hunt identified another uncial fragment as containing most of the first chapter of St. Matthew's Gospel. The evidence both of the handwriting and of the dated papyri with which they were found makes it certain that neither the "Logia" nor the St. Matthew fragment were written later than the third century A.D.; and they are therefore a century older than the oldest manuscripts of the New Testament. It is not improbable that they were the remains of a library belonging to some Christian who perished in the persecution during Diocletian's reign, and whose books were then thrown away. By a happy freak of fortune we had thus within a week of excavating in the town lit upon two examples of the kind of papyri which we most desired to find.

Since this rubbish mound had proved so fruitful I proceeded to increase the number of workmen gradually up to 110, and, as we moved northwards over other parts of the site, the flow of papyri soon became a torrent which it was difficult to cope with. Each lot found by a pair, man and boy, had to be kept separate; for the knowledge that papyri are found together is frequently of the greatest importance for determining their date, and since it is inevitable that so fragile a material should sometimes be broken in the process of extricating it from the closely-packed soil, it is imperative to keep together, as far as possible, fragments of the same document. We engaged two men to make tin boxes for storing the papyri, but for the next ten weeks they could hardly keep pace with us.

As I had anticipated, the remains of houses in the low ground between and outside the rubbish mounds were too shallow to be worth digging, and the rubbish mounds proved to cover very few traces of walls, much less any complete building. The papyri were, as a rule, not very far from the surface; in one patch of ground, indeed, merely turning up the soil with one's boot would frequently disclose a layer of papyri, and it was seldom that we found even tolerably well-preserved documents at a greater depth than ten feet. The explanation is that the damp soaking up from below, owing to the rise of the Nile bed, has proved fatal to what papyri there may have been in the lower levels. It was not uncommon to find at two or three feet from the surface in the

lower parts of mounds rolls which had been hopelessly spoiled
by damp.

The mounds divided themselves roughly into three classes:
those on the outside of the site producing first to early fourth
century papyri, those near the village being of the mediaeval
Arabic period, while the intermediate ones chiefly produced
papyri of the Byzantine period, varied occasionally by earlier
ones or by Arabic papyri of the eighth and ninth centuries. The
old town, founded probably on the river-bank where the modern
village stands, thus reached its widest extent in the Roman
period, and has been contracting ever since. As a rule, the papyri
found in one mound tended to be within a century or two of
each other; and where a mound had several layers of papyri at
different depths, the difference of date between the highest and
the lowest was generally not very marked, though two of the
highest mounds had a layer of Byzantine papyri on the top and
another of second to third century lower down. Some cases
where a mound was of a composite character, i.e. where it really
contained two or three smaller mounds heaped up at different
periods and then all covered over by later rubbish, produced
rather curious anomalies. One of these composite mounds had in
one part of it early first-century A.D. papyri quite close to the
surface; a few yards distant, but in the same mound, papyri five
or six centuries later were found at a much greater depth.

The papyri tended to run in layers rather than to be scattered
through several feet of rubbish, and as a rule were associated
with the particular kind of rubbish composed largely of pieces
of straw and twigs which the natives call *afsh*. It was not infre-
quent to find large quantities of papyri together, especially in
three mounds, where the mass was so great that these finds most
probably represent part of the local archives thrown away at different periods. It was the custom in Egypt to store up carefully
in the government record offices at each town official documents
of every kind dealing with the administration and taxation of the
country; and to these archives even private individuals used to
send letters, contracts, &c., which they wished to keep. After a
time, when the records were no longer wanted, a clearance became necessary, and many of the old papyrus rolls were put in

baskets or on wicker trays and thrown away as rubbish. In the first of these "archive" mounds, of which the papyri belong to the end of the first and beginning of the second century, we sometimes found not only the contents of a basket all together, but baskets themselves full of papyri. Unfortunately, it was the practice to tear most of the rolls to pieces first, and of the rest many had naturally been broken or crushed in being thrown away, or had been subsequently spoiled by damp, so that the amount discovered which is likely to be of use, though large in itself, bears but a small proportion to what the whole amount might have been. In the second find of archives the papyri belonged to the latter part of the third or early part of the fourth century, and several of them are large official documents which are likely to be of more than usual interest. The third and by far the greatest find, that of the Byzantine archives, took place on March 18th and 19th, and was, I suppose, a "record" in point of quantity. On the first of these two days we came upon a mound which had a thick layer consisting almost entirely of papyrus rolls. There was room for six pairs of men and boys to be working simultaneously at this storehouse, and the difficulty was to find enough baskets in all Behneseh to contain the papyri. At the end of the day's work no less than thirty-six good-sized baskets were brought in from this place, several of them stuffed with fine rolls three to ten feet long, including some of the largest Greek rolls I have ever seen. As the baskets were required for the next day's work, Mr. Hunt and I started at 9 P.M. after dinner to stow away the papyri in some empty packing-cases which we fortunately had at hand. The task was only finished at three in the morning, and on the following night we had a repetition of it, for twenty-five more baskets were filled before the place was exhausted.

This was our last great find of papyri. . . .

7. HOWARD CARTER

The finding of Tutankhamen's tomb in 1922 is still the greatest romance in the annals of archaeology. It has all the elements of a first-rate adventure story: the suspense of a long search; lurking doubts and flickering hopes; and, at the point of depair, sudden discovery. There is the triumph of a determined mind over all odds and against the predictions of the experts, and then the crowning achievement in the discovery of a fabulous treasure that even today has lost nothing of its luster. Like the greatest of adventures, it has the fairy-tale quality of being utterly improbable. Who would have believed in the existence of a pharaoh's grave, lavishly equipped and fully intact with the king resting in his golden coffin as he was buried almost 3,500 years ago? For once archaeology made the headlines when the news from Egypt was flashed to five continents. Struggling to be sober and scientific, archaeological spadework seemed to revert, at least in the public image, to its nineteenth-century preoccupation with treasure hunting. Yet the find was only possible because of the wholly scientific method and admirably well-reasoned plan of Howard Carter, whose greatest gift in the words of one of his colleagues was patience.

Who was the king whom Carter made one of the most celebrated of all Egyptian pharaohs? He was of little consequence, a boy king who died at the approximate age of eighteen; his ineffective regime of about six years overshadowed by the revived power of the priests of Thebes, who had recently triumphed over the apostate Akhenaten. Tutankhamen was actually the last of the once great Eighteenth Dynasty under which, during the sixteenth century B.C., Egypt had freed herself from the alien Hyksos and become an aggressive empire. He had apparently started his royal career in the new capital as Tutankhaten, or successor to Akhnaten, after the death of another prince who had been given in marriage to one of the pharaoh's daughters. The many likenesses of Tut in his tomb make it quite certain that he was closely related to Akhenaten; indeed, he may have been his son, although he acceded to the throne by marriage, since royal succession in Egypt followed the female line. His features show the same tired refinement and inbreeding, with slightly Negroid traits, as those of his predecessor. We have little information about the king. Perhaps because of his association with the heretic, monotheistic Akhenaten, the memory of Tut was systematically wiped out from later records. In Howard Carter's words: "Of the man himself—if indeed he ever arrived at the dignity of manhood—and of his personal character we know nothing. . . . In the present state of our knowledge we might say with truth that the one outstanding feature of his life was the fact that he died and was buried."

Actually in its layout and dimensions, the tomb is anything but imposing and compares unfavorably with those of Seti or Ramses VI above it. Their construction in later days may have covered up the entrance of Tut's sepulcher and perhaps explains why it was left unmolested for three millenniums. Thus the tomb is in some measure a reflection of the king's insignificance. In all likelihood, the splendor of its furnishings was not at all out of the ordinary and may have been easily outshone by other tombs. But as the latter had all suffered the misfortune of having been pillaged, we shall probably never know how they were furnished. Yet it will not do to minimize either the artistic merit or the historical value of the rich trove cleared by Carter and his assistants during several seasons. Artistically, little else found in Egypt surpasses it. While a few alabaster vases and other objects may be in doubtful taste, most of them are delicately beautiful, reflecting to some degree the short-lived freedom of the Amarna age.

Among the many exquisite pieces—pectorals, rugs, amulets, daggers, diadems, statuettes, chariots, lamps, fans, funerary furniture—perhaps finest are the magnificent golden throne in pure Amarna style and symbolism with its cloisonné decorations of faïence and precious stone, the third coffin of pure gold whose material value runs probably into hundreds of thousands of dollars, the wonderful gold masks of the king, and the enormous canopic chest of his viscera, guarded by the statuettes of four alluring goddesses. The majority of all the treasures are now housed in the Cairo National Museum where, somewhat to the regret of its curators, Tutankhamen steals the show, having become such an attraction that tourists are apt to disregard all the rest of that institution's outstanding exhibits.

Howard Carter's quest for Tut has been frequently told, but nowhere better than in his own book. Originally brought to Egypt as a draughtsman to the Egyptologist P. E. Newberry when still in his teens, he served as assistant to Petrie in 1892. During Maspero's second tenure as director of antiquities he was named chief of the monuments of Upper Egypt and Nubia. It was then that he began his first excavations in the Valley of the Kings. The discovery of the boy king's tomb was by no means his first archaeological success. He had previously opened or cleared the royal tombs of Thutmose IV, Hatshepsut, and Amenophis I. Again on Maspero's insistence, Carter was engaged as superintendent of excavations by George Herbert, fifth Earl of Carnarvon, a wealthy English sportsman who entered the field of Egyptian archaeology in 1907. At that time the concession for excavating in the Valley of the Kings was held by an American, Theodore Davis. However, by 1914 Davis was thoroughly convinced, as Belzoni had been earlier, that the Valley was fully exhausted and would yield no further tomb. Carnarvon was therefore able to take over from Davis.

Despite Maspero's warning, both Carter and Carnarvon remained hopeful. Carter was encouraged by several isolated minor finds made previously by Davis which carried inscriptions of an obscure king whose tomb had never been accounted for—Tutankhamen. Carter believed this king's tomb was somewhere in the vicinity, and with the aid of a map, he systematically narrowed down the sites in which exploratory excavation should be carried out. For six years, partially interrupted by World War I, the search proved unprofitable, though on two occasions Carter came within a hairsbreadth of the entrance to Tut's tomb. At one time he refrained from digging there any further in order not to interfere with the visitors to Ramses VI's tomb, one of the most popular in the Valley.

Full work was resumed in 1917, again without results. By 1921 Carnarvon tended to accept the verdict of Davis and Maspero. However, when Carter offered to shoulder the cost of excavating for another season himself, the Earl pledged his financial support for one more year. Barely a week after the reopening of the campaign on October 28, 1922, a flight of steps was laid bare. Refusing to be tempted by curiosity, Carter proceeded slowly and methodically, hampered by interference from the Egyptian government. Only in 1928, five years after Carnarvon's death, did Carter reach the pharaoh's sarcophagus and open its coffin of solid gold.

The Tomb of Tutankhamen

HOWARD CARTER

EVER SINCE my first visit to Egypt in 1890 it had been my ambition to dig in The Valley [of the Kings], and when, at the invitation of Sir William Garstin and Sir Gaston Maspero, I began to excavate for Lord Carnarvon in 1907, it was our joint hope that eventually we might be able to get a concession there. I had, as a matter of fact, when Inspector of the Antiquities Department, found, and superintended the clearing of, two tombs in The Valley for Mr. Theodore Davis, and this had made me the more anxious to work there under a regular concession. For the moment it was impossible, and for seven years we dug with varying fortune in other parts of the Theban necropolis. . . .

In 1914 our discovery of the tomb of Amen-hetep I, on the summit of the Drah abu'l Negga foothills, once more turned our attention Valleywards, and we awaited our chance with some impatience. Mr. Theodore Davis, who still held the concession,

From *The Tomb of Tut-Ankh-Amen* by Howard Carter and A. C. Mace (1923). Reprinted by permission of Cassell & Co., Ltd., and the executors of the estate of Howard Carter.

had already published the fact that he considered The Valley exhausted, and that there were no more tombs to be found, a statement corroborated by the fact that in his last two seasons he did very little work in The Valley proper, but spent most of his time excavating in the approach thereto, in the neighbouring north valley, where he hoped to find the tombs of the priest kings and of the Eighteenth Dynasty queens, and in the mounds surrounding the Temple of Medinet Habu. Nevertheless he was loath to give up the site, and it was not until June, 1914, that we actually received the long-coveted concession. Sir Gaston Maspero, Director of the Antiquities Department, who signed our concession, agreed with Mr. Davis that the site was exhausted, and told us frankly that he did not consider that it would repay further investigation. We remembered, however, that nearly a hundred years earlier Belzoni had made a similar claim, and refused to be convinced. We had made a thorough investigation of the site, and were quite sure that there were areas, covered by the dumps of previous excavators, which had never been properly examined.

Clearly enough we saw that very heavy work lay before us, and that many thousands of tons of surface debris would have to be removed before we could hope to find anything; but there was always the chance that a tomb might reward us in the end, and, even if there was nothing else to go upon, it was a chance that we were quite willing to take. As a matter of fact we had something more, and, at the risk of being accused of *post actum* prescience, I will state that we had definite hope of finding the tomb of one particular king, and that king Tut·ankh·Amen.

To explain the reasons for this belief of ours we must turn to the published pages of Mr. Davis's excavations. Towards the end of his work in The Valley he had found, hidden under a rock, a faïence cup which bore the name of Tut·ankh·Amen. In the same region he came upon a small pit-tomb, in which were found an unnamed alabaster statuette, possibly of Ay, and a broken wooden box, in which were fragments of gold foil, bearing the figures and names of Tut·ankh·Amen and his queen. On the basis of these fragments of gold he claimed that he had actually found the burial place of Tut·ankh·Amen. The theory was quite untenable, for the pit-tomb in question was small and insignificant, of a type that might very well belong to a member of the royal household in the Ramesside period, but ludicrously inadequate for a king's burial in the Eighteenth Dynasty. Obviously, the royal material found in it had been placed there at some later period, and had nothing to do with the tomb itself.

Some little distance eastward from this tomb, he had also found in one of his earlier years of work (1907–8), buried in an irregular hole cut in the side of the rock, a cache of large pottery jars, with sealed mouths, and hieratic inscriptions upon their shoulders. A cursory examination was made of their contents, and as these seemed to consist merely of broken pottery, bundles of linen, and other oddments, Mr. Davis refused to be interested in them, and they were laid aside and stacked away in the store-room of his Valley house. There, some while afterwards, Mr. Winlock noticed them, and immediately realised their importance. With Mr. Davis's consent the entire collection of jars was packed and sent to the Metropolitan Museum of Art, New York, and there Mr. Winlock made a thorough examination of their contents. Extraordinarily interesting they proved to be. There were clay seals, some bearing the name of Tut·ankh·Amen and others the impression of the royal necropolis seal, fragments of magnificent painted pottery vases, linen head-shawls—one inscribed with the latest known date of Tut·ankh·Amen's reign—floral collars, of the kind represented as worn by mourners in burial scenes, and a mass of other miscellaneous objects; the whole representing, apparently, the material which had been used during the funeral ceremonies of Tut·ankh·Amen, and afterwards gathered together and stacked away within the jars.

We had thus three distinct pieces of evidence—the faïence cup found beneath the rock, the gold foil from the small pit-tomb, and this important cache of funerary material—which seemed definitely to connect Tut·ankh·Amen with this particular part of The Valley. To these must be added a fourth. It was in the near vicinity of these other finds that Mr. Davis had discovered the famous Akh·en·Aten cache. This contained the funerary remains of heretic royalties, brought hurriedly from Tell el Amarna and hidden here for safety, and that it was Tut·ankh·Amen himself who was responsible for their removal and reburial we can be reasonably sure from the fact that a number of his clay seals were found.

With all this evidence before us we were thoroughly convinced in our minds that the tomb of Tut-ankh-Amen was still to find, and that it ought to be situated not far from the centre of The Valley. In any case, whether we found Tut-ankh-Amen or not, we felt that a systematic and exhaustive search of the inner Valley presented reasonable chances of success, and we were in the act of completing our plans for an elaborate campaign in the season of 1914–15 when war broke out, and for the time being all the plans had to be left in abeyance.

War-work claimed most of my time for the next few years, but there were occasional intervals in which I was able to carry out small pieces of excavation. In February 1915, for example, I made a complete clearance of the interior of the tomb of Amen-hetep III, partially excavated in 1799 by M. Devilliers, one of the members of Napoleon's "Commission d'Égypte," and re-excavated later by Mr. Theodore Davis. In the course of this work we made the interesting discovery, from the evidence of intact foundation-deposits outside the entrance, and from other material found within the tomb, that it had been originally designed by Thothmes IV, and that Queen Tyi had actually been buried there. . . .

In the autumn of 1917 our real campaign in The Valley opened. The difficulty was to know where to begin, for mountains of rubbish thrown out by previous excavators encumbered the ground in all directions, and no sort of record had ever been kept as to which areas had been properly excavated and which had not. Clearly the only satisfactory thing to do was to dig systematically right down to bedrock, and I suggested to Lord Carnarvon that we take as a starting-point the triangle of ground defined by the tombs of Rameses II, Mer-en-Ptah, and Rameses VI, the area in which we hoped the tomb of Tut-ankh-Amen might be situated.

It was rather a desperate undertaking, the site being piled high with enormous heaps of thrown-out rubbish, but I had reason to believe that the ground beneath had never been touched, and a strong conviction that we should find a tomb there. In the course of the season's work we cleared a considerable part of the upper layers of this area, and advanced our excavations right up to the foot of the tomb of Rameses VI. Here we came on a series of workmen's huts, built over masses of flint boulders, the latter usually indicating in The Valley the near proximity of a tomb. Our natural impulse was to enlarge our clearing in this direction, but by doing this we should have cut off all access to the tomb of Rameses above, to visitors one of the most popular tombs in the whole Valley. We determined to await a more convenient opportunity. So far the only results from our work were some *ostraca*, interesting but not exciting.

We resumed our work in this region in the season of 1919–20. Our first need was to break fresh ground for a dump, and in the course of this preliminary work we lighted on some small deposits of Rameses IV, near the entrance to his tomb. The idea this year was to clear the whole of the remaining part of the triangle already mentioned, so we started in with a fairly large gang of workmen. By the time Lord and Lady Carnarvon arrived in March the whole of the top debris had been removed, and we were ready to clear down into what we believed to be virgin ground below. We soon had proof that we were right, for we presently came upon a small cache containing thirteen alabaster jars, bearing the names of Rameses II and Mer·en·Ptah, probably from the tomb of the latter. As this was the nearest approach to a real find that we had yet made in The Valley, we were naturally somewhat excited, and Lady Carnarvon, I remember, insisted on digging out these jars—beautiful specimens they were —with her own hands.

With the exception of the ground covered by the workmen's huts, we had now exhausted the whole of our triangular area, and had found no tomb. I was still hopeful, but we decided to leave this particular section until, by making a very early start in the autumn, we could accomplish it without causing inconvenience to visitors.

For our next attempt we selected the small lateral valley in which the tomb of Thothmes III was situated. This occupied us throughout the whole of the two following seasons, and, though

nothing intrinsically valuable was found, we discovered an interesting archaeological fact. The actual tomb in which Thothmes
III was buried had been found by Loret in 1898, hidden in a
cleft in an inaccessible spot some way up the face of the cliff.
Excavating in the valley below, we came upon the beginning of
a tomb, by its foundation-deposits originally intended for the
same king. Presumably, while the work on this low-level tomb
was in progress, it occurred to Thothmes or to his architect that
the cleft in the rock above was a better site. It certainly presented better chances of concealment, if that were the reason for
the change; though probably the more plausible explanation
would be that one of the torrential downpours of rain which visit
Luxor occasionally may have flooded out the lower tomb, and
suggested to Thothmes that his mummy would have a more comfortable resting-place on a higher level.

Near by, at the entrance to another abandoned tomb, we came
upon foundation-deposits of his wife Meryt·Re·Hat·shep·sût,
sister of the great queen of that name. Whether we are to infer
that she was buried there is a moot point, for it would be contrary to all custom to find a queen in The Valley. In any case
the tomb was afterwards appropriated by the Theban official
Sen·nefer.

We had now dug in The Valley for several seasons with extremely scanty results, and it became a much debated question
whether we should continue the work, or try for a more profitable site elsewhere. After these barren years were we justified in
going on with it? My own feeling was that so long as a single
area of untouched ground remained the risk was worth taking.
It is true that you may find less in more time in The Valley than
in any other site in Egypt, but, on the other hand, if a lucky
strike be made, you will be repaid for years and years of dull
and unprofitable work.

There was still, moreover, the combination of flint boulders
and workmen's huts at the foot of the tomb of Rameses VI to be
investigated, and I had always had a kind of superstitious feeling
that in that particular corner of The Valley one of the missing
kings, possibly Tut·ankh·Amen, might be found. Certainly the
stratification of the debris there should indicate a tomb. Eventu-

ally we decided to devote a final season to The Valley, and, by making an early start, to cut off access to the tomb of Rameses VI, if that should prove necessary, at a time when it would cause the least inconvenience to visitors. . . .

The history of The Valley . . . has never lacked the dramatic element, and in this, the latest episode, it has held to its traditions. For consider the circumstances. This was to be our final season in The Valley. Six full seasons we had excavated there, and season after season had drawn a blank; we had worked for months at a stretch and found nothing, and only an excavator knows how desperately depressing that can be; we had almost made up our mind that we were beaten, and were preparing to leave The Valley and try our luck elsewhere; and then—hardly had we set hoe to the ground in our last despairing effort than we made a discovery that far exceeded our wildest dreams. Surely, never before in the whole history of excavation had a full digging season been compressed within the space of five days.

Let me try and tell the story of it all. It will not be easy, for the dramatic suddenness of the initial discovery left me in a dazed condition, and the months that have followed have been so crowded with incident that I have hardly had time to think. Setting it down on paper will perhaps give me a chance to realise what has happened and all that it means.

I arrived in Luxor on October 28th [1922], and by November 1st I had enrolled my workmen and was ready to begin. Our former excavations had stopped short at the north-east corner of the tomb of Rameses VI, and from this point I started trenching southwards. It will be remembered that in this area there were a number of roughly constructed workmen's huts, used probably by the labourers in the tomb of Rameses. These huts, built about three feet above bed-rock, covered the whole area in front of the Ramesside tomb, and continued in a southerly direction to join up with a similar group of huts on the opposite side of The Valley, discovered by Davis in connexion with his work on the Akh·en·Aten cache. By the evening of November 3rd we had laid bare a sufficient number of these huts for experimental purposes, so, after we had planned and noted them, they were removed, and we were ready to clear away the three feet of soil that lay beneath them.

Hardly had I arrived on the work next morning (November 4th) than the unusual silence, due to the stoppage of the work, made me realise that something out of the ordinary had happened, and I was greeted by the announcement that a step cut in the rock had been discovered underneath the very first hut to be attacked. This seemed too good to be true, but a short amount of extra clearing revealed the fact that we were actually in the entrance of a steep cut in the rock, some thirteen feet below the entrance to the tomb of Rameses VI, and a similar depth from the present bed level of The Valley. The manner of cutting was that of the sunken stairway entrance so common in The Valley, and I almost dared to hope that we had found our tomb at last. Work continued feverishly throughout the whole of that day and the morning of the next, but it was not until the afternoon of November 5th that we succeeded in clearing away the masses of rubbish that overlay the cut, and were able to demarcate the upper edges of the stairway on all its four sides.

It was clear by now beyond any question that we actually had before us the entrance to a tomb, but doubts, born of previous disappointments, persisted in creeping in. There was always the horrible possibility, suggested by our experience in the Thothmes III Valley, that the tomb was an unfinished one, never completed and never used: if it had been finished there was the depressing probability that it had been completely plundered in ancient times. On the other hand, there was just the chance of an untouched or only partially plundered tomb, and it was with ill-suppressed excitement that I watched the descending steps of the staircase, as one by one they came to light. The cutting was excavated in the side of a small hillock, and, as the work progressed, its western edge receded under the slope of the rock until it was, first partially, and then completely, roofed in, and became a passage, 10 feet high by 6 feet wide. Work progressed more rapidly now; step succeeded step, and at the level of the twelfth, towards sunset, there was disclosed the upper part of a doorway, blocked, plastered, and sealed.

A sealed doorway—it was actually true, then! Our years of

patient labour were to be rewarded after all, and I think my first feeling was one of congratulation that my faith in The Valley had not been unjustified. With excitement growing to fever heat I searched the seal impressions on the door for evidence of the identity of the owner, but could find no name: the only decipherable ones were those of the well-known royal necropolis seal, the jackal and nine captives. Two facts, however, were clear: first, the employment of this royal seal was certain evidence that the tomb had been constructed for a person of very high standing; and second, that the sealed door was entirely screened from above by workmen's huts of the Twentieth Dynasty was sufficiently clear proof that at least from that date it had never been entered. With that for the moment I had to be content.

While examining the seals I noticed, at the top of the doorway, where some of the plaster had fallen away, a heavy wooden lintel. Under this, to assure myself of the method by which the doorway had been blocked, I made a small peephole, just large enough to insert an electric torch, and discovered that the passage beyond the door was filled completely from floor to ceiling with stones and rubble—additional proof this of the care with which the tomb had been protected.

It was a thrilling moment for an excavator. Alone, save for my native workmen, I found myself, after years of comparatively unproductive labour, on the threshold of what might prove to be a magnificent discovery. Anything, literally anything, might lie beyond that passage, and it needed all my self-control to keep from breaking down the doorway, and investigating then and there.

One thing puzzled me, and that was the smallness of the opening in comparison with the ordinary Valley tombs. The design was certainly of the Eighteenth Dynasty. Could it be the tomb of a noble buried here by royal consent? Was it a royal cache, a hiding-place to which a mummy and its equipment had been removed for safety? Or was it actually the tomb of the king for whom I had spent so many years in search?

Once more I examined the seal impressions for a clue, but on the part of the door so far laid bare only those of the royal necropolis seal already mentioned were clear enough to read. Had I but known that a few inches lower down there was a perfectly clear and distinct impression of the seal of Tut·ankh·Amen, the king I most desired to find, I would have cleared on, had a much better night's rest in consequence, and saved myself nearly three weeks of uncertainty. It was late, however, and darkness was already upon us. With some reluctance I re-closed the small hole that I had made, filled in our excavation for protection during the night, selected the most trustworthy of my workmen— themselves almost as excited as I was—to watch all night above the tomb, and so home by moonlight, riding down The Valley.

Naturally my wish was to go straight ahead with our clearing to find out the full extent of the discovery, but Lord Carnarvon was in England, and in fairness to him I had to delay matters until he could come. Accordingly, on the morning of November 6th I sent him the following cable:—"At last have made wonderful discovery in Valley; a magnificent tomb with seals intact; recovered same for your arrival; congratulations."

My next task was to secure the doorway against interference until such time as it could finally be reopened. This we did by filling our excavation up again to surface level, and rolling on top of it the large flint boulders of which the workmen's huts had been composed. By the evening of the same day, exactly forty-eight hours after we had discovered the first step of the staircase, this was accomplished. The tomb had vanished. So far as the appearance of the ground was concerned there never had been any tomb, and I found it hard to persuade myself at times that the whole episode had not been a dream.

I was soon to be reassured on this point. News travels fast in Egypt, and within two days of the discovery congratulations, inquiries, and offers of help descended upon me in a steady stream from all directions. It became clear, even at this early stage, that I was in for a job that could not be tackled single-handed, so I wired to Callender, who had helped me on previous occasions, asking him if possible to join me without delay, and to my relief he arrived on the very next day. On the 8th I had received two messages from Lord Carnarvon in answer to my cable, the first of which read, "Possibly come soon," and the second, received a little later, "Propose arrive Alexandria 20th."

We had thus nearly a fortnight's grace, and we devoted it to making preparations of various kinds, so that when the time of re-opening came, we should be able, with the least possible delay, to handle any situation that might arise. On the night of the 18th I went to Cairo for three days, to meet Lord Carnarvon and make a number of necessary purchases, returning to Luxor on the 21st. On the 23rd Lord Carnarvon arrived in Luxor with his daughter, Lady Evelyn Herbert, his devoted companion in all his Egyptian work, and everything was in hand for the beginning of the second chapter of the discovery of the tomb. Callender had been busy all day clearing away the upper layer of rubbish, so that by morning we should be able to get into the staircase without any delay.

By the afternoon of the 24th the whole staircase was clear, sixteen steps in all, and we were able to make a proper examination of the sealed doorway. On the lower part the seal impressions were much clearer, and we were able without any difficulty to make out on several of them the name of Tut·ankh·Amen. This added enormously to the interest of the discovery. If we had found, as seemed almost certain, the tomb of that shadowy monarch, whose tenure of the throne coincided with one of the most interesting periods in the whole of Egyptian history, we should indeed have reason to congratulate ourselves.

With heightened interest, if that were possible, we renewed our investigation of the doorway. Here for the first time a disquieting element made its appearance. Now that the whole door was exposed to light it was possible to discern a fact that had hitherto escaped notice—that there had been two successive openings and re-closings of a part of its surface: furthermore, that the sealing originally discovered, the jackal and nine captives, had been applied to the reclosed portions, whereas the sealings of Tut·ankh·Amen covered the untouched part of the doorway, and were therefore those with which the tomb had been originally secured. The tomb then was not absolutely intact, as we had hoped. Plunderers had entered it, and entered it more than once—from the evidence of the huts above, plunderers of a date not later than the reign of Rameses VI—but that they had not rifled it completely was evident from the fact that it had been resealed. (From later evidence we found that this re-sealing could not have taken place later than the reign of Hor·em·neb, i.e., from ten to fifteen years after the burial.)

Then came another puzzle. In the lower strata of rubbish that filled the staircase we found masses of broken potsherd and boxes, the latter bearing the names of Akh·en·Aten, Smenkh·ka·Re and Tut·ankh·Amen, and, what was much more upsetting, a scarab of Thothmes III and a fragment with the name of Amen·hetep III. Why this mixture of names? The balance of evidence so far would seem to indicate a cache rather than tomb, and at this stage in the proceedings we inclined more and more to the opinion that we were about to find a miscellaneous collection of objects of the Eighteenth Dynasty Kings, brought from Tell el Amarna by Tut·ankh·Amen and deposited here for safety.

So matters stood on the evening of the 24th. On the following day the sealed doorway was to be removed, so Callender set carpenters to work making a heavy wooden grille to be set up in its place. Mr. Engelbach, Chief Inspector of the Antiquities Department, paid us a visit during the afternoon, and witnessed part of the final clearing of rubbish from the doorway.

On the morning of the 25th the seal impressions on the doorway were carefully noted and photographed, and then we removed the actual blocking of the door, consisting of rough stones carefully built from floor to lintel, and heavily plastered on their outer faces to take the seal impressions.

This disclosed the beginning of a descending passage (not a staircase), the same width as the entrance stairway, and nearly seven feet high. As I had already discovered from my hole in the doorway, it was filled completely with stone and rubble, probably the chip from its own excavation. This filling, like the doorway, showed distinct signs of more than one opening and re-closing of the tomb, the untouched part consisting of clean white chip, mingled with dust, whereas the disturbed part was composed mainly of dark flint. It was clear that an irregular tunnel had been cut through the original filling at the upper corner on the left side, a tunnel corresponding in position with that of the hole in the doorway.

As we cleared the passage we found, mixed with the rubble of the lower levels, broken potsherds, jar sealings, alabaster jars, whole and broken, vases of painted pottery, numerous fragments of smaller articles, and water skins, these last having obviously been used to bring up the water needed for the plastering of the doorways. These were clear evidence of plundering, and we eyed them askance. By night we had cleared a considerable distance down the passage, but as yet saw no sign of second doorway or of chamber.

The day following (November 26th) was the day of days, the most wonderful that I have ever lived through, and certainly one whose like I can never hope to see again. Throughout the morning the work of clearing continued, slowly perforce, on account of the delicate objects that were mixed with the filling. Then, in the middle of the afternoon, thirty feet down from the outer door, we came upon a second sealed doorway, almost an exact replica of the first. The seal impressions in this case were less distinct, but still recognisable as those of Tut·ankh·Amen and of the royal necropolis. Here again the signs of opening and re-closing were clearly marked upon the plaster. We were firmly convinced by this time that it was a cache that we were about to open, and not a tomb. The arrangement of the stairway, entrance passage and doors reminded us very forcibly of the cache of Akh·en·Aten and Tyi found in the very near vicinity of the present excavation by Davis, and the fact that Tut·ankh·Amen's seals occurred there likewise seemed almost certain proof that we were right in our conjecture. We were soon to know. There lay the sealed doorway, and behind it was the answer to the question.

Slowly, desperately slowly it seemed to us as we watched, the remains of passage debris that encumbered the lower part of the doorway were removed, until at last we had the whole door clear before us. The decisive moment had arrived. With trembling hands I made a tiny breach in the upper left hand corner. Darkness and blank space, as far as an iron testing-rod could reach, showed that whatever lay beyond was empty, and not filled like the passage we had just cleared. Candle tests were applied as a precaution against possible foul gases, and then, widening the hole a little, I inserted the candle and peered in, Lord Carnarvon, Lady Evelyn and Callender standing anxiously beside me to hear the verdict. At first I could see nothing, the hot air escaping from the chamber causing the candle flame to flicker, but presently, as my eyes grew accustomed to the light, details of the room within emerged slowly from the mist, strange animals, statues, and gold—everywhere the glint of gold. For the moment—an eternity it must have seemed to the others standing by—I was struck dumb with amazement, and when Lord Carnarvon, unable to stand the suspense any longer, inquired anxiously, "Can you see anything?" it was all I could do to get out the words, "Yes, wonderful things." Then widening the whole a little further, so that we both could see, we inserted an electric torch.

I suppose most excavators would confess to a feeling of awe—embarrassment almost—when they break into a chamber closed and sealed by pious hands so many centuries ago. For the moment, time as a factor in human life has lost its meaning. Three thousand, four thousand years maybe, have passed and gone since human feet last trod the floor on which you stand, and yet, as you note the signs of recent life around you—the half-filled bowl of mortar for the door, the blackened lamp, the finger-mark upon the freshly painted surface, the farewell garland dropped upon the threshold—you feel it might have been yesterday. The very air you breathe, unchanged throughout the centuries, you share with those who laid the mummy to its rest. Time is annihilated by little intimate details such as these, and you feel an intruder.

That is perhaps the first and dominant sensation, but others follow thick and fast—the exhilaration of discovery, the fever of suspense, the almost overmastering impulse, born of curiosity, to break down seals and lift the lids of boxes, the thought—pure joy to the investigator—that you are about to add a page to history, or solve some problem of research, the strained expectancy—why not confess it?—of the treasure-seeker. Did these thoughts actually pass through our minds at the time, or have I imagined them since? I cannot tell. It was the discovery that my memory was blank, and not the mere desire for dramatic chapter-ending, that occasioned this digression.

Surely never before in the whole history of excavation had such an amazing sight been seen as the light of our torch revealed to us. . . . imagine how they appeared to us as we looked down upon them from our spy-hole in the blocked doorway, casting the beam of light from our torch—the first light that had pierced the darkness of the chamber for three thousand years—from one group of objects to another, in a vain attempt to interpret the treasure that lay before us. The effect was bewildering, overwhelming. I suppose we had never formulated exactly in our minds just what we had expected or hope to see, but certainly we had never dreamed of anything like this, a roomful—a whole museumful it seemed—of objects, some familiar, but some the like of which we had never seen, piled one upon another in seemingly endless profusion.

Gradually the scene grew clearer, and we could pick out individual objects. First, right opposite to us—we had been conscious of them all the while, but refused to believe in them—were three great gilt couches, their sides carved in the form of monstrous animals, curiously attenuated in body, as they had to be to serve their purpose, but with heads of startling realism. Uncanny beasts enough to look upon at any time: seen as we saw them, their brilliant gilded surfaces picked out of the darkness by our electric torch, as though by limelight, their heads throwing grotesque distorted shadows on the wall behind them, they were almost terrifying. Next, on the right, two statues caught and held our attention; two life-sized figures of a king in black, facing each other like sentinels, gold kilted, gold sandalled, armed with mace and staff, the protective sacred cobra upon their foreheads.

These were the dominant objects that caught the eye first. Between them, around them, piled on top of them, there were countless others—exquisitely painted and inlaid caskets; alabaster vases, some beautifully carved in openwork designs; strange black shrines, from the open door of one a great gilt snake peeping out; bouquets of flowers or leaves; beds; chairs beautifully carved; a golden inlaid throne; a heap of curious white oviform boxes; staves of all shapes and designs; beneath our eyes, on the very threshold of the chamber, a beautiful lotiform cup of translucent alabaster; on the left a confused pile of overturned chariots, glistening with gold and inlay; and peeping from behind them another portrait of a king.

Such were some of the objects that lay before us. Whether we noted them all at the time I cannot say for certain, as our minds were in much too excited and confused a state to register accurately. Presently it dawned upon our bewildered brains that in all this medley of objects before us there was no coffin or trace of mummy, and the much-debated question of tomb or cache began to intrigue us afresh. With this question in view we re-examined the scene before us, and noticed for the first time that between the two black sentinel statues on the right there was another sealed doorway. The explanation gradually dawned upon us. We were but on the threshold of our discovery. What we saw was merely an antechamber. Behind the guarded door there were to be other chambers, possibly a succession of them, and in one of them, beyond any shadow of a doubt, in all his magnificent panoply of death, we should find the Pharaoh lying.

We had seen enough, and our brains began to reel at the thought of the task in front of us. We reclosed the hole, locked the wooden grille that had been placed upon the first doorway, left our native staff on guard, mounted our donkeys and rode home down The Valley, strangely silent and subdued. . . .

Mesopotamia

8. AUSTEN LAYARD

The memory of Nineveh, capital of the ruthless and boastful warrior race of the Assyrians, had grown dim since the mighty city had fallen. There were vivid reminders of it in the words of the Hebrew prophets exulting in the just punishment of the Assyrian scourge. But like the rest of Mesopotamia—with its many Biblical associations from Abraham or Ur and the Tower of Babel to the Babylonian Captivity—the existence of the splendid metropolis had been veiled by the mist of intervening millenniums. The great land of the two rivers, fallen into utter decline since the Mongol invasions and for centuries under Turks, showed none of its past glories as Egypt did. After the passing of many races and conquerors, the colorful magnificence of Mesopotamia was obliterated by history itself. Scattered over the parched and monotonous alluvial landscape there were a few mounds that little more than legend connected with such evocative names as Babylon, Ur, and Nineveh.

Only two hundred years after its destruction, which took place in 612 B.C., Xenophon, as he passed with his Ten Thousand, thought the ruins of Nineveh were those of a vanished Parthian city. Lucian, the Greco-Syrian satirist, speaking of Nineveh, says: "It is so completely destroyed that it is no longer possible to see where it stood. Not a single trace of it remains." The Danish scholar Karsten Niebuhr crossed the site in the 1760s, taking it for natural hills until the natives told him differently. However, local traditions die slowly. Medieval Arab and Jewish travelers, visiting Mosul near the junction of the Tigris and Khosar rivers, correctly identified the two hills of Kuyunjik and Nebi Yunus across the Tigris on its eastern bank with Nineveh; so did Leonhart Rauwolff in the sixteenth century. Slowly the conviction grew that the commanding mounds found all over Mesopotamia covered splendid palaces and monuments. From time to time natives quarrying them for building material hit upon strange statuary. Largely fired by their never-ending search for the Tower of Babel, visitors like Piero della Valle and the Abbé de Beauchamp carried away odd "inscribed bricks" that were correctly identified by some scholars as writings, while other equally respected scholars considered them merely decorative patterns that resembled "bird tracks on wet sand."

Biblical interest may then be named the chief stimulus to the rise of archaeology in the Tigris-Euphrates valley, where, without the fanfare of a Napoleonic expedition or the inspiration of such spectacular remains as the pyramids, archaeological studies began almost as early as in Egypt. And subsequently the development of the science was closely paralleled in the two regions.

Investigation of the Mesopotamian past began with studies of its more recent civilizations. The Assyrians were studied first, and it is for that reason the whole science of Mesopotamian antiquities is still, quite inappropriately, referred to as Assyriology. The archaeologists then proceeded back to the Babylonians and to the hitherto unknown Sumerians. Finally, in our day, they have reached the subsoil of the "cradle of human civilization," the proto- and pre-Sumerian cultures of al 'Ubaid and Hassuna.

The man who laid the foundations of Assyrian archaeology was Claudius James Rich (1787–1820), one of a long line of immensely versatile English civil servants of the nineteenth century. As British resident in Baghdad since 1808, he investigated the sites of Babylon and Nineveh, drew up a plan of the latter's ruins, and incorporated his observations in widely-read memoirs. Rich probably carried out some minor excavations. He collected a few tablets and cylinders, which, after his early death from cholera at Shiraz, reached the British Museum.

After reading Rich's writings, Paul-Émile Botta came to Mosul as French vice-consul in 1842 determined to carry out research. The son of an Italian historian and trained as a naturalist, Botta had long felt the call of archaeological excavation. Following a hint by Rich he dug first at the Nebi Yunus mound, which was said to contain Jonah's tomb; but Moslem opposition drove him to Kuyunjik, where he encountered little of interest. Then, after receiving promising information from natives, in March 1843 he shifted his attention to Khorsabad, fourteen miles to the north. There, in virtually no time, he found sculptured reliefs, cuneiform tablets, and the walls of a vast Assyrian palace. This shining success led him to reject Rich's identification of Nineveh and claim that he had rediscovered it at his own northern site. What he had actually unearthed was the new capital built by Sargon II (721–705 B.C.) and called Dûr Sharrukin or "Sargonburg." Botta was a royalist, and, in 1848, when the republican regime came into power, he was removed to a minor post in North Africa. His archaeological career was ended. Meanwhile, his mantle had fallen upon a young Englishman of parts, Austen Henry Layard, who had become acquainted with Botta when visiting Mosul in 1842.

The ebullient Layard, an English traveler and diplomat of Huguenot descent, is one of the titans of nineteenth-century archaeology. Independent, unconventional, active, and resourceful even as a schoolboy, he found it impossible to settle down to a legal career and, on the death of his father, jumped at the offer of an uncle, a coffee planter in Ceylon, to join him. But Layard took his time to reach his destination; in fact, he never got there. Having always entertained "a passionate desire for exploring the East," he set forth by land in order to see as many Oriental places as he could and traveled by way of the Balkan countries and Constantinople. He was able to move with the greatest freedom because he was willing to forgo official sanction and protection and the amenities of "civilized" travel. A true love for local custom and the personal qualities of the people he visited helped him make friends, learn languages, and acquire a profound knowledge of the Orient. He was robbed on several occasions, held as a slave by Bedouins, and plagued with bouts of disease; but his zest did not diminish.

Layard, who was a gifted draftsman, made some sketches of Botta's finds at Khorsabad, sent them to London, and hinted that, if provided with sufficient funds, he could furnish the British with equally exciting objects. In 1845 he persuaded Stratford Canning, the British ambassador at Constantinople, to finance excavations at Nimrud some twenty miles south of Mosul. Later the British Museum made him grants, stipulating that Layard was to "obtain the greatest possible number of well-preserved objects of art at the least possible outlay of time and money." After two previous visits to the hills across the Tigris from Mosul, Layard, like Botta, abandoned the view that Nineveh had been there. Layard, however, came to believe that Nineveh had been at Nimrud, and in this he proved to be as mistaken as Botta had been about Khorsabad. But Nimrud, the ancient city of Calah, nevertheless satisfied Layard's expectations most lavishly. Almost at once he turned up treasures of all kinds that are still the mainstay of the Assyrian collection of the British Museum.

Layard's methods were, of course, typical of his day, and his reports, like those of other contemporary archaeologists, contain casual references to objects disintegrating on exposure to air. During his first excavation Layard seems to have paid no attention at all to cuneiform tablets, but his discoveries excited Victorian fancy and made him a celebrity, a recipient of academic titles and other honors. Most notable of his finds at Nimrud were the royal palace of Assurnasipal (884–859 B.C.) with its wonderful wall reliefs, the celebrated winged bulls with bearded "Semitic" heads of men (the Cherubs of the Bible), and the Black Obelisk of Shalmaneser III (859–824 B.C.). On the latter Shalmaneser is depicted with a prisoner at his feet. Rawlinson's deciphering in 1850 identified the prisoner as King Jehu. This, the only known portrait of an Israelite king, is invaluable corroborative evidence for a Biblical account of Assyro-Israelite relations.

In spite of Layard's diplomatic skill and amiability, during his operations he ran into considerable difficulty with the local governor, who planted gravestones at the excavation site in order to stop the work by claiming infidels were desecrating a Moslem cemetery. Nevertheless the antiquities Layard found at Nimrud were transported to Basra and shipped from there by way of India around the Cape to England. In Bombay, the cases were opened by curiosity seekers and local pundits delivered fanciful lectures on them. At last, they reached the British Museum and part of the collection was even exhibited at the Crystal Palace.

Layard's luck held out when he returned to Kuyunjik in 1849.

He discovered both the palace of Sennacherib and, having enlightened himself during his visit to England on the value of clay tablets, a great library from the Temple of Nebo. Apart from resuming excavations at Nimrud, he also dug briefly at Ashur (modern Sharqat), Babylon, and at Nippur in southern Mesopotamia. By 1851 he considered his Assyrian studies completed and returned to London to begin an entirely new career. He served repeatedly as Liberal Member of Parliament and was for some time undersecretary for foreign affairs and commissioner of works. In 1869 he was sent to Spain as ambassador and from 1877 to 1880 held the same post at the Porte, where he was of considerable assistance to a new generation of archaeologists engaged in excavation on Turkish territory. At sixty-three he retired to Italy to collect Venetian paintings.

The Huge Mounds of Assyria

AUSTEN LAYARD

DURING the autumn of 1839 and winter of 1840, I had been wandering through Asia Minor and Syria, scarcely leaving untrod one spot hallowed by tradition, or unvisited one ruin consecrated by history. I was accompanied by one no less curious and enthusiastic than myself. We were both equally careless of comfort and unmindful of danger. We rode alone; our arms were our only protection; a valise behind our saddles was our wardrobe, and we tended our own horses, except when relieved from the duty by the hospitable inhabitants of a Turcoman village or an Arab tent. Thus unembarrassed by needless luxuries, and uninfluenced by the opinions and prejudices of others, we mixed among the people, acquired without effort their manners, and enjoyed without alloy those emotions which scenes so novel, and spots so rich in varied association, can not fail to produce.

From Layard's *A Popular Account of Discoveries at Nineveh* (1851).

I look back with feelings of grateful delight to those happy days when, free and unheeded, we left at dawn the humble cottage or cheerful tent, and lingering as we listed, unconscious of distance and of the hour, found ourselves, as the sun went down, under some heavy ruin tenanted by the wandering Arab, or in some crumbling village still bearing a well-known name. No experienced dragoman measured for distances, and appointed our stations. We were honored with no conversations by pashaws, nor did we seek any civilities from governors. We neither drew tears nor curses from villagers by seizing their horses, or searching their houses for provisions: their welcome was sincere; their scanty fare was placed before us; we ate, and came, and went in peace.

I had traversed Asia Minor and Syria, visiting the ancient seats of civilization, and the spots which religion has made holy. I now felt an irresistible desire to penetrate to the regions beyond the Euphrates, to which history and tradition point as the birth-place of the wisdom of the West. Most travelers, after a journey through the usually frequented parts of the East, have the same longing to cross the great river, and to explore those lands which are separated on the map from the confines of Syria by a vast blank stretching from Aleppo to the banks of the Tigris. A deep mystery hangs over Assyria, Babylonia, and Chaldea. With these names are linked great nations and great cities dimly shadowed forth in history; mighty ruins, in the midst of deserts, defying, by their very desolation and lack of definite form, the description of the traveler; the remnants of mighty races still roving over the land; the fulfilling and fulfillment of prophecies; the plains to which the Jew and the Gentile alike look as the cradle of their race. After a journey in Syria, the thoughts naturally turn eastward; and without treading on the remains of Nineveh and Babylon our pilgrimage is incomplete.

I left Aleppo, with my companion, on the 18th of March. We still traveled as we had been accustomed—without guide or servants. The road across the desert is at all times impracticable, except to a numerous and well-armed caravan, and offers no object of interest. We preferred that through Bir and Orfa. From the latter city we traversed the low country at the foot of the

Kurdish hills, a country little known, and abounding in curious remains. The Egyptian frontier, at that time, extended to the east of Orfa, and the war between the sultan and Mohammed Ali Pasha being still unfinished, the tribes took advantage of the confusion, and were plundering on all sides. With our usual good fortune, we succeeded in reaching Nisibin unmolested, although we ran daily risks, and more than once found ourselves in the midst of foraging parties, and of tents which, an hour before, had been pillaged by the wandering bands of Arabs. We entered Mosul on the 10th of April.

During a short stay in this town, we visited the great ruins on the east bank of the river, which have been generally believed to be the remains of Nineveh. We rode also into the desert, and explored the mound of Kalah Sherghat, a vast ruin on the Tigris, about fifty miles below its junction with the Zab. As we journeyed thither, we rested for the night at the small Arab village of Hammun Ali, around which are still the vestiges of an ancient city. From the summit of an artificial eminence we looked down upon a broad plain, separated from us by the river. A line of lofty mounds bounded it to the east, and one of a pyramidical form rose high above the rest. Beyond it could be faintly traced the waters of the Zab. Its position rendered its identification easy. This was the pyramid which Xenophon had described, and near which the ten thousand had encamped: the ruins around it were those which the Greek general saw twenty-two centuries before, and which were even then the remains of an *ancient* city. Although Xenophon had confounded a name, spoken by a strange race, with one familiar to a Greek ear, and had called the place Larissa, tradition still points to the origin of the city, and, by attributing its foundation to Nimrod, whose name the ruins now bear, connect it with one of the first settlements of the human race.

Kalah Sherghat, like Nimroud, was an Assyrian ruin: a vast, shapeless mass, now covered with grass, and showing scarcely any traces of the work of man except where the winter rains had formed ravines down its almost perpendicular sides, and had thus laid open its contents. A few fragments of pottery and inscribed bricks, discovered after a careful search among the rubbish which had accumulated around the base of the great mound, served to prove that it owed its construction to the people who had founded the city of which Nimroud is the remains. There was a tradition current among the Arabs, that strange figures, carved in black stone, still existed among the ruins; but we searched for them in vain, during the greater part of a day in which we were engaged in exploring the heaps of earth and bricks covering a considerable extent of country on the right bank of the Tigris. At the time of our visit, the country had been abandoned by the Bedouins, and was only occasionally visited by a few plunderers from the Shammar or Aneyza tents. We passed the night in the jungle which clothes the banks of the river, and wandered during the day undisturbed by the tribes of the desert. A cawass, who had been sent with us by the Pashaw of Mosul, alarmed at the solitude, and dreading the hostile Arabs, left us in the wilderness, and turned homeward. But he fell into the danger he sought to avoid. Less fortunate than ourselves, at a short distance from Kalah Sherghat, he was met by a party of horsemen, and fell a victim to his timidity.

Were the traveler to cross the Euphrates to seek for such ruins in Mesopotamia and Chaldea as he had left behind him in Asia Minor or Syria, his search would be vain. The graceful column rising above the thick foliage of the myrtle, ilex, and oleander; the gradines of the amphitheater covering a gentle slope, and overlooking the dark blue waters of a lakelike bay; the richly-carved cornice or capital half hidden by luxuriant herbage,—are replaced by the stern, shapeless mound rising like a hill from the scorched plain, the fragments of pottery, and the stupendous mass of brick-work occasionally laid bare by the winter rains. He has left the land where nature is still lovely, where, in his mind's eye, he can rebuild the temple or the theater, half doubting whether they would have made a more grateful impression upon the senses than the ruin before him. He is now at a loss to give any form to the rude heaps upon which he is gazing. Those of whose works they are the remains, unlike the Roman and the Greeks, have left no visible traces of their civilization, or of their arts: their influence has long since passed away. The more the conjectures, the more vague the results appear. The scene around is worthy of the ruin he is contemplating; desolation meets desolation; a feeling of awe succeeds to wonder; for there is nothing to relieve the mind, to lead to hope, or to tell of what has gone by. These huge mounds of Assyria made a deeper impression upon me, gave rise to more serious thoughts, and more earnest reflection, than the temple of Balbec, and the theaters of Ionia. . . .

My first step on reaching Mosul was to present my letters to Mohammed Pashaw, the governor of the province. Being a native of Candia, he was usually known as Keritli Oglu (the son of the Cretan), to distinguish him from his celebrated predecessor of the same name. The appearance of his excellency was not prepossessing, but it matched his temper and conduct. Nature had placed hypocrisy beyond his reach. He had one eye and one ear; he was short and fat, deeply marked by the small-pox, uncouth in gestures and harsh in voice. His fame had reached the seat of his government before him. On the road he had revived many good old customs and impositions, which the reforming spirit of the age had suffered to fall into decay. He particularly insisted on *dish-parasi;* or a compensation in money, levied upon all villages in which a man of such rank is entertained, for the wear and tear of his teeth in masticating the food he condescends to receive from the inhabitants. On entering Mosul, he had induced several of the principal aghas, who had fled from the town on his approach, to return to their homes; and having made a formal display of oaths and protestations, cut their throats to show how much his word could be depended upon. At the time of my arrival, the population was in a state of terror and despair. Even the appearance of a casual traveler led to hopes, and reports were whispered about the town of the disgrace of the tyrant. Of this the pashaw was aware, and hit upon a plan to test the feelings of the people toward him. He was suddenly taken ill one afternoon, and was carried to his harem almost lifeless. On the following morning the palace was closed, and the attendants answered inquiries by mysterious motions, which could only be interpreted in one fashion. The doubts of the Mosuleeans gradually gave way to general rejoicings; but at mid-day his excellency, who had posted his spies all over the town, appeared in perfect

health in the market-place. A general trembling seized the inhabitants. His vengeance fell principally upon those who possessed
property, and had hitherto escaped his rapacity. They were
seized and stripped, on the plea that they had spread reports
detrimental to his authority.

The villages, and the Arab tribes, had not suffered less than
the townspeople. The pashaw was accustomed to give instructions to those who were sent to collect money, in three words—
"Go, destroy, eat"; and his agents were not generally backward
in entering into the spirit of them. The tribes, who had been attacked and plundered, were retaliating upon caravans and travelers, or laying waste the cultivated parts of the pashawlic. The
villages were deserted, and the roads were little frequented and
very insecure.

Such was the pashaw to whom I was introduced two days
after my arrival by the British vice-consul, Mr. Rassam. He read
the letter which I presented to him, and received me with that
civility which a traveler generally expects from a Turkish func-
tionary of high rank. His anxiety to know the object of my
journey was evident, but his curiosity was not gratified for the
moment.

Many reasons rendered it necessary that my plans should be
concealed, until I was ready to put them into execution. Although
I had always experienced from M. Botta the most friendly assistance, there were others who did not share his sentiments;
from the authorities and the people of the town I could only
expect the most decided opposition. On the 8th of November,
having secretly procured a few tools, I engaged a mason at the
moment of my departure, and carrying with me a variety of
guns, spears, and other formidable weapons, declared that I was
going to hunt wild boars in a neighboring village, and floated
down the Tigris on a small raft constructed for my journey. I was
accompanied by Mr. Ross (a British merchant of Mosul), my
cawass, and a servant.

At this time of the year nearly seven hours are required to
descend the Tigris, from Mosul to Nimroud. It was sunset before
we reached the awai, or dam across the river. We landed and
walked to the village of Naifa. No light appeared as we ap-

proached, nor were we even saluted by the dogs, which usually abound in an Arab village. We had entered a heap of ruins. I was about to return to the raft, upon which we had made up our minds to pass the night, when the glare of a fire lighted up the entrance to a miserable hovel. Through a crevice in the wall, I saw an Arab family crouching round a heap of half-extinguished embers. The dress of the man, the ample cloak and white turban, showed that he belonged to one of the tribes which cultivate a little land on the borders of the Desert, and are distinguished, by their more sedentary habits, from the Bedouins. Near him were three women, lean and haggard, their heads almost concealed in black handkerchiefs, and the rest of their persons enveloped in the striped aba. Some children, nearly naked, and one or two mangy greyhounds, completed the group. As we entered, all the party rose, and showed some alarm at this sudden appearance of strangers. The man, however, seeing Europeans, bid us welcome, and spreading some corn-sacks on the ground, invited us to be seated. The women and children retreated into a corner of the hut. Our host, whose name was Awad or Abd-Allah, was a sheikh of the Jehesh. His tribe having been plundered by the pashaw, and being now scattered in different parts of the country, he had taken refuge in this ruined village. He had learnt a little Turkish, and was intelligent and active. Seeing, at once, that he would be useful, I acquainted him with the object of my journey; offering him the prospect of regular employment in the event of the experiment proving successful, and assigning him fixed wages as superintendent of the workmen. He volunteered to walk, in the middle of the night, to Selamiyah, a village three miles distant, and to some Arab tents in the neighborhood, to procure men to assist in the excavations.

I had slept little during the night. The hovel in which we had taken shelter, and its inmates, did not invite slumber; but such scenes and companions were not new to me: they could have been forgotten, had my brain been less excited. Hopes, long cherished, were now to be realized, or were to end in disappointment. Visions of palaces under-ground, of gigantic monsters, of sculptured figures, and endless inscriptions, floated before me. After forming plan after plan for removing the earth, and extricating these treasures, I fancied myself wandering in a maze of chambers from which I could find no outlet. Then, again, all was reburied, and I was standing on the grass-covered mound. Exhausted, I was at length sinking into sleep, when hearing the voice of Awad, I rose from my carpet, and joined him outside the hovel. The day already dawned; he had returned with six Arabs, who agreed for a small sum to work under my direction.

The lofty cone and broad mound of Nimroud broke like a distant mountain on the morning sky. But how changed was the scene since my former visit! The ruins were no longer clothed with verdure and many-colored flowers; no signs of habitation, not even the black tent of the Arab, were seen upon the plain. The eye wandered over a parched and barren waste, across which occasionally swept the whirlwind, dragging with it a cloud of sand. About a mile from us was the small village of Nimroud, like Naifa, a heap of ruins.

Twenty minutes' walk brought us to the principal mound. The absence of all vegetation enabled me to examine the remains with which it was covered. Broken pottery and fragments of bricks, both inscribed with the cuneiform character, were strewed on all sides. The Arabs watched my motions as I wandered to and fro, and observed with surprise the objects I had collected. They joined, however, in the search, and brought me handfuls of rubbish, among which I found with joy the fragment of a bas-relief. The material on which it was carved had been exposed to fire, and resembled, in every respect, the burnt gypsum of Khorsabad. Convinced from this discovery, that sculptured remains must still exist in some part of the mound, I sought for a place where excavations might be commenced with a prospect of success. Awad led me to a piece of alabaster which appeared above the soil. We could not remove it, and on digging downward, it proved to be the upper part of a large slab. I ordered all the men to work around it, and they shortly uncovered a second slab. Continuing in the same line, we came upon a third; and, in the course of the morning, discovered ten more, the whole forming a square, with a slab missing at one corner. It was evident that we had entered a chamber, and that the gap was its entrance. I now dug down the face of one of the stones, and an inscription in the cuneiform character was soon exposed to view. Similar inscriptions occupied the center of all the slabs, which were in the best preservation; but plain, with the exception of the writing. Leaving half the workmen to remove the rubbish from the chamber, I led the rest to the S. W. corner of the mound, where I had observed many fragments of calcined alabaster.

A trench, opened in the side of the mound, brought me almost immediately to a wall, bearing inscriptions in the same character as those already described. The slabs, which had been almost reduced to lime by exposure to intense heat, threatened to fall to pieces as soon as uncovered.

Night interrupted our labors. I returned to the village well satisfied with their result. It was now evident that the remains of buildings of considerable extent existed in the mound; and that although some had been injured by fire, others had escaped the conflagration. As inscriptions, and the fragment of a basrelief had been found, it was natural to conclude that sculptures were still buried under the soil. I determined, therefore, to explore the N. W. corner, and to empty the chamber partly uncovered during the day.

On returning to the village, I removed from the crowded hovel in which we had passed the night. With the assistance of Awad, who was no less pleased than myself with our success, we patched up with mud the least ruined house in the village, and restored its falling roof. We contrived at least to exclude, in some measure, the cold night winds; and to obtain a little privacy for my companion and myself.

Next morning my workmen were increased by five Turcomans from Selamiyah who had been attracted by the prospect of regular wages. I employed half of them in emptying the chamber, and the rest in following the wall at the S. W. corner of the mound. Before evening, the work of the first party was completed, and I found myself in a room paneled with slabs about eight feet high, and varying from six to four feet in breadth. Upon one of them, which had fallen backward from its place, was rudely inscribed, in Arabic characters, the name of Ahmed Pashaw, one of the former hereditary governors of Mosul. A na-

tive of Selamiyah remembered that some Christians were employed to dig into the mound about thirty years before, in search
of stone for the repair of the tomb of Sultan Abd-Allah, a Mus-
sulman saint, buried on the left bank of the Tigris, a few miles
below its junction with the Zab. They uncovered this slab; but
being unable to move it, they cut upon it the name of their employer, the pashaw. My informant further stated that, in another
part of the mound, he had forgotten the precise spot, they had
found sculptured figures, which they broke in pieces to carry
away the fragments.

The bottom of the chamber was paved with smaller slabs than
those which lined the walls. They were covered with inscriptions
on both sides, and had been placed upon a layer of bitumen,
which, having been used in a liquid state, had retained a perfect
impression in relief of the characters carved upon the stone. The
inscriptions on the upright slabs were about twenty lines in
length, and all were precisely similar.

In the rubbish near the bottom of the chamber, I found several objects in ivory, upon which were traces of gilding; among
them were the figure of a king carrying in one hand the Egyptian crux ansata, or emblem of life, part of a crouching sphinx,
and an elegant ornamental border of flowers. Awad, who had his
own suspicions of the object of my search, which he could
scarcely persuade himself was limited to mere stones, carefully
collected all the scattered fragments of gold leaf he could find
in the rubbish; and, calling me aside in a mysterious and con-
fidential fashion, produced them wrapped up in a piece of dingy
paper. "O bey," said he, "Wallah! your books are right, and the
Franks know that which is hid from the true believer. Here is
the gold, sure enough, and please God, we shall find it all in a
few days. Only don't say any thing about it to those Arabs, for
they are asses and can not hold their tongues. The matter will
come to the ears of the pashaw." The sheikh was much surprised,
and equally disappointed, when I generously presented him with
the treasures he had collected, and all such as he might here-
after discover. He left me, muttering "Yia Rubbi!" and other
pious ejaculations, and lost in conjectures as to the meaning of
these strange proceedings.

At the foot of the slabs in the S. W. corner, we found a great accumulation of charcoal, proving that the building of which they had formed part had been destroyed by fire. I dug also in several directions in this part of the mound, and in many places came upon the calcined remains of walls.

On the third day, I opened a trench in the high conical mound, but found only fragments of inscribed bricks. I also dug at the back of the north side of the chamber first explored, in the expectation of coming upon other walls beyond, but unsuccessfully. As my chief aim was to ascertain the existence, as soon as possible, of sculptures, all my workmen were moved to the S. W. corner, where the many remains of walls already discovered evidently belonging to the same edifice, promised speedier success. I continued the excavations in this part of the mound until the 13th, still finding inscriptions, but no sculptures. . . .

It was nearly the middle of February before I thought it prudent to make fresh experiments among the ruins. To avoid notice I employed only a few men, and confined myself to the examination of such parts of the mound as appeared to contain buildings. My first attempt was in the S. W. corner, where a new wall was speedily discovered, all the slabs of which were sculptured, and uninjured by fire, though they had, unfortunately, been half destroyed by long exposure to the atmosphere. On three consecutive slabs was one bas-relief; on others were only parts of a subject. It was evident from the costume, the ornaments, and the general treatment, that these sculptures did not belong either to the same building, or to the same period as those previously discovered. I recognized in them the style of Khorsabad, and in the inscriptions certain characters, which were peculiar to monuments of that age. The slabs, like those in other parts of the edifice, had been brought from elsewhere.

The most perfect of the bas-reliefs was, in many respects, interesting. It represented a king, distinguished by his high conical tiara, raising his extended right hand and resting his left upon a bow. At his feet crouched a warrior, probably a captive enemy or rebel, but more likely the latter as he wore the pointed helmet peculiar to the Assyrians. An eunuch held a fly-flapper or fan over the head of the king, who appeared to be conversing or performing some ceremony with an officer standing in front of him—probably his vizier or minister. Behind this personage, who differed from the king by his head-dress—a simple fillet confining the hair—were two attendants, the first an eunuch, the second a bearded figure. This bas-relief was separated from a second above, by an inscription; the upper sculpture had been almost totally destroyed, and I could with difficulty trace a wounded figure, wearing a helmet with a curved crest, resembling the Greek, and horsemen engaged in battle. Both subjects were continued on the adjoining slabs, but they were broken off near the bottom, and the feet of a row of figures, probably other attendants, standing behind the king and his minister, could alone be distinguished.

On the same wall, which had completely disappeared in some places, could be traced a group resembling that just described, and several colossal winged figures in low relief.

Several deep trenches led me to two new walls, the sculptures on which were not better preserved than those previously discovered in this part of the mound. Of the lower parts of several colossal figures, some had been purposely defaced by a sharp instrument, others, from long exposure, had been worn almost smooth.

These experiments were sufficient to prove that the building I was exploring had not been entirely destroyed by fire, but had been partly exposed to gradual decay. No sculptures had hitherto been discovered in a perfect state of preservation, and only one or two could bear removal. I determined, therefore, to abandon this corner, and to resume excavations in the north-west ruins near the chamber first opened, where the slabs were uninjured. The workmen were directed to dig behind the remains of the small lions, which appeared to have formed an entrance; and after removing much earth, they discovered a few unsculptured slabs, fallen from their places, and broken in many pieces. The walls of the room of which they had originally formed part could not be traced.

As this part of the building stood on the very edge of the mound, it had probably been more exposed, and had consequently sustained more injury, than any other. I determined, therefore, to open a trench more in the center of the edifice, and chose for the purpose a deep ravine, which, apparently worn by the winter rains, extended far into the ruins. In two days the workmen reached the top of an entire slab, standing in its original position. On one face of it I discovered, to my great satisfaction, two human figures, considerably above the natural size, in low relief, and in admirable preservation. In a few hours the earth and rubbish were completely removed from the sculpture. The ornaments delicately graven on the robes, the tassels and fringes, the bracelets and armlets, the elaborate curls of the hair and beard, were all entire. The figures were back to back, and from the shoulders of each sprang two wings. They appeared to represent divinities, presiding over the seasons, or over particular religious ceremonies. The one, whose face was turned to the east, carried a fallow deer on his right arm, and in his left hand a branch bearing five flowers. Around his temples was a fillet, adorned in front with a rosette. The other held a square vessel, or basket, in the left hand, and an object [a] rounded cap, ornamented at the lower part by a kind of horn curved upward in front. The garments of both, consisting of a stole falling from the shoulders to the ankles, and a short tunic underneath, descending to the knee, were richly and tastefully decorated with embroideries and fringes. Their hair fell in a profusion of ringlets on their shoulders, and their beards were elaborately arranged in alternate rows of curls. Although the relief was lower, yet the outline was perhaps more careful, and true, than that of the sculptures of Khorsabad. The limbs were delineated with peculiar accuracy, and the muscles and bones faithfully, though somewhat too strongly, marked. In the center of the slab, and crossing the figures, was an inscription.

Adjoining this slab, was a second, cut so as to form a corner, sculptured with an elegant device, in which curved branches, springing from a kind of scroll-work, terminated in flowers of graceful form. As one of the figures last described was turned, as if [in an] act of adoration, toward this device, it was evidently a sacred emblem; and I recognized in it the holy tree, or tree of life, so universally adored at the remotest periods in the East, and which was preserved in the religious systems of the Persians to the final overthrow of their empire by the Arabian conquerors. The flowers were formed by seven petals springing from two tendrils, or a double scroll; thus in all its details resembling that tasteful ornament of Ionic architecture known as the honeysuckle. The alternation of this flower with an object resembling a tulip in the embroideries on the garments of the two winged figures just described, and in other bas-reliefs subsequently discovered, establishes, beyond a doubt, the origin of one of the most favorite and elegant embellishments of Greek art. We are also reminded, by the peculiar arrangement of the intertwining branches, of the "network of pomegranates," which was one of the principal ornaments of the temple of Solomon. This sculpture and the two winged figures resembled in their style and details several of the fragments built into the S. W. palace, proving at once, from whence the greater part of the materials used in the construction of that building had been obtained.

Adjoining this corner-stone was a figure of singular form. A human body, clothed in robes similar to those of the winged men already described, was surmounted by the head of an eagle or of a vulture. The curved beak, of considerable length, was half open, and displayed a narrow pointed tongue, on which were still the remains of red paint. On the shoulders fell the usual curled and bushy hair of the Assyrian images, and a comb of feathers rose on the top of the head. Two wings sprang from the back, and in either hand was the square vessel and fir-cone. In a kind of girdle were three daggers, the handle of one being in the form of the head of a bull. They may have been of precious metal, but more probably of copper, inlaid with ivory or enamel, as a few days before a copper dagger-handle, precisely similar in form to one of those carried by this figure, hollowed to receive an ornament of some such material, had been discovered in the S.W. ruins, and is now preserved in the British Museum.

This effigy, which probably typified by its mythic form the union of certain divine attributes, may perhaps be identified with the god Nisroch, in whose temple Sennacherib was slain by his sons after his return from his unsuccessful expedition against

Jerusalem; the word Nisr signifying, in all Semitic languages, an eagle.

On all these figures were traces of color, particularly on the hair, beard, eyes, and sandals, and there can be no doubt that they had been originally painted. The slabs on which they were sculptured had sustained no injury, and they evidently formed part of a chamber, which could be completely explored by digging along the wall, now partly uncovered.

On the morning following these discoveries, I had ridden to the encampment of Sheikh Abd-ur-rahman, and was returning to the mound, when I saw two Arabs of his tribe urging their mares to the top of their speed. On approaching me they stopped. "Hasten, O Bey," exclaimed one of them—"hasten to the diggers, for they have found Nimrod himself. Wallah! it is wonderful, but it is true! we have seen him with our eyes. There is no God but God"; and both joining in this pious exclamation, they galloped off, without further words, in the direction of their tents.

On reaching the ruins I descended into the new trench, and found the workmen, who had already seen me, as I approached, standing near a heap of baskets and cloaks. While Awad advanced and asked for a present to celebrate the occasion, the Arabs withdrew the screen they had hastily constructed, and disclosed an enormous human head sculptured in full out of the alabaster of the country. They had uncovered the upper part of a figure, the remainder of which was still buried in the earth. I saw at once that the head must belong to a winged lion or bull, similar to those of Khorsabad and Persepolis. It was in admirable preservation. The expression was calm, yet majestic, and the outline of the features showed a freedom and knowledge of art, scarcely to be looked for in works of so remote a period. The cap had three horns, and, unlike that of the human-headed bulls hitherto found in Assyria, was rounded and without ornament at the top.

I was not surprised that the Arabs had been amazed and terrified at this apparition. It required no stretch of imagination to conjure up the most strange fancies. This gigantic head, blanched with age, thus rising from the bowels of the earth, might well have belonged to one of those fearful beings which are pictured in the traditions of the country, as appearing to mortals, slowly ascending from the regions below. One of the workmen, on catching the first glimpse of the monster, had thrown down his basket and had run off toward Mosul as fast as his legs could carry him. I learned this with regret, as I anticipated the consequences.

While I was superintending the removal of the earth, which still clung to the sculpture, and giving directions for the continuation of the work, a noise of horsemen was heard, and presently Abd-ur-rahman, followed by half his tribe, appeared on the edge of the trench. As soon as the two Arabs had reached the tents, and published the wonders they had seen, every one mounted his mare and rode to the mound to satisfy himself of the truth of these inconceivable reports. When they beheld the head they all cried together, "There is no God but God, and Mohammed is his Prophet!" It was some time before the sheikh could be prevailed upon to descend into the pit, and convince himself that the image he saw was of stone. "This is not the work of men's hands," exclaimed he, "but of those infidel giants of whom the Prophet, peace be with him! has said, that they were higher than the tallest date-tree; this is one of the idols which Noah, peace be with him! cursed before the flood." In this opinion, the result of a careful examination, all the by-standers concurred.

I now ordered a trench to be dug due south from the head in the expectation of finding a corresponding figure, and before night-fall reached the object of my search about twelve feet distant. Engaging two or three men to sleep near the sculptures, I returned to the village, and celebrated the day's discovery by a slaughter of sheep, of which all the Arabs near partook. As some wandering musicians chanced to be at Selamiyah, I sent for them, and dances were kept up during the greater part of the night. On the following morning Arabs from the other side of the Tigris, and the inhabitants of the surrounding villages, congregated on the mound. Even the women could not repress their curiosity, and came in crowds, with their children, from afar. My cawass was stationed during the day in the trench, into which I would not allow the multitude to descend.

As I had expected, the report of the discovery of the gigantic head, carried by the terrified Arab to Mosul, had thrown the town into commotion. He had scarcely checked his speed before reaching the bridge. Entering breathless into the bazars, he announced to every one he met that Nimrod had appeared. The news soon got to the ears of the cadi, who called the mufti and the ulema together, to consult upon this unexpected occurrence. Their deliberations ended in a procession to the governor, and a formal protest, on the part of the Mussulmans of the town, against proceedings so directly contrary to the laws of the Koran. The cadi had no distinct idea whether the bones of the mighty hunter had been uncovered, or only his image; nor did Ismail Pashaw very clearly remember whether Nimrod was a true-believing prophet, or an infidel. I consequently received a somewhat unintelligible message from his excellency, to the effect that the remains should be treated with respect, and be by no means further disturbed; that he wished the excavations to be stopped at once, and desired to confer with me on the subject.

I called upon him accordingly, and had some difficulty in making him understand the nature of my discovery. As he requested me to discontinue my operations until the sensation in the town had somewhat subsided, I returned to Nimroud and dismissed the workmen, retaining only two men to dig leisurely along the walls without giving cause for further interference. I ascertained by the end of March the existence of a second pair of winged human-headed lions, differing from those previously discovered in form, the human shape being continued to the waist, and being furnished with human arms, as well as with the legs of the lion. In one hand each figure carried a goat or stag, and in the other, which hung down by the side, a branch with three flowers. They formed a northern entrance into the chamber of which the lions previously described were the western portal. I completely uncovered the latter, and found them to be entire. They were about twelve feet in height, and the same number in length. The body and limbs were admirably portrayed; the muscles and bones, although strongly developed to display the strength of the animal, showed at the same time a correct knowledge of its anatomy and form. Expanded wings sprung from the shoulder and spread over the back; a knotted girdle, ending in tassels, encircled the loins. These sculptures, forming an entrance, were partly in full and partly in relief. The head and fore-part, facing the chamber, were in full; but only one side of the rest of the slab was sculptured, the back being placed against the wall of sun-dried bricks. That the spectator might have both a perfect front and side view of the figures, they were furnished with five legs; two were carved on the end of the slab to face the chamber, and three on the side. The relief of the body and limbs was high and bold, and the slab was covered, in all parts not occupied by the image, with inscriptions in the cuneiform character. The remains of color could still be traced in the eyes—the pupils being painted black, and the rest filled up with an opaque white pigment; but on no other parts of the sculpture. These magnificent specimens of Assyrian art were in perfect preservation, the most minute lines in the details of the wings and in the ornaments had been retained with their original freshness.

I used to contemplate for hours these mysterious emblems, and muse over their intent and history. What more noble forms could have ushered the people into the temple of their gods? What more sublime images could have been borrowed from nature, by men who sought, unaided by the light of revealed religion, to embody their conception of the wisdom, power, and ubiquity of a Supreme Being? They could find no better type of intellect and knowledge than the head of the man; of strength, than the body of the lion; of ubiquity, than the wings of the bird. Those winged human-headed lions were not idle creations, the offspring of mere fancy; their meaning was written upon them. They had awed and instructed races which flourished 3000 years ago. Through the portals which they guarded, kings, priests, and warriors had borne sacrifices to their altars, long before the wisdom of the East had penetrated to Greece, and had furnished its mythology with symbols recognized of old by the Assyrian votaries. They ·may have been buried, and their existence may have been unknown, before the foundation of the eternal city. For twenty-five centuries they had been hidden from the eye of man, and they now stood forth once more in their ancient majesty. But how changed was the scene around them! The luxury and civilization of a mighty nation had given place to the wretchedness and ignorance of a few half-barbarous tribes. The wealth of temples, and the riches of great cities, had been succeeded by ruins and shapeless heaps of earth. Above the spacious hall in which they stood, the plow had passed and the corn now waved. Egypt has monuments no less ancient and no less wonderful; but they have stood forth for ages to testify her early power and renown; while those before me had but now appeared to bear witness, in the words of the prophet, that once "the Assyrian was a cedar in Lebanon with fair branches and with a shadowing shroud of an high stature; and his top was among the thick boughs . . . his height was exalted above all the trees of the field, and his boughs were multiplied, and his branches became long, because of the multitude of waters when he shot forth. All the fowls of heaven made their nests in his boughs, and under his branches did all the beasts of the fields bring forth their young, and under his shadow dwelt all great nations"; for now is "Nineveh a desolation, and dry like a wilderness, and flocks lie down in the midst of her: all the beasts of the nations, both the cormorant and bittern, lodge in the upper lintels of it; their voice sings in the windows; and desolation is in the threshold."

The entrance formed by the human-headed lions led into a chamber round which were sculptured winged figures, such as I have already described. They were in pairs facing one another, and separated by a sacred tree. These bas-reliefs were inferior in execution, and finish, to those previously discovered.

During the month of March I received visits from the principal sheikhs of the Jebour Arabs, whose followers had now partly crossed the Tigris, and were pasturing their flocks in the neighborhood of Nimroud, or cultivating millet on the banks of the river. The Jebours are a branch of the ancient tribe of Obeid, and their pasture-grounds are on the banks of the Khabour, from its junction with the Euphrates,—from the ancient Carchemish or Circesium, to its source at Ras-el-Ain. Having been suddenly attacked and plundered a year or two before by the Aneyza, they had left their haunts, and taken refuge in the districts around Mosul. They were at this time divided into three branches obeying different sheikhs. The names of the three chiefs were Abd' rubbou, Mohammed-Emin, and Mohammed-ed-Dagher. Although all three visited me at Nimroud, it was the first with whom I was best acquainted, and who rendered me most assistance. I thought it necessary to give to each a few small presents, a silk dress, or an embroidered cloak, with a pair of capacious boots, as in case of any fresh disturbances in the country, it would be as well to be on friendly terms with the tribe.

The middle of March in Mesopotamia is the brightest epoch of spring. A new change had come over the face of the plain of Nimroud. Its pasture lands, known as the "Jaif," are renowned for their rich and luxuriant herbage. In times of quiet, the studs of the pashaw and of the Turkish authorities, with the horses of the cavalry and of the inhabitants of Mosul, are sent here to graze. Day by day they arrived in long lines. The Shemutti and Jehesh left their huts, and encamped on the greensward which surrounded the villages. The plain, as far as the eye could reach, was studded with the white pavilions of the hytas and the black tents of the Arabs. Picketed around them were innumerable horses in gay trappings, struggling to release themselves from the bonds which restrained them from ranging over the green pastures.

Flowers of every hue enameled the meadows; not thinly scattered over the grass as in northern climes, but in such thick and gathering clusters that the whole plain seemed a patchwork of many colours. The dogs, as they returned from hunting, issued from the long grass dyed red, yellow, or blue, according to the flowers through which they had last forced their way.

The villages of Naifa and Nimroud were deserted, and I remained alone with Said (my host) and my servants. The houses now began to swarm with vermin; we no longer slept under the roofs, and it was time to follow the example of the Arabs. I accordingly encamped on the edge of a large pond on the outskirts of Nimroud. Said accompanied me; and Salah, his young wife, a bright-eyed Arab girl, built up his shed, and watched and milked his diminutive flock of sheep and goats.

I was surrounded with Arabs, who had either pitched their tents, or, too poor to buy the black goat-hair cloth of which they are made, had erected small huts of reeds and dry grass.

In the evening, after the labour of the day, I often sat at the door of my tent, and giving myself up to the full enjoyment of that calm and repose which are imparted to the senses by such scenes as these, gazed listlessly on the very group before me. As the sun went down behind the low hills which separate the river from the desert—even their rocky sides had struggled to emulate the verdant clothing of the plain—its receding rays were gradually withdrawn, like a transparent veil of light, from the landscape. Over the pure, cloudless sky was the glow of the last light. The great mound threw its dark shadow far across the plain. In the distance, and beyond the Zab, Keshaf, another venerable ruin, rose indistinctly into the evening mist. Still more distant, and still more indistinct was a solitary hill overlooking the ancient city of Arbela. The Kurdish mountains, whose snowy summits cherished the dying sunbeams, yet struggled with the twilight. The bleating of sheep and lowing of cattle, at first faint, became louder as the flocks returned from their pastures, and wandered among the tents. Girls hurried over the greensward to seek their fathers' cattle, or crouched down to milk those which had returned alone to their well-remembered folds. Some were coming from the river bearing the replenished pitcher on their heads or shoulders; others, no less graceful in their form, and erect in their carriage, were carrying the heavy load of long grass which they had cut in the meadows. Sometimes a party of horsemen might have been seen in the distance slowly crossing the plain, the tufts of ostrich feathers which topped their long spears showing darkly against the evening sky. They would ride up to my tent, and give me the usual salutation, "Peace be with you, O Bey," or, "Allah Aienak, God help you." Then driving the end of their lances into the ground, they would spring from their mares, and fasten their halters to the still quivering weapons. Seating themselves on the grass, they related deeds of war and plunder, or speculated on the site of the tents of Sofuk, until the moon rose, when they vaulted into their saddles and took the way of the desert.

The plain now glittered with innumerable fires. As the night advanced, they vanished one by one until the landscape was wrapped in darkness and in silence, only disturbed by the barking of the Arab dog.

9. HENRY RAWLINSON

The real breakthrough in Near Eastern archaeology came with the deciphering of Egyptian and Mesopotamian scripts. In both regions a vast quantity of inscriptions was readily obtainable, but they were in two entirely unknown forms of writing and, there was every reason to believe, in unfamiliar languages as well. The unlocking of these scripts by Champollion and Rawlinson, aided by significant contributions from a host of predecessors and contemporaries, is one of the supreme achievements of nineteenth-century scholarship.

As long as it was impossible to read the literature and records left by the ancient inhabitants of Egypt and Mesopotamia, knowledge of them remained altogether haphazard. Indeed, it extended only a little beyond such fragmentary and hopelessly inadequate sources as Herodotus or the Bible. The unearthed monuments meant comparatively little without understandable written testimony, and their epochs were relegated to the shadowy realm of prehistory. But with the discovery of the key to these ancient peoples' writings, dead generations came suddenly to life as their attitudes, hopes, and achievements were revealed in their accounts, religious writings, poems, letters, official decrees, lists of kings, commercial transactions, and legal codes. The frontiers of history were pushed back by thousands of years. In Egypt, for instance, deciphering has made it possible to know more about life in the New Kingdom in the second millennium B.C. than that of early medieval England.

Widely adopted all over the Near East—even by non-Mesopotamian people, the Tell el-Amarna tablets testify—the Mesopotamian type of writing had fallen into disuse around the beginning of our era, probably because of the Alexandrian conquest and the advent of the far less complicated Phoenician alphabetic script, which was spread by Aramaean traders. As in the case of the Egyptian hieroglyphs, the ability to read the Mesopotamian script was quickly forgotten. Yet Mesopotamian inscriptions in this wedge-shaped or cuneiform character had occasionally attracted the attention of travelers since the days of the Greeks. Apart from the giant rock inscriptions in the Persian foothills, the Tigris-Euphrates region had yielded an increasing number of baked clay tablets since the seventeenth century, and the nature of the markings on them had been much debated.

One of the pioneers in the deciphering of cuneiform was Karsten Niebuhr, a geographer of wide interests from Danish Holstein. He transcribed some of the large-scale inscriptions at Persepolis and compiled a list of what seemed to him individual symbols. In addition, he correctly assumed that the texts carved on reliefs represented distinct languages; later they were equated with Old Persian, Elamite, and Assyrian. Niebuhr's account of his travels in the Near East, written in German and published in Copenhagen in 1774–8, stimulated the interest of a number of scholars in solving the riddle of the cuneiform script. The most significant advance was made by a Göttingen schoolteacher, Georg Grotefend (1775–1853), who had no knowledge of Oriental languages. The Greek text on the Rosetta Stone had provided Champollion with a key from the known to the unknown, but Grotefend had no version of the same text in a known language. All three passages of the trilingual at his disposal were written in the same unknown cuneiform script. Nevertheless, his deductions, announced in 1802, were amazingly ingenious and sound, enabling him to identify the title "King of Kings" and the names of Darius Hystaspes and Xerxes. Thereupon he was able to single out a great many letters and to identify twelve of them correctly. Like Gregor Mendel's discoveries in genetics, however, Grotefend's remarkable contribution was unrecognized, buried in obscure publications, and virtually forgotten. It was left to Henry Creswicke Rawlinson to rediscover some of Grotefend's brilliant intuitions and complete the solution.

Like Layard, Rawlinson was a happy combination of scholar and man of action. After entering the army of the East India Company at the age of seventeen, he devoted much of his free time to Oriental studies. In 1835, when he was transferred as a military adviser to Persia, he learned the language and toured the country extensively, exploring its many antiquities. Cuneiform inscriptions, of which he copied two at Mount Alwand, became his consuming interest. Soon, by methods akin to Grotefend's, he tackled the names of ancient Persian kings. He heard of the giant Behistun inscription, a Mesopotamian Rosetta Stone, perched high up on a cliff on the road from Babylon to Ecbatana. After having suppressed domestic uprisings, Darius I had had it carved in 516 B.C. to proclaim the might and extent of his now-consolidated empire. This unique record measured about 150 by 100 feet, high above the floor of the valley.

The trilingual's first column in ancient Persian was within comparatively easy reach and was also the first to be translated (it was independently deciphered by Dr. Edward Hincks, an Anglican clergyman). The most inaccessible and recalcitrant column was the third, in Babylonian (Babylonian III or Assyrian), from which Rawlinson finally obtained squeezes with the help of an agile Kurdish boy in a marvelous feat of acrobatics. By 1847 squeezes from all the sections had been taken and the texts could be made more widely available. Rawlinson was now joined by other scholars—among them Hincks, Oppert, and Fox Talbot—in mastering the Babylonian inscription. His own version was published in 1851. Skepticism concerning the deciphering of Babylonian cuneiform was neatly dispelled in 1857, when the Royal Asiatic Society invited four Assyriologists to translate independently a British Museum inscription from a cylinder of Tiglath-Pileser I. The key had indeed been discovered and the vast records of Mesopotamian civilization were now an open book. In time, cuneiform writings in Sumerian and Hittite would also be cracked.

Climbing After Cuneiform

HENRY RAWLINSON

. . . This rock of Behistun is a very remarkable natural object on the high road between Ecbatana and Babylon. It was probably in the very earliest times invested with a holy character; for the Greek physician, Ctesias, who must have visited this spot in the fourth century before Christ, ascribes the most remarkable of the antiquities to be found there to the Assyrian queen Semiramis . . . The rock of Behistun doubtless preserved its holy character in the age of Darius, and it was on this account chosen by the monarch as a fit part for the commemoration of his warlike achievements. The name itself, *Bhagistán*, signifies "the place of the god"; and the figures of Osmazd, the chief of the "Bhagas," or gods of the old Persian theogony, is thus depicted on the tablet as the presiding local divinity.

The rock, or, as it is usually called by the Arab geographers, the mountain of Behistun is not an isolated hill, as has been sometimes imagined. It is merely the terminal point of a long, narrow range which bounds the plain of Kermanshah to the eastward. This range is rocky and abrupt throughout, but at the extremity it rises in height, and becomes a sheer precipice. The altitude I found by careful triangulation to be 3,807 feet, and the height above the plain at which occur the tablets of Darius is perhaps 500 feet, or sometimes more. Notwithstanding that a French antiquarian commission in Persia described it a few years back to be impossible to copy the Behistun inscriptions, I certainly do not consider it any great feat in climbing to ascend to the spot where the inscriptions occur. When I was living at Ker-

From Rawlinson's "Notes on some Paper Casts of Cuneiform Inscriptions upon the sculptured Rock at Behistun, exhibited to the Society of Antiquaries," *Archaeologia*, XXXIV (1852).

manshah fifteen years ago, and was somewhat more active than I am at present, I used frequently to scale the rock three or four times a day without the aid of a rope or a ladder: without any assistance, in fact, whatever. During my late visits I have found it more convenient to ascend and descend by the help of ropes where the track lies up a precipitate cleft, and to throw a plank over these chasms where a false step in leaping across would probably be fatal. On reaching the recess which contains the Persian text of the record, ladders are indispensable in order to examine the upper portion of the tablet; and even with ladders there is considerable risk, for the footledge is so narrow, about eighteen inches or at most two feet in breadth, that with a ladder long enough to reach the sculptures sufficient slope cannot be given to enable a person to ascend, and, if the ladder be shortened in order to increase the slope, the upper inscriptions can only be copied by standing on the topmost step of the ladder, with no other support than steadying the body against the rock with the left arm, while the left hand holds the note-book, and the right hand is employed with the pencil. In this position I copied all the upper inscriptions, and the interest of the occupation entirely did away with any sense of danger.

To reach the recess which contains the Scythic translation of the record of Darius is a matter of far greater difficulty. On the left-hand side of the recess alone is there any foot-ledge whatever; on the right hand, where the recess, which is thrown a few feet further back, joins the Persian tablet, the face of the rock presents a sheer precipice, and it is necessary therefore to bridge this intervening space between the left-hand Persian tablet and the foot-ledge on the left-hand of the recess. With ladders of sufficient length, a bridge of this sort can be constructed without difficulty; but my first attempt to cross the chasm was unfortunate, and might have been fatal, for, having previously shortened my only ladder in order to obtain a slope for copying the Persian upper legends, I found, when I came to lay it across to the recess in order to get at the Scythic translation, that it was not sufficiently long to lie flat on the foot-ledge beyond. One side of the ladder would alone reach the nearest point of the ledge, and, as it would of course have tilted over if a person had

attempted to cross it in that position, I changed it from a horizontal to a vertical direction, the upper side resting firmly on
the rock at its two ends, and the lower hanging over the precipice, and I prepared to cross, walking on the lower side, and
holding to the upper side with my hands. If the ladder had been
a compact article, this mode of crossing, although far from comfortable, would have been at any rate practicable; but the Persians merely fit in the bars of their ladders without pretending
to clench them outside, and I had hardly accordingly begun to
cross over when the vertical pressure forced the bars out of their
sockets, and the lower and unsupported side of the ladder thus
parted company from the upper, and went crashing down over
the precipice. Hanging on to the upper side, which still remained
firm in its place, and assisted by my friends, who were anxiously watching the trial, I regained the Persian recess, and did
not again attempt to cross until I had made a bridge of comparative stability. Ultimately I took the cast of the Scythic writings, which are suspended against the walls of the room, by laying one long ladder, in the first instance, horizontally across the
chasm, and by then placing another ladder, which rested on the
bridge, perpendicularly against the rock.

The Babylonian transcript at Behistun is still more difficult to
reach than either the Scythic or the Persian tablets. The writing
can be copied by the aid of a good telescope from below, but I
long despaired of obtaining a cast of the inscription; for I found
it quite beyond my powers of climbing to reach the spot where
it was engraved, and the cragsmen of the place, who were accustomed to track the mountain goats over the entire face of
the mountain, declared the particular block inscribed with the
Babylonian legend to be unapproachable. At length, however, a
wild Kurdish boy, who had come from a distance, volunteered
to make the attempt, and I promised him a considerable award
if he succeeded. The mass of the rock in question is scarped,
and it projects some feet over the Scythic recess, so that it cannot be approached by any of the ordinary means of climbing.
The boy's first move was to squeeze himself up a cleft in the
rock a short distance to the left of the projecting mass. When he
had ascended some distance above it, he drove a wooden peg

firmly into the cleft, fastened a rope to this, and then endeavoured to swing himself across to another cleft at some distance
on the other side; but in this he failed, owing to the projection
of the rock. It then only remained for him to cross over to the
cleft by hanging on with his toes and fingers to the slight in-
equalities on the bare face of the precipice, and in this he succeeded, passing over a distance of twenty feet of almost smooth
perpendicular rock in a manner which to a looker-on appeared
quite miraculous. When he had reached the second cleft the real
difficulties were over. He had brought a rope with him attached
to the first peg, and now, driving in a second, he was enabled to
swing himself right over the projecting mass of rock. Here with
a short ladder he formed a swinging seat, like a painter's cradle,
and, fixed upon this seat, he took under my direction the paper
cast of the Babylonian translation of the records of Darius which
is now at the Royal Asiatic Society's rooms, and which is almost
of equal value for the interpretation of the Assyrian inscriptions
as was the Greek translation on the Rosetta Stone for the intelligence of the hieroglyphic texts of Egypt. I must add, too,
that it is of the more importance that this invaluable Babylonian
key should have been thus recovered, as the mass of rock on
which the inscription is engraved bore every appearance, when
I last visited the spot, of being doomed to a speedy destruction,
water trickling from above having almost separated the overhanging mass from the rest of the rock, and its own enormous
weight thus threatening very shortly to bring it thundering down
into the plain, dashed into a thousand fragments.

10. GEORGE SMITH

Archaeological spadework is not always carried out in the field. Champollion, the decipherer of the hieroglyphs, was an armchair archaeologist who pursued his greatest researches in his own study, though later he participated in Egyptian exploration. Another remarkable man who accomplished his most important work at home was George Smith. In fact, he did most of his digging at the British Museum. That institution had been enriched by an enormous haul of clay tablets and inscribed slabs and cylinders from the Mesopotamian sites. From 1849 to 1854, when Rawlinson and his assistant, Hormuzd Rassam, discovered two libraries at Nineveh, a total of about 26,000 tablets had been obtained. Most of these were gathered negligently, since their discoverers were more intrigued by winged bulls and other potential exhibits, and failed to recognize the tablets' full worth. For a long time, Layard had actually regarded them as "bits of pottery decorated in an unusual manner." The tablets were not shipped with proper care and a number disintegrated during transportation and unpacking. It has been said they were more detrimentally affected by their rediscoverers than by the Medes who ransacked Nineveh and its libraries before them. However, because of the astonishing advances being made in the deciphering of cuneiform by Rawlinson and others, the inscriptions soon came to be looked upon with greater respect and interest. But it was a titanic job to repair, classify, and translate them.

A godsend appeared on the scene in the person of George Smith, an unprepossessing young man of twenty-one, who had been spending his lunch hours and most of his spare time at the British Museum studying Assyrian objects. By profession an engraver of banknotes, he was entirely self-educated. Books and articles by Layard and Rawlinson had kindled his enthusiasm for Babylon and Assyria. Offered a minor job as "repairer" by

Dr. Birch, Keeper of the Oriental Department, he set out in 1863 to piece together and classify the Kuyunjik tablets. He soon proved to have almost uncanny skill in joining clay pieces and developed as well such a genius for deciphering them that he soon became one of the leading Assyriologists of his day. His early researches, published in learned journals, gained him the respect of established scholars.

In 1872, while examining the tablets he had already grouped under the heading "Legends and Mythology," he made his signal discovery of a Chaldean account of the Deluge: "On looking down the third column, my eye caught the statement that the ship rested on the mountains of Nizir, followed by the account of the sending forth of the dove, and its finding no resting-place and returning. I saw at once that I had here discovered a portion at least of the Chaldean account of the Deluge." Later, he was invited to read the first part of a paper on his discovery before the Society of Biblical Archaeology. Gladstone and Rawlinson were on the platform. The announcement of the close resemblance between the Biblical version of the Flood and that given in the cuneiform inscriptions inaugurated a new era in the study of the Bible. Theologians, scholars, and the general public were aroused; the junior assistant of the British Museum's Assyrian department found himself famous. To both fundamentalists and rationalists Smith's disclosures came as a shock. The latter could no longer maintain that the Flood was nothing but a Bible story concocted by Hebrew myth-makers. It was left to Leonard Woolley in 1928 to find such possible physical evidence of the Flood in lower Mesopotamian fluvial layers.

As the Museum's Deluge record lacked a salient passage of what Smith estimated to be fifteen lines, an enterprising London newspaper, aware of the headline potential of this Assyrian story and hoping for an archaeological scoop, offered the sum of one thousand guineas to finance an expedition to Nineveh under George Smith's direction to search for the missing fragment. How by lucky chance the missing portion—consisting of seventeen instead of fifteen lines—turned up within a week after the excavation began is told by Smith himself in his popular book *Assyrian Discoveries*. Smith cabled the good news to his patron, the *Daily Telegraph*, but was somewhat surprised, when he obtained a copy of the newspaper, to read inserted in the printed text of his cable the ominous words: "as the season is closing." Being thus advised that the paper considered his mission completed, he had little choice but to return. The British Museum financed another campaign under his aegis in 1874. On his third expedition in 1876 he met with reversals from the very beginning. Abandoning Nineveh, he traveled during the summer heat across the desert to the Mediterranean and died from dysentery in a peasant's hut at the age of thirty-six.

Lacking the vitality and urbanity of a Layard, Smith was perhaps ill-suited for arduous archaeological field work in Oriental countries and should have been retained at the museum, as Sir Frederic Kenyon, a later director of the British Museum, suggests. Be this as it may, his contributions to the development of Assyriology were of the first rank. Smith's work was not limited to identifying the Chaldean version of the Flood, which turned out to be only an episode from *Gilgamesh*, probably the world's oldest epic and one of its most impressive. In 1875 he discovered in the museum collection a Chaldean account of the Genesis story contained in tablets which reported a "continuous series of legends, giving the history of the world from the Creation down to some period after the Fall of Man."

Largely as a result of Smith's epoch-making researches, Flood and Creation myths came to be accepted as part of a universal tradition of mankind. From now on, Biblical scholarship and Higher Criticism were compelled to consider Babylonian similarities and affinities with the Hebrew revelations in Genesis. In the study of Hebrew origins and Judaic religion, the older Babylonian heritage had to be taken into account.

To Nineveh for the Daily Telegraph

GEORGE SMITH

EVERYONE has some bent or inclination which, if fostered by favorable circumstances, will colour the rest of life. My own taste has always been for Oriental studies, and from my youth I have taken a great interest in Eastern explorations and discoveries, particularly in the great work in which Layard and Rawlinson were engaged.

For some years I did little or nothing, but in 1866, seeing the unsatisfactory state of our knowledge of those parts of Assyrian history which bore upon the history of the Bible, I felt anxious to do something towards settling a few of the questions involved. I saw at the time that the key of some of the principal difficulties in the case lay in the annals of Tiglath Pileser, and I wrote to Sir Henry Rawlinson to ask him if the casts and fragments of the inscriptions of this reign were available for reference and examination. Sir Henry Rawlinson, with whom I had corresponded before, took a generous interest in any investigations likely to throw light on the studies in which he held so distinguished a place, and he at once accorded me permission to examine the large store of paper casts in his workroom at the British Museum.

The work I found one of considerable difficulty, as the casts were most of them very fragmentary, and I was quite inexperienced, and had little time at my disposal.

In this my first examination of original texts, I did not obtain much of consequence belonging to the period I was in search of; but I lighted on a curious inscription of Shalmaneser III, which formed my first discovery in Assyrian. On a remarkable obelisk of black stone, discovered by Layard in the centre of the

From Smith's *Assyrian Discoveries* (1875).

mound of Nimroud, there are five lines of sculpture, representing the tribute received by the Assyrian monarch from different countries; and attached to the second one is an inscription which was deciphered independently by Sir Henry Rawlinson and the late Dr. Hincks, and which reads "Tribute of Jehu, son of Omri (*here follow the names of the articles*), I received." It was recognized that this was the Jehu of the Bible, but the date of the transaction could not be determined from the inscription. The new text which I had found gave a longer and more perfect account of the war against Hazael king of Syria, and related that it was in the eighteenth year of Shalmaneser when he received the tribute from Jehu.

A short account of this text I published in the "Athenaeum," 1866, and being encouraged to proceed in my researches by Sir Henry Rawlinson and Dr. Birch, the keeper of the Oriental department of the British Museum, I next set to work on the cylinders containing the history of Assurbanipal, the Sardanapalus of the Greeks. The annals of this monarch were then in considerable confusion, through the mutilated condition of the records; but by comparing various copies, I soon obtained a fair text of the earlier part of these inscriptions, and Sir Henry Rawlinson proposed that I should be engaged by the trustees of the British Museum to assist him in the work of preparing a new volume of "Cuneiform Inscriptions." Thus, in the beginning of 1867, I entered into official life, and regularly prosecuted the study of the cuneiform texts. I owed my first step to Sir Henry Rawlinson, whose assistance has been to me of the greatest value throughout my work . . .

I now again took up the examination of the annals of Tiglath Pileser, and had the good fortune to find several new fragments of the history of this period, and discovered notices of Azariah king of Judah, Pekah king of Israel, and Hoshea king of Israel.

In the same year, I found some new portions of the Assyrian canon, one with the name of the Shalmaneser who, according to the Second Book of Kings, attacked Hoshea king of Israel. In 1868, continuing my investigations, I discovered several accounts of an early conquest of Babylonia by the Elamites. This conquest is stated to have happened 1635 years before Assurbanipal's conquest of Elam, or B.C. 2280, which is the earliest date yet found in the inscriptions.

In the year 1869, I discovered among other things a curious calendar of the Assyrians, in which every month is divided into four weeks, and the seventh days, or "Sabbaths," are marked out as days on which no work should be undertaken. . . .

My next discoveries were in the field of early Babylonian history, and these were published in the first volume of the "Transactions of the Society of Biblical Archaeology."

In 1872, I had the good fortune to make a far more interesting discovery, namely, that of the tablets containing the Chaldean account of the Deluge. The first fragment I discovered contained about half of the account; it was the largest single fragment of these legends.

As soon as I recognized this, I began a search among the fragments of the Assyrian library to find the remainder of the story.

This library was first discovered by Mr. Layard, who sent home many boxes full of fragments of terra-cotta tablets, and after the close of Mr. Layard's work, Mr. Hormuzd Rassam and Mr. Loftus recovered much more of this collection. The fragments of clay tablets were of all sizes, from half an inch to a foot long, and were thickly coated with dirt, so that they had to be cleaned before anything could be seen on the surface. Whenever I found anything of interest, it was my practice to examine the most likely parts of this collection, and pick out all the fragments that would join, or throw light on the new subject. My search for fragments of the Deluge story was soon rewarded by some good finds, and I then ascertained that this tablet, of which I obtained three copies, was the eleventh in a series of tablets giving the history of an unknown hero, named Izdubar; and I subsequently ascertained that this series contained in all twelve tablets. These tablets were full of remarkable interest, and a notice of them being published, they at once attracted a considerable amount of attention, both in England and abroad. . . .

In consequence of the wide interest taken at the time in these discoveries, the proprietors of the "Daily Telegraph" newspaper came forward and offered to advance a sum of one thousand guineas for fresh researches at Nineveh, in order to recover more of these interesting inscriptions, the terms of agreement being that I should conduct the expedition, and should supply the "Telegraph" from time to time with accounts of my journeys and discoveries in the East in return.

The offer of the proprietors of the "Daily Telegraph" being accepted by the trustees of the British Museum, I received leave of absence for six months and directions to proceed to the East and open excavations for the recovery of further cuneiform inscriptions. It would have been better to have waited until the next autumn before starting, but I desired that there should be no disappointment to the proprietors of the "Daily Telegraph," who had generously offered to pay the expenses, and who naturally wished some letters in return while the subject was fresh in the public mind, so I resolved to start at once, and after receiving much advice and assistance from my friend Mr. Edwin Arnold, himself an old Eastern traveller, I got off from London on the evening of the 20th of January, 1873. . . .

I started before sunrise [on the second of March], and arrived about nine in the morning at the ruins of Nineveh. I cannot well describe the pleasure with which I came in sight of this memorable city, the object of so many of my thoughts and hopes. My satisfaction was all the greater as I thought that my journeys were over, and I had only to set to work in order to disinter the treasures I was seeking. . . .

The ruins of Nineveh are situated on the eastern bank of the Tigris; they consist now of a large enclosure covered with low mounds surrounded by the ruins of a magnificent wall, about eight miles in circuit, and broken on the western side by two great artificial mounds, Kouyunjik or Tel Armush, and Nebbi Yunas. Through the middle of the city flows the stream of the Khosr, entering through the eastern wall and passing out through the western wall by the southern corner of the mound of Kouyunjik.

The mounds of the wall of Nineveh are said to be in some places even now nearly 50 ft. high, while the breadth of the débris at the foot is from 100 ft. to 200 ft.

Diodorus states that the walls of Nineveh were 100 ft. high, which was probably not beyond truth; but, as the upper part of the wall is everywhere destroyed, it is impossible to prove the matter at present. The breadth of the wall was probably 50 ft.— excavation, however, might determine this with certainty.

The western face of the wall of Nineveh is over two and a half miles long; it faces towards the town of Mosul and the river Tigris. At the northern and southern corners the river closely approaches the wall, but, between the two points the Tigris bends out to the west, making a bow-shaped flat of land about a mile broad between the wall and the river. On the western side, with their outer border in a line with the wall, lie the two palace mounds called Kouyunjik and Nebbi Yunas, to be described later.

Where the western wall at its northern corner abuts on the Tigris it is joined by the northern wall, which is about a mile and one-third long. There is a considerable mound in one part of this wall, which makes the site of a tower and of the great northern gate of Nineveh. The entrance, which was excavated by Mr. Layard, is adorned by colossal winged bulls and mythological figures, and paved with large slabs of limestone; it appears to have been under the centre of the tower, which had a depth from front to back of 130 ft. The northern wall is continued from the north-eastern corner by the eastern wall, which is three and a quarter miles long. Nearly half way along this side the wall is broken by the stream of the Khosr, which, coming from the east, passes right through the site of Nineveh and runs into the Tigris. Where the stream of the Khosr breaks through the wall the floods have destroyed a portion of the defences; enough remains, however, to show that the lower part of the wall in this part is built of large blocks of stone, probably to resist the water; and in the river itself, in a line with the wall, stand fragmentary blocks of solid masonry, which Captain Jones, who made the best survey of the ruins, considers to be remains of a dam to turn the Khosr into the ditch. I am rather inclined to think that they are part of a bridge over which the wall was carried.

South of the Khosr, where the road to Ervil and Baghdad passes through the eastern wall, stands a double mound, marking the site of the Great Gate of Nineveh, the scene of so many triumphal entries and pageants of the Assyrian kings.

As this was the grandest gate in the wall of Nineveh, it would be an important spot to excavate. Outside the eastern wall Nineveh was shielded by four walls and three moats, making this side of the fortification exceptionally strong. The eastern and western walls are connected at their southern extremities by the south wall, which is the shortest and least important of the defences of Nineveh, measuring little more than half a mile in length.

The two palace mounds, called Kouyunjik and Nebbi Yunas, are situated on the western side of the city, and at one time joined the wall. Nebbi Yunas is a triangular-shaped mound, crowned by a village and burying-ground. It is called Nebbi Yunas from the supposed tomb of Jonah, over which a mosque is erected.

Excavations were made here by Mr. Layard, and afterwards by the Turkish Government. The works showed the existence of palaces here, the first built by Vul-nirari, B.C. 812, the next by Sennacherib, B.C. 705, who, after finishing his great palace on the Kouyunjik mound, built a new one here late in his reign. From this building came the fine memorial cylinder, with the account of the expedition against Hezekiah, king of Judah. The third palace at Nebbi Yunas was built by Esarhaddon, son of Sennacherib, B.C. 681, and from here came three memorial cylinders, containing the history of this reign. North of Nebbi Yunas, just above the stream of the Khosr, lies the largest mound, on the site of Nineveh, Kouyunjik.

The eastern and southern faces of the mound, from the northeast to the south-west corner, are bounded by the stream of the Khosr, which has been artificially diverted to flow round it. The mound at one time was surrounded by a casing of large squared stones, and some former excavator had cleared a considerable space of this facing at the northern part of the mound. The Turks have since built a bridge part of the way across the Tigris, and for this purpose they pulled down and carried away the exposed facing wall of Kouyunjik, and the basement wall of the palace of Assurbanipal.

The northern part of the Kouyunjik mound is occupied by the palace of Assurbanipal, called the North Palace, and the southwestern part by the palace of Sennacherib. Between the two palaces, and on the eastern part of the mound, there exists a wide space of ground, on which no Assyrian building has been discovered. According to the Assyrian inscriptions, there were at least four temples in this space—two temples to Ishtar, the goddess of Nineveh, a temple to Nebo and Merodach, and a ziggurat or temple-tower. . . .

On the 7th of May I commenced work at Kouyunjik on the library space of the south-west palace, the building raised by Sennacherib, and on the 9th of May I started some trenches at the south-eastern corner of the north palace built by Assurbanipal. There was nothing of interest in the trenches at first, as all the sculptures had been discovered by former excavators, and my object was the recovery of inscribed terra-cotta tablets. . . . My trenches in the palace of Sennacherib proceeded slowly and produced little result, the ground being so cut up by former excavations that it was difficult to secure good results without more extensive operations than my time or means would allow; inscriptions, the great object of my work, were however found, and served as compensation for the labour.

In the north palace the results were more definite. Here was a large pit made by former excavators from which had come many tablets; this pit had been used since the close of the last excavations for a quarry, and stones for the building of the Mosul bridge had been regularly extracted from it. The bottom of the pit was now full of massive fragments of stone from the basement wall of the palace jammed in between heaps of small fragments of stone, cement, bricks, and clay, all in utter confusion. On removing some of these stones with a crowbar, and digging in the rubbish behind them, there appeared half of a curious tablet copied from a Babylonian original, giving warnings to kings and judges of the evils which would follow the neglect of justice in the country. On continuing the trench some distance further, the other half of this tablet was discovered, it having evidently been broken before it came among the rubbish.

On the 14th of May, my friend, Mr. Charles Kerr, whom I had left at Aleppo, visited me at Mosul, and as I rode into the khan where I was staying, I met him. After mutual congratulations I sat down to examine the store of fragments of cuneiform inscriptions from the day's diggings, taking out and brushing off the earth from the fragments to read their contents. On cleaning one of them I found to my surprise and gratification that it contained the greater portion of seventeen lines of inscription belonging to the first column of the Chaldean account of the Deluge and fitting into the only place where there was a serious blank in the story. When I had first published the account of this tablet I had conjectured that there were about fifteen lines wanting in this part of the story, and now with this portion I was enabled to make it nearly complete.

After communicating to my friend the contents of the fragment I copied it, and a few days later telegraphed the circumstance to the proprietors of the "Daily Telegraph." Mr. Kerr desired to see the mound at Nimroud, but, as the results from Kouyunjik were so important, I could not leave the site to go with him, so I sent my dragoman to show him the place, remaining myself to superintend the Kouyunjik excavations.

The palace of Sennacherib also steadily produced its tribute of objects, including a small tablet of Esarhaddon, king of Assyria, some new fragments of one of the historical cylinders of Assurbanipal, and a curious fragment of the history of Sargon, king of Assyria, relating to his expedition against Ashdod, which is mentioned in the twentieth chapter of the Book of Isaiah. On the same fragment was also part of the list of Median chiefs who paid tribute to Sargon. Part of an inscribed cylinder of Sennacherib, and half of an amulet in onyx with the name and titles of this monarch, subsequently turned up, and numerous impressions in clay of seals, with implements of bronze, iron, and glass. There was part of a crystal throne, a most magnificent article of furniture, in too mutilated condition to copy, but as far as it is preserved closely resembling in shape the bronze one discovered by Mr. Layard at Nimroud. . . .

I have said I telegraphed to the proprietors of the "Daily Telegraph" my success in finding the missing portion of the Deluge tablet. This they published in the paper on the 21st of May, 1873; but from some error unknown to me, the telegram as published differs materially from the one I sent. In particular, in the published copy occurs the words "as the season is closing," which led to the inference that I considered that the proper season for excavating was coming to an end. My own feeling was the contrary of this, and I did not send this. I was at the time waiting instructions, and hoped that as good results were being obtained, the excavations would be continued. The proprietors of the "Daily Telegraph," however, considered that the discovery of the missing fragment of the Deluge text accomplished the object they had in view, and they declined to prosecute the excavations further, retaining, however, an interest in the work, and desiring to see it carried on by the nation. I was disappointed myself at this, as my excavations were so recently commenced; but I felt I could not object to this opinion, and therefore prepared to finish my excavations and return. . . .

11. LEONARD WOOLLEY

When, in the mid-nineteenth century, archaeological excavation began in ancient Mesopotamia, the findings were invariably associated with the Assyrians and Babylonians, nations familiar from Biblical sources and classical writers. Only gradually did an entirely unknown people, much older than either, emerge, the Sumerians. No one had heard of them barely a hundred years ago, for they had long vanished from the scene by the time Alexander the Great appeared in western Asia. Yet they were the very fountainhead of human progress in the Tigris-Euphrates valley and represented perhaps the oldest civilization on earth. Today they are credited with some of the world's greatest innovations in mathematics, agriculture, technology, government, jurisprudence, architecture, literature, religion, and, above all, that prerequisite of civilized life, writing. Somewhat like the prediction of an undiscovered planet on the basis of irregularities in the orbits of known planets, it was through the study of the peculiarities of cuneiform scripts that scholars first postulated the existence of a more ancient people as the originators of this type of writing. Thus, without knowing their name or character, circumstantial evidence pointed to a mysterious people. Corroborative proof was not wanting for long.

The first step was taken by Edward Hincks, one of the pioneers in cuneiform deciphering, who, on philological grounds, demonstrated cogently that cuneiform could not have been evolved by the Semitic Assyrians and Babylonians, but by its structure and devices represented an adaptation from an antecedent people of non-Semitic tongue. That such a people had definitely existed was put on firmer basis by Jules Oppert in 1869. He supplemented the linguistic evidence by testimony from physical relics, insisting that these people were the Sumerians who had occupied sites of great antiquity in southern Mesopotamia, where some digs had already been made in the 1850s—at Warka by N. K. Loftus and at Tell el-Muqayyar by the British vice-consul at Basra, J. E. Taylor. Oppert's identification of the ancient inhabitants of southern Mesopotamia, the Biblical Shinar, as Sumerians depended largely on the deciphering of the Kuyunjik cuneiform tablets in which occasional reference was made to royal personages with the title of King of Sumer and Akkad. In addition, the Assurbanipal library had included syllabaries and bilinguals in a non-Semitic tongue. Apparently Sumerian continued to be used as a ceremonial language somewhat as Latin is in the Roman Catholic Church. George Smith also had pointed out that the text he had found of the Deluge account from the time of Assurbanipal must have been derived from an earlier southern Mesopotamian original. Conclusive proof of Oppert's hypothesis was provided by archaeological digging that began with Ernest de Sarzac's excavations at Telloh from 1877 to 1900 and culminated triumphantly in the work of Leonard Woolley.

It was at Telloh, which was recognized as the ancient city of Lagash, that the Sumerians were brought to light. De Sarzac's methods of excavation are open to severe criticism and his early work suffered "from interference or molestation by Rassam's gangs," who indulged on behalf of the British Museum in a kind of minor warfare against the French; but his results were revolutionary. He came up with a splendid archaic style of unknown art exemplified by such statues as that of Gudea, governor of Lagash, about 2,600 B.C., and the celebrated Stela of the Vultures, probably some 400 years older. Of still greater importance for our knowledge of the Sumerians were the quantities of cuneiform tablets that were excavated, often illegally by local dealers.

American archaeologists entered the picture at Nippur, the religious center of the Sumerians. Their campaigns began in 1887 under the sponsorship of the University of Pennsylvania. The Sumerian cuneiform inscriptions found at Nippur were extremely valuable, since many represented rare literary texts, among them a Sumerian account of the Flood. However, they were not published until much later.

With the aid of cylinder inscriptions, Tell el-Muqayyar was already established in 1853 by Rawlinson as Ur, the Ur of the

Chaldees of the Old Testament and the birthplace of Abraham. Today it is about a hundred miles inland, but 5,000 years ago it was a flourishing port at the head of the Persian Gulf. After Taylor's dig there in the 1850s, large-scale excavation was not initiated until the end of World War I. In 1922, after the University of Pennsylvania and the British Museum had joined hands in sharing in further campaigns, Leonard Woolley was named to direct the work. Thus began one of the most exciting archaeological investigations in our century, investigations that very nearly equaled the discovery of Tutankhamen's tomb in popular appeal. Only now was the age and depth of the great Sumerian civilization made fully manifest. The legendary first dynasty of Ur was established as historic when Woolley found a foundation tablet with the names of A-annipadda and his father Mesannipadda at nearby al 'Ubaid. The most remarkable of all the finds, the royal tombs of Ur, were apparently even older, possibly pre-dynastic; they may have preceded Abraham by nearly a thousand years. Wonderful objects, such as golden inlaid daggers, harps, elaborate headdresses in lapis lazuli and carnelian with characteristic golden beech leaves, and much more, were found. Almost equaling Tutankhamen's tomb in art treasures and precious materials, the royal graves of Ur are in some ways more notable, for they brought forth objects of surprising refinement of style and workmanship. Tutankhamen's tomb brightened our eyes, but added relatively little to our knowledge of Egyptian civilization; Woolley's Ur changed our whole concept of the Mesopotamian past.

The royal graves had their gruesome side. The body of the queen and the grave which had held the king's body were surrounded by the bodies of their retainers—servants, grooms, guards, courtiers, and entertainers—who had obviously been killed. It has been proposed, but rejected by Woolley, that the king and queen, Abargi and Shubad, buried in the royal cemetery were not really rulers, but a priest and priestess who were sacrificed as the climax of an annual fertility ceremony.

Woolley's campaign at Ur also established the layout of the temple and that of the great, fairly well-preserved ziggurat on which it stood. In addition, his excavations helped to throw light on the daily life and surroundings of the average Sumerian, which were surprisingly similar to those of the present-day Iraqi. These campaigns, which Woolley directed almost single-handedly at Ur from 1922 to 1934 were, moreover, distinguished for the careful handling, minute observation, and ingenious techniques for recovery and preservation of disintegrated objects that characterized his methods. And the field work at Ur was complemented and guided at all times by well-reasoned plans and deductions. It was, in fact, a model of modern scientific archaeology.

In 1929 Woolley drove a shaft at Ur through the various layers of thousands of years of human occupation to the virgin soil of alluvial silt. While doing so, he hit upon an intervening thick stratum of water-deposited sediments, evidence that, at least locally, there had been a catastrophic flood. However, it could be shown that the artifacts above and below the flood-layers were of much the same kind—the so-called al 'Ubaid ware, which later was succeeded by the more recent Uruk and Jemdet Nasr type of pottery. The latter indicated the influx of a new people, perhaps the Sumerians, who were not indigenous to the area and may not have arrived, according to some scholars, much earlier than 3,000 B.C. Where they came from is still a question. Various theories suggest that they came from Malaya, from the Indus Valley via the Bahrein Islands, and even from Mongolia; but probably they came from the adjacent northeastern highlands. It is conceivable that future research may take away some of the Sumerians' luster, since we now know that they too had their predecessors in Mesopotamia from whom they may have borrowed freely.

Sir Leonard Woolley, who died in 1960 at the age of 79, had a long and distinguished career as one of the outstanding twentieth-century archaeologists. The son of a clergyman, he received his training at New College, Oxford and served for two years as assistant keeper of the Ashmolean Museum there. From 1907 on he participated in various excavations in Britain, Italy, Sinai, Nubia, and, after 1911, at Carchemish in Turkey, an ancient Hittite site where he was assisted by T. E. Lawrence. While Woolley was doing intelligence work during World War I, he was captured by the Turks and remained a prisoner until the end of hostilities. He resumed his investigations at Carchemish in 1919. From 1922 to 1934, he conducted his celebrated excavations at Ur, then he transferred in 1935 to a site at Tel Atchana (ancient Alalakh), not far from Antioch in the Turkish Hatay. There a forgotten kingdom was revealed, which had been at the crossroads of Mesopotamian, Hittite, Minoan, and Mycenaean influences. During World War II, Woolley was attached to the Allied armies in Italy and helped to preserve ancient monuments exposed to the hazards of modern warfare.

The Graves of the Kings of Ur

LEONARD WOOLLEY

UR LIES about half-way between Baghdad and the head of the Persian Gulf, some ten miles west of the present course of the Euphrates. A mile and a half to the east of the ruins runs the single line of railway which joins Basra to the capital of Iraq, and between the rail and the river there is sparse cultivation and little villages of mud huts or reed-mat shelters are dotted here and there; but westwards of the line is desert blank and unredeemed. Out of this waste rise the mounds which were Ur, called by the Arabs after the highest of them all, the Ziggurat hill, 'Tel al Muqayyar,' the Mound of Pitch.

Standing on the summit of this mound one can distinguish along the eastern skyline the dark tasselled fringe of the palm-gardens on the river's bank, but to north and west and south as far as the eye can see stretches a waste of unprofitable sand. To the southwest the flat line of the horizon is broken by a grey upstanding pinnacle, the ruins of the staged tower of the sacred city of Eridu which the Sumerians believed to be the oldest city upon earth, and to the north-west a shadow thrown by the low sun may tell the whereabouts of the low mound of al 'Ubaid; but otherwise nothing relieves the monotony of the vast plain over which the shimmering heat-waves dance and the mirage spreads its mockery of placid waters. It seems incredible that such a wilderness should ever have been habitable for man, and yet the weathered hillocks at one's feet cover the temples and houses of a very great city. . . .

The greater part of three seasons' work has been devoted to the clearing of the great cemetery which lay outside the walls of the old town and occupied the rubbish heaps piled up between them and the water-channel, and the treasures which have been unearthed from the graves during that time have revolutionised our ideas of the early civilisation of the world.

The cemetery (there are really two cemeteries, one above the other, but I am speaking now only of the lower and older) consists of burials of two sorts, the graves of commoners and the tombs of kings. Because the latter have yielded the richest works of art one is inclined to think of them alone, but the graves of the common folk, as well as being a hundred-fold as many in number, have also produced very fine objects, and have afforded precious evidence for the dating of the cemetery.

The tombs of the kings appear to be on the whole earlier in date than the graves of their subjects, and this is not so much because they lie at a deeper level, for that might be explained as a natural precaution, the larger and richer graves being dug deeper as a protection against robbers, but because of their relative positions. It is a common sight to see in a Moslem graveyard the tomb of some local saint surrounded by its little domed chapel and the other graves crowded round this as close as may be, as if the occupants sought the protection of the holy man. So it is with the royal tombs at Ur. The older private graves are clustered around them; later it seems as if the visible monuments of the dead kings vanished and their memory faded, leaving only a vague tradition of this being holy ground, and we find the newer graves invading the shafts of the royal tombs and dug right down into them.

The private graves are found at very varying levels, partly perhaps because there was no regular standard of depth, partly because the ground surface of the cemetery was far from uniform; but, generally speaking, the higher graves are the later, and this is due to the rise in the ground-level, which went on steadily throughout the time that the graveyard was in use. The result of this rise obliterating the position of the older graves was that a new grave might be placed directly above an old but, being started from a higher level, would not go quite so far down, and we may find as many as half a dozen graves superimposed one above the other. When this is so, the position in the ground necessarily corresponds to the order in time, and from these superimposed graves we get most valuable evidence for chronology.

Judging from the character of their contents, pottery, etc., the later graves seem to come just before the beginning of the First Dynasty of Ur, which we date to about 2700 B.C., and a few are actually contemporary with that dynasty; for the cemetery age as a whole I think that we must allow a period of at least 200 years. The first of the royal tombs then, may be dated soon after 3000 B.C., and by 2700 B.C. the graveyard was falling out of use. There is not space here to go into all the arguments, but everyone, I think, will agree that some time must have elapsed before the kings, buried as they were with such ghastly pomp, could be forgotten and the sanctity of the tomb-shafts be invaded by the common dead; and if we find above them six or more superimposed burials, between each of which there must have been a decent lapse of time, and the topmost of these dates before 2700 B.C., then the chronology which I suggest will not seem exaggeratedly long. . . .

The first of the royal tombs proved a disappointment. At the very end of the season 1926–7 two important discoveries were made. At the bottom of an earth shaft, amongst masses of copper weapons, there was found the famous gold dagger of Ur, a wonderful weapon whose blade was gold, its hilt of lapis lazuli decorated with gold studs, and its sheath of gold beautifully worked with an openwork pattern derived from plaited grass; with it was another object scarcely less remarkable, a cone-shaped reticule of gold ornaments with a spiral pattern and containing a set of little toilet instruments, tweezers, lancet, and pencil, also of gold. Nothing like these things had ever before come from the soil of Mesopotamia; they revealed an art hitherto unsuspected and they gave promise of future discoveries out-stripping all our hopes.

The other discovery was less sensational. Digging down in another part of the cemetery we found what at first appeared to be walls of *terre pisée*, i.e. of earth not moulded into bricks but used as concrete is used for building. As the sun dried the soil and brought out the colours of its stratification, it became evident that these were not built walls but the clean-cut sides of a pit sunk in the rubbish; the looser filling of the pit had fallen away as we worked and had left the original face exactly as the first diggers had made it. As the excavation continued we came on slabs and blocks of rough limestone which seemed to form a paving over the pit's base. This was an astonishing thing, because there is no stone in the Euphrates delta, not so much as a pebble in its alluvium, and to obtain blocks of limestone such as these it is necessary to go some thirty miles away into the higher desert. The cost of transport would be considerable, and the result is that stone is scarcely ever found in buildings at Ur: a stone pavement underground would therefore be an unheard of ex-travagance. As the season was just at its end we could no more than clear the surface of the "pavement" and leave its fuller examination for the next autumn.

Thinking the matter over during the summer, we came to the conclusion that the stones might be not the floor of a building but its roof, and that we might have discovered a royal grave. It was with high hopes that we resumed work in the following autumn and very soon we could assure ourselves that our forecast was correct: we had found a stone-built underground structure which had indeed been the tomb of a king, but a rubbish-filled tunnel led from near the surface to the broken roof, robbers had been there before us, and except for a few scattered fragments of a gold diadem and some decayed copper pots there was noth-ing left for us to find.

But in spite of that disappointment the discovery was most important. We had laid bare the ruins of a two-chambered struc-ture built of stone throughout with one long and narrow chamber vaulted with stone and a square room which had certainly once been covered with a stone dome, though the collapse of the roof made it difficult to establish the exact method of construction. A doorway, blocked with rubble masonry, afforded entrance to the tomb and was approached by a slanting ramp cut down from the ground surface in the hard soil. Nothing of the sort had ever been found before, and the light thrown on the architectural knowledge of this remote period might well atone for the loss of the tomb's contents; moreover, there was no reason to suppose that this was an isolated tomb, and we could hope for others to which the plunderers had not made their way.

During that season (1927–8) and in the course of last winter more royal tombs came to light, and it is curious to find that never more than two of them are alike. Two large tombs, both plundered, consist of a four-roomed building occupying the whole area of the excavated shaft at the bottom of which they lie; walls and roofs alike are of limestone rubble, and in each case there are two long outer chambers which are vaulted and two smaller central chambers crowned with domes; a ramp leads to the arched door in the outer wall, and arched doors give communication between the rooms. Two graves, those of Queen Shub-ad and her supposed husband, consist of a pit open to the sky and approached by a sloped ramp, at one end of which is a single-chamber tomb with limestone walls and a roof constructed of burnt brick, vaulted and with apsidal ends; the chamber was destined to receive the royal body, the open pit was for offerings and subsidiary burials, and was simply filled in with earth. In another case the pit was found, but the tomb chamber did not lie inside it, but seems to have been close by on a different level. A small grave found last winter consists of a single stone-built domed chamber with a little front court at the bottom of the shaft and, higher up in the shaft, mud-brick buildings for the subsidiary burials and offerings, the whole being covered with earth; another has the same general arrangement, but instead of the domed stone chamber there was a vaulted chamber of mud brick.

There is variety enough therefore in the actual structures, but underlying all there was a common ritual for which different generations provided in different ways; what that ritual was can best be explained by describing the excavation of the graves.

In 1927–8, soon after our disappointment with the plundered stone tomb, we found, in another part of the field, five bodies lying side by side in a shallow sloping trench; except for the copper daggers at their waists and one or two small clay cups, they had none of the normal furniture of a grave, and the mere fact of there being a number thus together was unusual. Then, below them, a layer of matting was found, and tracing this along we came to another group of bodies, those of ten women carefully arranged in two rows; they wore head-dresses of gold, lapis lazuli, and carnelian, and elaborate bead necklaces, but they too possessed no regular tomb furnishings. At the end of the row lay the remains of a wonderful harp, the wood of it decayed but its decoration intact, making its reconstruction only a matter of care; the upright wooden beam was capped with gold, and in it were fastened the gold-headed nails which secured the strings; the sounding-box was edged with a mosaic in red stone, lapis lazuli and white shell, and from the front of it projected a splendid head of a bull wrought in gold with eyes and beard of lapis lazuli; across the ruins of the harp lay the bones of the gold-crowned harpist.

By this time we had found the earth sides of the pit in which the women's bodies lay and could see that the bodies of the five men were on the ramp which led down to it. Following the pit along, we came upon more bones which at first puzzled us by being other than human, but the meaning of them soon became clear. A little way inside the entrance to the pit stood a wooden sledge chariot decorated with red, white, and blue mosaic along the edges of the framework and with golden heads of lions having manes of lapis lazuli and shell on its side panels; along the top rail were smaller gold heads of lions and bulls, silver lionesses' heads adorned the front, and the position of the vanished swingle-tree was shown by a band of blue and white inlay and two smaller heads of lionesses in silver. In front of the chariot lay the crushed skeletons of two asses with the bodies of the grooms by their heads, and on the top of the bones was the double ring, once attached to the pole, through which the reins had passed;

it was of silver, and standing on it was a gold 'mascot' in the form of a donkey most beautifully and realistically modelled.

Close to the chariot were an inlaid gaming-board and a collection of tools and weapons, including a set of chisels and a saw made of gold, big bowls of gray soapstone, copper vessels, a long tube of gold and lapis which was a drinking tube for sucking up liquor from the bowls, more human bodies, and then the wreckage of a large wooden chest adorned with a figured mosaic in lapis lazuli and shell which was found empty but had perhaps contained such perishable things as clothes. Behind this box were more offerings, masses of vessels in copper, silver, stone (including exquisite examples of volcanic glass, lapis lazuli, alabaster, and marble), and gold; one set of silver vessels seemed to be in the nature of a communion-service, for there was a shallow tray or platter, a jug with tall neck and long spout such as we know from carved stone reliefs to have been used in religious rites, and tall slender silver tumblers nested one inside another; a similar tumbler in gold, fluted and chased, with a fluted feeding-bowl, a chalice, and a plain oval bowl of gold lay piled together, and two magnificent lions' heads in silver, perhaps the ornaments of a throne, were amongst the treasures in the crowded pit. The perplexing thing was with all this wealth of objects we had found no body so far distinguished from the rest as to be that of the person to whom all were dedicated; logically our discovery, however great, was incomplete.

The objects were removed and we started to clear away the remains of the wooden box, a chest some 6 feet long and 3 feet across, when under it we found burnt bricks. They were fallen, but at one end some were still in place and formed the ring-vault of a stone chamber. The first and natural supposition was that here we had the tomb to which all the offerings belonged, but further search proved that the chamber was plundered, the roof had not fallen from decay but had been broken through, and the wooden box had been placed over the hole as if deliberately to hide it. Then, digging round the outside of the chamber, we found just such another pit as that 6 feet above. At the foot of the ramp lay six soldiers, orderly in two ranks, with copper spears by their sides and copper helmets crushed flat on the

broken skulls; just inside, having evidently been backed down
the slope, were two wooden four-wheeled waggons each drawn
by three oxen—one of the latter so well preserved that we were
able to lift the skeleton entire; the waggons were plain, but the
reins were decorated with long beads of lapis and silver and
passed through silver rings surmounted with mascots in the form
of bulls; the grooms lay at the oxen's heads and the drivers in
the bodies of the cars; of the cars themselves only the impression
of the decayed wood remained in the soil, but so clear was this
that a photograph showed the grain of the solid wooden wheel
and the grey-white circle which had been the leather tyre.

Against the end wall of the stone chamber lay the bodies of
nine women wearing the gala head-dress of lapis and carnelian
beads from which hung golden pendants in the forms of beech
leaves, great lunate earrings of gold, silver "combs" like the palm
of a hand with three fingers tipped with flowers whose petals are
inlaid with lapis, gold, and shell, and necklaces of lapis and
gold; their heads were leaned against the masonry, their bodies
extended on to the floor of the pit, and the whole space between
them and the waggons was crowded with other dead, women
and men, while the passage which led along the side of the
chamber to its arched door was lined with soldiers carrying
daggers, and with women. Of the soldiers in the central space
one had a bundle of four spears, and by another there was a
remarkable relief in copper with a design of two lions trampling
on the bodies of two fallen men which may have been the
decoration of a shield.

On the top of the bodies of the "court ladies" against the
chamber wall had been placed a wooden harp, of which there
survived only the copper head of a bull and the shell plaques
which had adorned the sounding-box; by the side wall of the
pit, also set on the top of the bodies, was a second harp with a
wonderful bull's head in gold, its eyes, beard, and horn-tips of
lapis, and a set of engraved shell plaques not less wonderful;
there are four of them with grotesque scenes of animals playing
the parts of men, and while the most striking feature about them
is that sense of humour which is so rare in ancient art, the grace
and balance of the design and the fineness of the drawing make

of these plaques one of the most instructive documents that we possess for the appreciation of the art of early Sumer.

Inside the tomb the robbers had left enough to show that it had contained bodies of several minor people as well as that of the chief person, whose name, if we can trust the inscription on a cylinder seal, was A-bar-gi; overlooked against the wall we found two more model boats, one of copper now hopelessly decayed, the other of silver wonderfully well preserved; some 2 feet long, it has high stern and prow, five seats, and amidships an arched support for the awning which would protect the passenger, and the leaf-bladed oars are still set in the thwarts; it is a testimony to the conservatism of the East that a boat of identical type is in use to-day on the marshes of the Lower Euphrates, some 50 miles from Ur.

The king's tomb-chamber lay at the far end of his open pit; continuing our search behind it we found a second stone chamber built up against it either at the same time or, more probably, at a later period. This chamber, roofed like the king's with a vault of ring arches in burnt brick, was the tomb of the queen to whom belonged the upper pit with its ass chariot and other offerings: her name, Shub-ad, was given us by a fine cylinder seal of lapis lazuli which was found in the filling of the shaft a little above the roof of the chamber and had probably been thrown into the pit at the moment when the earth was being put back into it. The vault of the chamber had fallen in, but luckily this was due to the weight of earth above, not to the violence of tomb-robbers; the tomb itself was intact.

At one end, on the remains of a wooden bier, lay the body of the queen, a gold cup near her hand; the upper part of the body was entirely hidden by a mass of beads of gold, silver, lapis lazuli, carnelian, agate, and chalcedony, long strings of which, hanging from a collar, had formed a cloak reaching to the waist and bordered below with a broad band of tubular beads of lapis, carnelian, and gold: against the right arm were three long gold pins of lapis heads and three amulets in the form of fish, two of gold and one of lapis, and a fourth in the form of two seated gazelles, also of gold.

The head-dress whose remains covered the crushed skull was

a more elaborate edition of that worn by the court ladies: its basis was a broad gold ribbon festooned in loops round the hair—and the measurement of the curves showed that this was not the natural hair but a wig padded out to an almost grotesque size; over this came three wreaths, the lowest hanging down over the forehead, of plain gold ring pendants, the second of beech leaves, the third of long willow leaves in sets of three with gold flowers whose petals were of blue and white inlay; all these were strung on triple chains of lapis and carnelian beads. Fixed into the back of the hair was a golden "Spanish comb" with five points ending in lapis-centred gold flowers. Heavy spiral rings of gold wire were twisted into the side curls of the wig, huge lunate ear-rings of gold hung down to the shoulders, and apparently from the hair also hung on each side a string of large square stone beads with, at the end of each, a lapis amulet, one shaped as a seated bull and the other as a calf. Complicated as the head-dress was, its different parts lay in such good order that it was possible to reconstruct the whole and exhibit the likeness of the queen with all her original finery in place.

For the purposes of exhibition a plaster cast was made from a well-preserved female skull of the period (the queen's own skull was too fragmentary to be used), and over this my wife mod-elled the features in wax, making this as thin as possible so as not to obliterate the bone structure; the face was passed by Sir Arthur Keith, who has made a special study of the Ur and al 'Ubaid skulls, as reproducing faithfully the character of the early Sumerians. On this head was put a wig of the correct dimensions dressed in the fashion illustrated by terra-cotta figures which, though later in date, probably represent an old tradition. The gold hair-ribbon had been lifted from the tomb without disturb-ing the arrangement of the strands, these having been first fixed in position by strips of glued paper threaded in and out between them and by wires twisted round the gold; when the wig had been fitted on the head, the hair-ribbon was balanced on the top and the wires and paper bands were cut, and the ribbon fell naturally into place and required no further arranging. The wreaths were re-strung and tied on in the order noted at the time of excavation. Though the face is not an actual portrait of the queen, it gives at least the type to which she must have conformed, and the whole reconstructed head presents us with the most accurate picture we are likely ever to possess of what she looked like in her lifetime.

By the side of the body lay a second head-dress of a novel sort. On to a diadem made apparently of a strip of soft white leather had been sewn thousands of minute lapis lazuli beads, and against this background of solid blue were set a row of exquisitely fashioned gold animals, stags, gazelles, bulls, and goats, with between them clusters of pomegranates, three fruits hanging together shielded by their leaves, and branches of some other tree with golden stems and fruit or pods of gold and carnelian, while gold rosettes were sewn on at intervals, and from the lower border of the diadem hung palmettes of twisted gold wire.

The bodies of two women attendants were crouched against the bier, one at its head and one at its foot, and all about the chamber lay strewn offerings of all sorts, another gold bowl, vessels of silver and copper, stone bowls, and clay jars for food, the head of a cow in silver, two silver tables for offerings, silver lamps, and a number of large cockle-shells containing green paint; such shells are nearly always found in women's graves, and the paint in them, presumably used as a cosmetic, may be white, black, or red, but the normal colour is green. Queen Shub-ad's shells were abnormally big, and with them were found two pairs of imitation shells, one in silver and one in gold, each with its green paint.

The discovery was now complete and our earlier difficulty was explained: King A-bar-gi's grave and Queen Shub-ad's were exactly alike, but whereas the former was all on one plane, the queen's tomb-chamber had been sunk below the general level of her grave-pit. Probably they were husband and wife: the king had died first and been buried, and it had been the queen's wish to lie as close to him as might be; for this end the grave-diggers had reopened the king's shaft, going down in it until the top of the chamber vault appeared; then they had stopped work in the main shaft but had dug down at the back of the chamber's pit in which the queen's stone tomb could be built. But the treasures known to lie in the king's grave were too great a tempta-

tion for the workmen; the outer pit where the bodies of the
court ladies lay was protected by 6 feet of earth which they
could not disturb without being detected, but the richer plunder
in the royal chamber itself was separated from them only by the
bricks of the vault; they broke through the arch, carried off their
spoil, and placed the great clothes-chest of the queen over the
hole to hide their sacrilege.

Nothing else would account for the plundered vault lying
immediately below the untouched grave of the queen, and the
connecting of Shub-ad's stone chamber with the upper "death-
pit," as we came to call these open shafts in which the subsidiary
bodies lay, made an exact parallel to the king's grave and, in a
lesser degree, to the other royal tombs. Clearly, when a royal
person died, he or she was accompanied to the grave by all the
members of the court: the king had at least three people with
him in his chamber and sixty-two in the death-pit; where there
was a larger stone building with two or four rooms, then one of
these was for the royal body and the rest for the followers sacrificed in precisely the same way; the ritual was identical, only the
accommodation for the victims differed in different cases.

On the subject of human sacrifice more light was thrown by
the discovery of a great death-pit excavated last winter. At about
26 feet below the surface we came upon a mass of mud brick
not truly laid but rammed together and forming, as we guessed,
not a floor but the stopping, as it were, of a shaft. Immediately
below this we were able to distinguish the clean-cut earth sides
of a pit, sloping inwards and smoothly plastered with mud; following these down, we found the largest death-pit that the cemetery has yet produced. The pit was roughly rectangular and
measured 37 feet by 24 at the bottom, and was approached as
usual by a sloped ramp. In it lay the bodies of six men-servants
and sixty-eight women; the men lay along the side by the door,
the bodies of the women were disposed in regular rows across
the floor, every one lying on her side with legs slightly bent and
hands brought up near the face, so close together that the heads
of those in one row rested on the legs of those in the row above.
Here was to be observed even more clearly what had been
fairly obvious in the graves of Shub-ad and her husband, the

neatness with which the bodies were laid out, the entire absence of any signs of violence or terror.

We have often been asked how the victims in the royal graves met their death, and it is impossible to give a decisive answer. The bones are too crushed and too decayed to show any cause of death, supposing that violence had been used, but the general condition of the bodies does supply a strong argument. Very many of these women wear head-dresses which are delicate in themselves and would easily be disarranged, yet such are always found in good order, undisturbed except by the pressure of the earth; this would be impossible if the wearers had been knocked on the head, improbable if they had fallen to the ground after being stabbed, and it is equally unlikely that they could have been killed outside the grave and carried down the ramp and laid in their places with all their ornaments intact; certainly the animals must have been alive when they dragged the chariots down the ramp, and if so, the grooms who led them and the drivers in the cars must have been alive also; it is safe to assume that those who were to be sacrificed went down alive into the pit.

That they were dead, or at least unconscious, when the earth was flung in and trampled down on the top of them is an equally safe assumption, for in any other case there must have been some struggle which would have left its traces in the attitude of the bodies, but these are always decently composed; indeed, they are in such good order and alignment that we are driven to suppose that after they were lying unconscious someone entered the pit and gave the final touches to their arrangement—and the circumstances that in A-bar-gi's grave, the harps were placed on the top of the bodies proves that someone did enter the grave at the end. It is most probable that the victims walked to their places, took some kind of drug—opium or hashish would serve—and lay down in order; after the drug had worked, whether it produced sleep or death, the last touches were given to their bodies and the pit was filled in. There does not seem to have been anything brutal in the manner of their deaths.

None the less, the sight of the remains of the victims is gruesome enough with the gold leaves and the coloured beads lying thick on the crushed and broken skulls, but in excavating a great death-pit such as that of last winter we do not see it as a whole, but have to clear it a little at a time. The soil was removed until the bodies were almost exposed, covered only by the few inches of broken brick which had been the first of the filling thrown over the dead; here and there a pick driven too deep might bring to view a piece of gold ribbon or a golden beech leaf, showing that everywhere there were bodies richly adorned, but these would be quickly covered up again and left until more methodical work should reveal them in due course. Starting in one corner of the pit, we marked out squares such as might contain from five to six bodies, and all these were cleared, noted, and the objects belonging to them collected and removed before the next square was taken in hand.

It was slow work, and especially so in those cases where we decided to remove the entire skull with all its ornaments in position on it. The wreaths and chains and necklaces re-strung and arranged in a glass case may look very well, but it is more interesting to see them as they were actually found, and therefore a few heads on which the original order of the beads and gold-work was best preserved were laboriously cleaned with small knives and brushes, the dirt being removed without disturbing any of the ornaments—a difficult matter as they are loose in the soil—and then boiling paraffin wax was poured over them, solidifying them in one mass. The lump of wax, earth, bone, and gold was then strengthened by waxed cloth pressed carefully over it, so that it could be lifted from the ground by undercutting. Mounted in plaster, with the superfluous wax cleaned off, these heads form an exhibit which is not only of interest in itself but proves the accuracy of the restorations which we have made of others.

Of the sixty-eight women in the pit, twenty-eight wore hair-ribbons of gold. At first sight it looked as if the others had nothing of the kind, but closer examination showed that many, if not all, had originally worn exactly similar ribbons of silver. Unfortunately silver is a metal which ill resists the action of the acids in the soil, and where it was but a thin strip and, being worn on the head, was directly affected by the corruption of the flesh, it generally disappears altogether, and at most there may be detected on the bone of the skull slight traces of a purplish colour which is silver chloride in a minutely powdered state: we could be certain that the ribbons were worn, but we could not produce material evidence of them.

But in one case we had better luck. The great gold ear-rings were in place, but not a sign of discoloration betrayed the existence of any silver head-dress, and this negative evidence was duly noted: then, as the body was cleared, there was found against it, about on the level of the waist, a flat disk a little more than 3 inches across of a grey substance which was certainly silver; it might have been a small circular box. Only when I was cleaning it in the house that evening, hoping to find something which would enable me to catalogue it more in detail, did its real nature come to light: it was the silver hair-ribbon, but it had never been worn—carried apparently in the woman's pocket, it was just as she had taken it from her room, done up in a tight coil with the ends brought over to prevent its coming undone; and since it formed thus a comparatively solid mass of metal and had been protected by the cloth of her dress, it was very well preserved and even the delicate edges of the ribbon were sharply distinct. Why the owner had not put it on one could not say; perhaps she was late for the ceremony and had no time to dress properly, but her haste has in any case afforded us the only example of a silver hair-ribbon which we are likely ever to find.

Another thing that perishes utterly in the earth is cloth, but occasionally on lifting a stone bowl which has lain inverted over a bit of stuff and has protected it from the soil one sees traces which, although only of fine dust, keep the texture of the material, or a copper vessel may by its corrosion preserve some fragment which was in contact with it. By such evidence we were able to prove that the women in the death-pit wore garments of bright red woollen stuff; and as many of them had at the wrists one or two cuffs made of beads which had been sewn on to cloth, it was tolerably certain that these were sleeved coats rather than cloaks. It must have been a very gaily dressed crowd that assembled in the open mat-lined pit for the royal obsequies, a blaze of colour with the crimson coats, the silver, and the gold; clearly these people were not wretched slaves killed as oxen might be killed, but persons held in honour, wearing their robes of office, and coming, one hopes, voluntarily to a rite which would in their belief be but a passing from one world to another, from the service of a god on earth to that of the same god in another sphere.

This much I think we can safely assume. Human sacrifice was confined exclusively to the funerals of royal persons, and in the graves of commoners, however rich, there is no sign of anything of the sort, not even such substitutes, clay figurines, etc., as are so common in Egyptian tombs and appears there to be reminiscent of an ancient and more bloody rite. In much later times Sumerian kings were deified in their lifetime and honoured as gods after their death: the prehistoric kings of Ur were in their obsequies so distinguished from their subjects because they too were looked upon as superhuman, earthly deities; and when the chroniclers wrote in the annals of Sumer that "after the Flood kingship again descended from the gods," they meant no less than this. If the king, then, was a god, he did not die as men die, but was translated; and it might therefore be not a hardship but a privilege for those of his court to accompany their master and continue in his service. . . .

This is the story of the excavations at Ur, not a history of the Sumerian people, but something must be said here to show how important those excavations have been for our knowledge of early civilisations. The contents of the tombs illustrate a very highly developed state of society of an urban type, a society in which the architect was familiar with all the basic principles of construction known to us to-day. The artist, capable at times of a most vivid realism, followed for the most part standards and conventions whose excellence had been approved by many generations working before him; the craftsman in metal possessed a knowledge of metallurgy and a technical skill which few ancient peoples ever rivalled; the merchant carried on a far-flung trade and recorded his transactions in writing; the army was well organised and victorious, agriculture prospered, and great wealth gave scope to luxury. Our tombs date, as has already been said, between 2900 and 2700 B.C., and, as the nature of the civilisation would lead one to expect, and as has been demonstrated by the discoveries in the rubbish below the tombs . . . by 2900 B.C. this civilisation was already many centuries old.

Until recently it was thought that the Egyptian civilisation was the oldest in the world and that it was the fountain-head wherefrom the latter civilisations of other Western countries drew at any rate the inspiration which informed them. But up to 3400 B.C. Egypt was still barbarous, divided into petty kingdoms not yet united by "Menes," the founder of the First Dynasty, into a single state. Egypt and Sumer therefore are more or less contemporary in origin and when Egypt makes a real start forward under Menes the beginnings of a new age are marked by the introduction of models and ideas which derive from that older civilisation which, as we know now, had long been developing and flourishing in the Euphrates valley; and to the Sumerians we can trace also much that is at the root of Babylonian, Assyrian, Hebrew, and Phoenician art and thought, and so see that the Greeks too were in debt to this ancient and for long forgotten people, the pioneers of the progress of Western man. It is this that makes excavation in the oldest levels at Ur of such absorbing interest, the knowledge that almost every object found is not merely an illustration of the achievement of a particular race at a particular time, but also a new document helping to fill up the picture of those beginnings from which is derived our modern world.

12. SAMUEL NOAH KRAMER

George Smith's discoveries revealed Mesopotamian myths with definite resemblances to the Biblical descriptions of the Creation and Flood. Another find at the turn of the century clearly showed Hebrew dependence on Mesopotamian contributions. Like Smith's discoveries, it redirected Old Testament studies. The new find was the Code of Hammurabi, consisting of three fragments of an enormous black diorite slab unearthed by Jacques de Morgan at the ancient city of Susa, the administrative capital of the Persian Empire; it had probably been carried off by an Elamite conqueror of the Babylonian town of Sippar. Today it is one of the most prized possessions of the Louvre. The longest cuneiform inscription known, it has at its top the figure of the powerful Babylonian king Hammurabi who is receiving the laws from the seated god Shamash. When the translation was published in 1902, the response of scholars everywhere was profound. Once again, archaeology had made necessary a reassessment of accepted doctrines, and repercussions were felt in the fields of Hebrew history, Old Testament theology, ancient comparative jurisprudence, and Mesopotamian civilization in general.

Hammurabi, Babylonian king of the Semitic Amorites in the eighteenth century B.C., was an empire-builder who so effectively subdued the Sumerian cities in the south that henceforth they vanished from the scene as political powers. Hammurabi was roughly contemporaneous with Abraham and lived several centuries before the Mosaic law was given. Any reader who compares the 280-odd legal clauses in Hammurabi's Code with those of the laws of Moses in Exodus, Deuteronomy, and Leviticus, cannot help being struck by the similarities in wording and content. Both codes subscribe to the legal principle of an eye for an eye; both are divinely inspired and were granted under conspicuously similar circumstances. Nevertheless, there are as significant differences as similarities. All that can be asserted is that the Hebrew code, like several other concepts and narratives of the Bible, may have grown out of Mesopotamian heritage. Whether the legal tradition was introduced by Abraham of Ur into Hebrew religion or whether, as seems more likely, the invading Hebrews found Canaanite codes of Semitic-Babylonian background when they entered Palestine, is still a question. However, quite unlike Egypt, codes of law were an accepted principle by which society was ordered in Babylonia and over much of western Asia, including the land of the Hittites. And this may be taken as a clear indication of the persuasiveness of the Mesopotamian legacy. In the words of the Italian Semitic scholar, Sabatino Moscati: "A natural tendency to distinguish and to codify lies behind the vast system of jurisprudence which was developed by Babylonian and Assyrian civilization and which served in its turn as one of the chief vehicles for the extension of that civilization to the surrounding world."

The modern study of Mesopotamian law has followed the same retrograde direction as that of the uncovering of civilization in the Tigris-Euphrates valley at large. Here, too, a start was made with the Assyrians, chronologically among the more recent of the ancient peoples of the area. But before the code of Hammurabi had been dug up, a German Assyriologist, Friedrich Delitzsch, had predicted its existence from evidences in the Assurbanipal library. The Hammurabi code long remained supreme and was looked upon as a unique creation until it too had to yield to more ancient Sumerian precursors. Older tablets were found at Nippur and Warka, but actual Sumerian, and earlier Semitic, law codes were not identified until immediately after World War II.

Samuel Noah Kramer, probably the leading Sumerologist in mid-twentieth-century America, helped to decipher the first such Sumerian law code encountered, the Lipit Ishtar code. He was also instrumental in bringing to light what is so far the oldest known code, that of Ur-Nammu, which is at least three hundred years earlier than Hammurabi's. But Kramer, quite aware of the quickening pace in his chosen field, is the first to assert that still older codes may come to light.

As Kramer points out, the spirit of Sumerian legal thought is far milder and more humane than that of the Semites. The Semitic Hammurabi subscribes to a legal rigorism that was still further intensified hundreds of years later by the Assyrians. Of the fused Sumerian-Semitic tradition that evolved in Mesopotamia, the law code of the Hebrews came to stress the Semitic-Babylonian element, while the code of the Hittites in Asia Minor, for instance, tended toward the milder Sumerian outlook.

The Sumerian law codes were discovered by investigating a vast number of cuneiform tablets in some of the great museum and university collections. Actually the tablets had been excavated decades earlier, but, until their deciphering, were lost among the yet undeciphered and unclassified pieces. The cuneiform tablets from Nippur, where an American expedition began excavations in 1887, played a major role in Kramer's discoveries.

Kramer has devoted most of his life to the exacting but exciting science of Sumerology, a subbranch of cuneiform studies. From 1919 to 1931, he was actively engaged in excavations in Iraq sponsored by the University of Pennsylvania. He has spent much of his time copying and translating tablets at the University Museum of the University of Pennsylvania, where he is Clark Professor of Assyriology and curator of the tablet collections. He has paid special attention to epic poems and other literary texts of Sumerian origin. His work has also led him, as a kind of wandering Sumerologist, on Guggenheim and Fulbright fellowships, to examine the cuneiform collections at such overseas institutions as the Louvre, the Friedrich-Schiller University in Jena, and, most fruitfully, the Museum of the Ancient Orient in Istanbul. His researches have thrown light on the whole range of Sumerian achievement.

Older Than Hammurabi's Code

SAMUEL NOAH KRAMER

UPON ARRIVAL in Istanbul [in 1946], I called immediately upon Mr. Aziz Ogan, the Director of the Archaeological museums of that city, who informed me that the Directorate of Antiquities, located in Ankara, had once again generously granted me permission to continue my research. As in the case of my earlier visits, the genial and sympathetic director gave his enthusiastic approval and cooperative support to the highly specialized project, for he fully realized that not only did it promise to result in a not insignificant contribution to humanistic studies, but it also served as an instructive example of Turkish-American cooperation on the cultural level. I was given comfortable and well-lighted space in the Tablet Archives section of the museum, which, I was happy to learn, was now under the capable charge of two young Turkish cuneiformists, Hatice Kizilyay and Muazzez Çig. Both had studied in the University of Ankara under Benno Landsberger, the most creative cuneiform scholar of our times, and under the eminent Hittitologist, F. G. Güterbock. In more recent years they had worked closely with F. R. Kraus who had been curator of the Tablet Archives for many years, and who, among other achievements, had prepared in the course of his stay in the museum, a highly detailed catalogue of the entire Nippur collection of the museum, consisting of some seventeen thousand tablets and fragments, which will prove invaluable to all who plan to do research in the museum's Tablet Archives. Moreover, under Güterbock's tutelage, these two ladies had copied and published quite a number of Hittite texts, while in

From Kramer's "A 'Fulbright' in Turkey," *The University Museum Bulletin,* XVII, No. 2. (December 1952), University of Pennsylvania. Reprinted by permission of the author.

the course of more recent years they had copied a considerable number of Sumerian legal documents; these are now in press. Fortunately for me they were also eager to try their hand at copying Sumerian literary texts, and as will soon become apparent, they made a highly important contribution to the project.

All was now set for the work to begin. The first step, before copying, consisted of course of selecting from among the thousands of tablets and fragments in the museum's Nippur collection those which were inscribed with the Sumerian belles lettres. Fortunately this was now, as a direct result of Kraus's painstaking catalogue, a relatively simple matter. For the catalogue divided the Nippur tablets into a number of categories, one of which was that of Sumerian literature. All that had to be done therefore was to have the pieces which were marked in the catalogue as containing unpublished literary inscriptions brought to my working desk. I soon realized, however, that it would be impossible to copy *all* the unpublished pieces—there were some eight hundred of them according to Kraus's catalogue—and it became necessary first to identify the types of composition inscribed on them in order to select for copying those which promised to prove most fruitful for the restoration of the more significant Sumerian compositions. I, therefore, asked that the tablets be brought to my desk drawer by drawer in numerical order, and then proceeded to study each of the eight hundred pieces more or less cursorily in order to place it in its proper literary category, and when possible, actually to assign it to the composition to which it belonged. After all these data were jotted down, the drawers were returned to their proper place in the cupboards, and I was now ready to begin copying them category by category, beginning with the proverbs and wisdom texts which were the largest and most significant single group and ending with the few and relatively far less important fragments inscribed with parts of the Sumerian epic tales. The results of the year's labor may now be summarized as follows:

Of the approximately eight hundred unpublished pieces in the Istanbul museum, some four hundred and fifty turned out to be tiny fragments inscribed with but a few broken lines of text, and it was not possible therefore to assign them to a particular composition. I therefore decided to leave this group for the very last in the hope—unfulfilled, as it turned out—that there might be time to copy at least a part of them towards the end of my stay in Istanbul. For the importance of a literary fragment is not always to be measured by its size; there are some well-preserved tablets which merely duplicate material already published and are therefore of relatively little value, whereas some of the smaller pieces may have the very lines and phrases which are missing from texts otherwise nearly complete.

Of the remaining pieces, about 350 in number, I myself copied two hundred and thirty-two, arranged on one hundred and eleven plates, eleven by seven and one-half inches in size. The majority are rather small fragments, but quite a number are large and middle-sized pieces, and not a few are four, six and eight column tablets in various states of preservation. . . .

One of the pieces contains a copy of the oldest law-code so far known to man, that promulgated by Ur-Nammu, the founder of the Third Dynasty of Ur who began his reign according to the "short" chronology [the chronology now favored by most Orientalists] about 2050 B.C. The tablet . . . contributes an unexpected piece of historical information which indirectly will help to set straight at last the approximate date of one of Sumer's best-known figures, that of Gudea, the *Ishakku* or "prince" of Lagash. Hitherto, the reign of Gudea, whose face and features are well known from his numerous statues excavated by the French years ago in Lagash and now on display in a number of museums including our own, has generally been placed by scholars before that of Ur-Nammu, although some inscriptional evidence to the contrary had to be explained away to make the date fit. The new law-code, however, now makes it certain that Gudea is to be placed *after* and not *before* Ur-Nammu, that is, that he was prince over Lagash while one of the rulers of the Third Dynasty of Ur, probably Shulgi, held sway over Sumer as a whole. For the prologue to the code mentions the defeat by Ur-Nammu of a prince of Lagash by the name Namhani, whom all scholars place a generation or two before Gudea [In the light of recent evidence, Dr. Kramer now dates Gudea before rather than after Ur-Nammu]. . . .

Were it not for Kraus's letter, I probably would have missed the tablet altogether. I had met F. R. Kraus a number of years ago in the course of my earlier Sumerological researches in the Istanbul Museum of the Ancient Orient, where he was curator for many years. Recently he had gone to Austria as professor of oriental studies in the University of Vienna. Hearing that I was once again in Istanbul, this time as Fulbright research scholar, he wrote me a letter reminiscing of olden days. But one paragraph "talked shop." Some years ago, in the course of his duties as curator in the Istanbul museum, he wrote, he had come upon two fragments of a tablet inscribed with Sumerian laws, had made a "join" of the two pieces, and had catalogued the resulting tablet as number 3191 of the Nippur collection of the museum. I might be interested in its contents, he added, and perhaps want to copy it.

Since Sumerian law tablets are extremely rare, I had number 3191 brought to my working table at once. There it lay, a sun-baked tablet, light brown in color, twenty centimeters by ten in size. More than half of the writing was destroyed, and what was preserved, at first, seemed hopelessly unintelligible. But after several days of concentrated study, its contents began to clarify and take shape, and I realized with no little excitement that what I held in my hand was a copy of the oldest law-code as yet known to man. It was promulgated by Ur-Nammu, the Sumerian king who founded what is commonly known in the history books as the Third Dynasty of Ur. According to the very lowest chronological estimates, Ur-Nammu reigned about 2050 B.C., some three hundred years before the now well-known and far-famed Semitic law-giver, Hammurabi.

Until only five years ago, the Hammurabi code, written in the cuneiform script and in the Semitic language known as Babylonian, was by all odds the most ancient brought to light. Sandwiched in between a boastful prologue and a curse-laden epilogue are close to three hundred laws which run the gamut of man's possible deeds and misdeeds. The diorite stele on which the code is inscribed now stands solemn and impressive in the Louvre for all to see and admire. From the point of view of fullness of legal detail and state of preservation, it is still by all odds the most impressive ancient law document as yet uncovered —but not from the point of view of age and antiquity. For in the year 1947, there came to light a law code promulgated by a king named Lipit-Ishtar who preceded Hammurabi by more than one hundred and fifty years.

The Lipit-Ishtar code, as it is now generally named, is not inscribed on a stele but on a sun-baked clay tablet. It is written in the cuneiform script, but in the non-Semitic Sumerian language. The tablet was excavated some fifty years ago, but for various reasons had remained unidentified and unpublished all these years. As reconstructed and translated with my help by Francis Steele, assistant curator in the University Museum, it is seen to have contained a prologue, epilogue, and an unknown number of laws of which thirty-seven are preserved wholly or in part.

But Lipit-Ishtar's claim to fame as the world's first law-giver was short-lived. For the very next year, Taha Baqir, the curator of the Iraq Museum in Baghdad, who was digging in an obscure mound called Harmal, announced the discovery of two tablets inscribed with an older law-code, written, like the Hammurabi code, in the Semitic Babylonian language. The documents were studied and copied that very year by the well-known Yale cuneiformist, Albrecht Goetze. In the brief prologue which precedes the laws—there is no epilogue—a king is mentioned by the name of Bilalama who lived some seventy years before Lipit-Ishtar. It is this Semitic Bilalama code, therefore, which seemed to be entitled to priority honors until this year, when as a result of F. R. Kraus's communication, the Istanbul tablet, inscribed with Ur-Nammu's Sumerian law-code, came to light. For Ur-Nammu, a far more important ruler than Bilalama, preceded the latter by at least one hundred years.

The Istanbul tablet was divided by the ancient scribe into eight columns, four on the obverse and four on the reverse. Each of the columns contained about forty-five small ruled spaces; less than half of these are now legible. The obverse contains a long prologue which is only partially intelligible because of the numerous breaks in the text. Briefly put, it runs as follows:

After the world had been created, and after the fate of the land Sumer and of the city Ur—the Biblical Ur of the Chaldees—

had been decided, An and Enlil, the two leading deities of the
Sumerian pantheon, appointed the moon-god Nanna as the king
of Ur. Then one day, Ur-Nammu was selected by the god to rule
over Sumer and Ur as his earthly representative. The new king's
first acts had to do with the political and military safety of Ur
and Sumer. In particular he found it necessary to do battle with
the bordering city-state of Lagash which was expanding at Ur's
expense. He defeated and put to death its ruler, Namhani, and
then "with the power of Nanna, the king of the city" he reestab-
lished Ur's former boundaries.

Now came the time to turn to internal affairs and to institute
social and moral reforms. He removed the "chiselers" and the
grafters, or as the code itself describes them, the "grabbers" of
the citizens' oxen, sheep, and donkeys. He then established and
regulated honest and unchangeable weights and measures. He
saw to it that "the orphan did not fall a prey to the wealthy,"
"the widow did not fall a prey to the powerful," "the man of one
shekel did not fall a prey to the man of one *mina* (sixty *shek-
els*)." And, though the relevant passage is destroyed on the tablet, it was no doubt to insure justice in the land and to promote
the welfare of its citizens that he promulgated the laws which
followed.

The laws themselves probably began on the reverse of the tablet, and are so badly damaged that only the contents of five of
them can be restored with some degree of certainty. One of them
seems to involve a trial by the water ordeal; another seems to
treat of the return of a slave to his master. But it is the other
three laws, fragmentary and difficult as their contents are, which
are of very special importance for the history of man's social and
spiritual growth. For they show that even before 2000 B.C., the
law of "eye for eye" and "tooth for tooth"—still prevalent to a
large extent in the Biblical laws of a much later day—had already given way to the far more humane approach in which a
money fine was substituted as a punishment. Because of their
historical significance these three laws are here quoted in the
original Sumerian, transcribed into our alphabet, together with
their literal translation:

tukum-bi	If
[lu-lu-ra	[a man to a man
gish- . . . -ta]	with a . . . -instrument]
. . . -a-ni	his . . .
gir in kud	the foot has cut off,
10-gin-ku-babbar	10 silver shekels
i-la-e	he shall pay.

tukum-bi	If
lu-lu-ra	a man to a man
gish-tukul-ta	with a weapon
gir-pad-du	his bones
al-mu-ra-ni	of . . .
in-zi-ir	severed,
1-ma-na-ku-babbar	1 silver mina
i-la-e	he shall pay.

tukum-bi	If
lu-lu-ra	a man to man
geshpu-ta	with a geshpu-instrument
ka- . . . in-kud	the nose (?) has cut off,
⅔-ma-na-ku-babbar	⅔ of a silver mina
i-la-e	he shall pay.

How long will Ur-Nammu retain his crown as the world's first law-giver? Not for long, I fear. There are indications that there were law-givers in Sumer long before Ur-Nammu was born. Sooner or later a lucky "digger" will come up with a copy of a law-code preceding that of Ur-Nammu by a century or more.

Syria and Palestine

13. CLAUDE SCHAEFFER

In the long-settled country sometimes called the Fertile Crescent there was much cultural interchange throughout antiquity. It stretches in a semicircle between desert, mountains, and the sea from the Persian Gulf along the Euphrates and Tigris northwestward to the Mediterranean and then follows southwest along the coast to Palestine. There the roots of human efforts go back to the Neolithic Age; mankind probably first advanced toward settled, agricultural life along its fringes. During the fourth millennium B.C., Mesopotamian civilization made itself strongly felt in the western Mediterranean part of the area we refer to as Syria. Excavations in the northernmost section of the Syrian littoral at Ras Shamra have now fully borne out the extent of Mesopotamian cultural, political, and commercial ascendancy in the third millennium B.C.

The unity of the area is indicated by the kindred Semitic elements that held increasing sway over the entire region. It is within the whole expanse of the Fertile Crescent that Abraham, setting out from his native Ur, moved up to Haran in the north and then further south to Hebron. Still earlier, Sargon of Akkad probably reached the Mediterranean coast near Ras Shamra, where he reputedly washed his sword in the sea water, and may have sailed across to Cyprus, a hundred miles away. He was preceded by the legendary Sumerian hero Gilgamesh, who, with his bosom friend and former foe, Enkidu, had visited the mountains "where the great cedars grow"—obviously the Lebanon ranges. In these parts a Mesopotamian-based civilization evolved, and under the Semitic Canaanites, a people virtually identical with the Phoenicians and closely related to the Amorites, retained a remarkable cultural uniformity along the 400-mile-long coastland from present-day Turkey down into the Negev of Palestine. Situated at the strategic and commercial crossroads from the Tigris-Euphrates valley to Egypt and from the latter to Anatolia, and open to invasions and trade from the Aegean and the nearby islands of Crete and Cyprus, Syria-Palestine was, even in antiquity, destined to become a battleground.

Chance discovery in 1928 of an old tomb at Ras Shamra opened up a vista to the past of this area. The finds there threw a new light on the culture of the Canaanites, particularly on their art, religion, and epic and spiritual literature. Of the latter's existence no one had previously had more than an inkling. Biblical studies were once again modified when the indebtedness of Hebrew religious concepts and texts to their Canaanite enemies was demonstrated. It had already been known that archaic Hebrew was virtually identical with early Phoenician. Now it was seen that the lofty ideals of justice and the sublime moral tone of the Hebrew Prophets had not evolved in splendid isolation, but had had Canaanite precedents. Even so familiar a figure as Daniel appears in a Canaanite poem as an "upright" man, who sits before the gate "judging the cause of the widow, adjudicating the case of the fatherless." There are surprising Canaanite parallels to Old Testament psalms. Some scholars have found in the Ras Shamra texts references to the Garden of Eden and to Adam and Eve, who were probably Near-Eastern historical personages. And the Old Testament godhead of El or Elohim is found in Canaanite literature, which also occasionally gravitates toward monotheism. Important as well to Old Testament scholarship was the fact that the Ras Shamra writings helped to explain passages in the Bible which were hard to understand without a knowledge of the Canaanite background. Hitherto known only through the accounts of the Hebrews, who had a stake in setting themselves up as wholly different from their idol-worshiping, sensuous rivals, we now have an inside view of the Canaanites and their religion. And in the light of these documents it seems likely that until the time of Moses the Israelites were indistinguishable from their Canaanite neighbors.

The impact of the Ras Shamra explorations on Old Testament studies by no means exhausts the results of the findings there. The Canaanite-Phoenician civilization that was brought to light in its creative wealth deserves to be studied for its own sake, despite its great debt to the Babylonians, Egyptians, Minoans, and Mycenaeans. At Ras Shamra its evolution can be followed in chronological and physical cross section. The beginning of Phoenician seapower can be seen, too, probably induced by the maritime incursions of early Achaeans and Cretans. Above all, the excavations give a wonderful glimpse of the polyglot, cosmopolitan character of the ancient Mediterranean port, a kind of Shanghai of the mid-second millennium B.C. It welcomed foreign traders, shippers, and craftsmen, and the Achaeans and Mycenaeans among them changed the city's character.

The multi-national nature of the city is best revealed in the texts dug up in 1929. Both in subject matter and language, these records from the library of Nimged reflect the lively and diverse activities of this maritime city. Among the languages encountered, besides the native Canaanite, were Sumerian (used mainly in legal documents), Akkadian (the international diplomatic language), Hurrian, Egyptian, Hittite, and two hitherto unknown idioms. To ease the confusion, the Canaanites had compiled word-lists, dictionaries, and lists of synonyms. Of all the different language texts, the Canaanite writings, which were not immediately identified as such, aroused the greatest interest; naturally they represented the majority of tablets. Their deciphering within little more than a year by French and German scholars was an astonishing performance, especially since it had to be done without the aid of bilinguals.

The script was cuneiform. Almost immediately, however, it was noticed that, because of the limited number of symbols employed, the signs could not stand for syllables or ideograms as in Babylonian or Sumerian cuneiform. In short, the script's symbols—at first believed to number twenty-six, then twenty-eight and later established as thirty—represented an alphabet, the earliest known. But what were the values of these alphabetic letters? Statistical evidence in the form of peculiarities of distribution and frequency pointed to a Semitic tongue. Here then were Canaanite—"proto-Phoenician"—records written in an alphabetic cuneiform. This disclosure made Ras Shamra famous. Once its texts could be read, the site was firmly identified as ancient Ugarit, long sought for by archaeologists. Ugarit had been by no means the most prominent Phoenician city—Tyre, Sidon, and Byblos loomed much larger—nevertheless it was widely known in antiquity and had figured in the Tell el-Amarna tablets, in Babylonian references, and in the Hittite (Boghazköy) and Mari archives.

Ugarit is located along the Mediterranean coast of northern Syria, about ten miles north of Latakia and near the present harbor of Minet-el-Beida. The northernmost of the maritime Phoenician cities, it occupies a mound about half a mile from the water. In the course of the past 2,500 years or so Ugarit has been entirely covered up. In fact, the Arab name Ras Shamra means fennel-head, an allusion to its aromatic overgrowth. In pre-classical antiquity, its location exposed the city to continuous inroads and influences from all areas of the Near East. In the third millennium it was occupied by Semitic (Canaanite) groups, who established its historic identity and, possibly, its name. During the age of Hammurabi, Ugarit looked to Babylon for leadership. But once the Amorites of the first Babylonian dynasty declined under Hittite and Kassite pressure, the power vacuum was filled by the Twelfth Egyptian Dynasty, which left many artifacts at the site. Among them were statuettes of pharaohs, queens, and sphinxes. After the Hyksos interregnum, Indo-European-speaking Hurrians seem to have entered the melting pot and to have promoted an attachment to the kindred Mitannis. But in the fifteenth and fourteenth century the Egyptian Eighteenth Dynasty reasserted its overlordship, and Ugarit entered its most flourishing period, from which its literary and religious texts survive, preserved in an extensive, well-classified library. At this time Mycenaean influences were strongly felt, too. In the ensuing duel between Hittites and Egyptians, Ugarit suffered an eclipse, perhaps hastened by a catastrophic earthquake, evidence of whose destructiveness has been found all around the eastern Mediterranean. Like the Hittites themselves, the city received its death-blow from the mysterious, marauding Sea Peoples and was eventually abandoned.

Since the nearby necropolis was accidentally discovered in 1928 when a peasant's plough struck a stone slab covering a funeral crypt, there have been some twenty campaigns at Ugarit.

But the city has still not given up all its riches. In 1953, for instance, its diplomatic archives were found. It is impossible to say on what aspect of the ancient preclassical world Ugarit made the greatest impression, since so many have been affected. It is a reflection of the importance of the site that the research connected with its material has led to a new field of scholarship and academic discipline: Ugaritic studies.

Claude F. A. Schaeffer, a French archaeologist who had made a name for himself as a student of European prehistory, has won international acclaim for the expert direction and the care with which he has handled the excavations of this mound. He has worked out a reasonably complete sequence of artifacts for about 2,000 years of successive strata at Ugarit that, in Leonard Woolley's words, puts "all archaeologists in his debt." In his stratigraphic work Schaeffer introduces geophysical data like earthquakes to arrive at an absolute chronology for prehistoric developments in the Near East. Since 1954, he has been a professor of the Collège de France in Paris. In addition to his research at Ras Shamra, he has led several archaeological campaigns in Cyprus and at Malatya, Turkey.

The Oldest Alphabet

CLAUDE SCHAEFFER

It was in the Seraglio of Lattakia, in the capital of the Alaouite State (North Syria), that this strange story was told me. Long before the war an English captain passing through Lattakia had invited the agent of his company to accompany him to his boat at Alexandretta. About ten miles north of Lattakia he drew the agent's attention to a cove, surrounded by white rocks, which

From Schaeffer's articles in *The Illustrated London News,* November 2, 1929, and November 29, 1930. Reprinted by permission of the author, Professor C. F. A. Schaeffer, Collège de France, France.

could be seen from starboard. Near the cove, which is an excellent little natural port, now abandoned, there were several small hillocks, which one of his grandfathers, also a sailor, had advised him to excavate when he had retired from the Navy. "There must be many valuable things in those hillocks," was the captain's conclusion. This story is, doubtless, not an invention. While I was making my purchases in the *souks* at Lattakia, where the report that a French archaeologist intended to make excavations near Minet-el-Beida had spread rapidly, several merchants told me that the natives who lived in the neighbourhood of the cove had found antique objects of gold.

These tales were first corroborated in March 1928. An Alaouite, working in his field not far from the bay, lifted a flagstone which was found to cover the entrance to a subterranean passage leading to a rectangular chamber vaulted with corbels. When he emptied it he found several things, some of gold, but no one else saw them. They have disappeared amongst the antiquities for sale. The news of this discovery reached the ears of M. Schoeffler, the present French Governor of the Alaouite State. He went to the spot himself, and informed the Director of Antiquities at Beyrouth, M. Virolleaud. Researches made, by someone attached to this service, in the chamber and its approaches, resulted only in the discovery of some terra-cotta vases, partly broken, which the native finder had not thought worth taking. But these vases, in the opinion of M. René Dussaud, a member of the Institut, date from the thirteenth century B.C., and are of Cypriot and Mycenean origin. On the other hand, the plan of the sepulchre reminded one of the Royal Tombs at Knossos, found by Sir Arthur Evans.

Up till then, no such discovery had been made on the Syrian coast. M. René Dussaud did not doubt that Minet-el-Beida was an ancient port, and a Cyprio-Cretan colony, which traded in merchandise from Cyprus, Crete, and Egypt, destined for the powerful centres of civilisation in Mesopotamia. Minet-el-Beida, in fact, situated just opposite the extreme point of Cyprus, is the starting point of many roads leading to the interior. Copper especially, coming from the Cyprus mines, which was used for making arms instead of iron, at that time a precious metal, must have played an important part in this trade. At the request of M. Dussaud, the Institut de France sent an archaeological mission to the spot, whose aim was to try and find the ancient maritime town of Minet-el-Beida and its necropolis. The leadership of this mission was entrusted to the present writer, who chose as his collaborator his good friend, M. G. Chenet, an archaeologist from the Argonne. The caravan of the expedition, consisting of seven camels carrying the luggage, and several donkeys and horses, reached Minet-el-Beida at the end of March 1929. The excavations began immediately after the camp was installed. After a week of soundings and digging, the supposed necropolis was found, and it proved very rich in archaeological treasure. Within an area of 3000 square metres, situated at 150 metres from the shore at Minet-el-Beida, the first discoveries brought to light were 80 funerary deposits consisting of various vases in the local ceramic style, Cyprian or Mycenean, or simply of a few pebbles and shells from the neighbouring beach; in one instance the pebbles were replaced by weights in polished or rough-hewn stone, the exact equivalents of the Egyptian *mina* of 437 grammes and its fractions. In other places there were enormous stone tablets, round slabs shaped like millstones, pierced in the centre, stone cubes or large *phalli,* also in stone, and very naturalistic. The bones discovered here were all those of animals, and not of human beings.

About the middle of this ground, at the foot of a little wall only 50 cm. high, and quite hidden in the soil, we discovered an important treasure of statuettes and jewels of great artistic and historical value. The first trace of these was the discovery of a bronze figure of a hawk, with the double crown of Upper and Lower Egypt, like that of Horus; it was lying amongst the remains of a rough vase and fragments of a classical Cyprian bowl. Quite near this hawk another was found, smaller, but encrusted with gold, a delightful little gem of ancient goldsmith's art, Egyptian in inspiration, but executed by an artist who no longer followed the models of the Nile Valley too closely, for there are no examples of the Horus hawk holding the uraeus between his claws, as does the hawk of Minet-el-Beida.

About 50 cm. away was found a statuette of a seated god. His profile was Egyptian, and the eyes were encrusted in enamel and silver. Close by was an upright statuette of a god, 22 cm. in height, in a walking attitude. On his head he wears a tall cap, plated in gold, resembling the *pschent* of the Pharaohs, or the head-gear of the Hittite kings. A mask of finely wrought gold covers the god's face; his body is silver-plated, and on his right arm there is a gold bracelet. It is, undoubtedly, the finest effigy of the Phoenician god Reshef which has been found up to the present. Besides him was a gold pendant, showing in relief the beautiful goddess Astarte, standing upright and holding a lotus in each hand. In the soil around the statuettes were found numerous single beads of a necklace, polished olives in cornelian, cylinders in pink quartz, and pears in cat's-eye stone.

At about twenty metres south of these treasures we found a large subterranean chamber, which was rectangular, and had enormous flagstones carefully matched; doubtless this was an important tomb, but unfortunately it was unfinished and empty. We then investigated on the western side, and came across a series of very curious monuments, in the form of wells, the opening of which was vaulted and shaped like a hive, and covered with a large pierced flagstone; there were also water-pipes for funerary water leading to a great jar or to a pierced stone. These monuments seem to have been connected with an edifice of rather important dimensions, of which only the flagstones and the foundations remain today. Below the flagstones we discovered a new tomb, this time a completed one, with a passage and staircase leading towards the actual sepulchre, vaulted in corbels. This corridor, formed of large flagstones, contained numerous painted vases, lamps with wicks which had been left burning (their smoke had blackened the adjacent wall), and a marvellous two-handled vase in Egyptian alabaster, quite intact. In front of the sepulchre was found the skull of a very young person, perhaps a servant killed at the door of his master's tomb.

When we entered the tomb proper, however, we discovered that it had been violated at a very distant period. It seems that the desecrators, evidently well informed as to the means of entry, had displaced one of the key-stones of the vault, and slipped through this narrow aperture. They had stripped the skeletons of their ornaments in precious metals, and had thrown the bones into a corner. There were at least four corpses in the sepulchre, but no sarcophagus. The funerary furniture was extraordinarily rich, as can be realised by the remains left or forgotten by the desecrators. Amongst beads in gold and hard stones, many vases of terra-cotta, with Mycenean or Cyprian paintings, goblets in glass paste, and Egyptian jugs in alabaster, we found also a gold ring and a hematite cylinder. Most interesting of all was an ivory casket, the lid of which, miraculously preserved intact, has an image of a seated goddess, with nude torso, and wearing a full skirt with a bustle, between two goats standing on their hind-legs. The whole work, which has an almost heraldic aspect, is very beautifully composed, and shows a very advanced form of art. The goddess appears to be akin to the Cretan and Mycenean fertility goddesses of Knossos and Tiryns in the thirteenth and fourteenth centuries B.C. The ivory is undoubtedly the finest and best-preserved that has come down to us from that remote period. It has been given a place of honour among the collections of Eastern antiquities in the Louvre.

In their richness and importance the tombs of Minet-el-Beida can be compared to the royal tombs of Isopata and of Zafer Papoura in Crete. Undoubtedly they contained the bodies of a princely dynasty, as yet unknown, of Northern Syria. It was now a question of finding the palace and the town to which the royal necropolis of Minet-el-Beida belonged. At a distance of 1000 metres from the shore, there is a mound (*tell*) 20 metres high; 1000 metres long, and 500 metres wide. It is called by the natives Ras Shamra, or Cape Fennel. For our excavations I chose the highest point of the mound facing the sea, where I supposed the palace to have been. As soon as the superficial layers were removed important foundations of fine stone appeared, amongst which we found a bronze dagger and the remains of a granite statue of a Pharaoh, as well as Egyptian *stelae* covered with hieroglyphics of the New Empire epoch. One of them is dedicated to the god Seth of Supuna. These discoveries enabled us to ascertain immediately the period of the palace, showing that it dates back to the second millennium B.C.; and they prove, moreover, that the kings who resided in this palace were friends or allies of Egypt. We ought soon to be enlightened regarding the importance of their diplomatic relations through the discovery of an entire library of terra-cotta tablets covered with cuneiform texts. Amongst these texts there are letters very like those of Tell el Amarna, which comprise, as is well known, the diplomatic correspondence of the Pharaohs of the Eighteenth Dynasty with the Syrian rulers. One of these letters, found at Ras Shamra, addressed to a king called Akinni, mentions the conclusion of a treaty between three towns, the names of which were hitherto unknown: Panashtai, Hazilou, and Halbini. But what makes this discovery particularly interesting—indeed, quite sensational—is that most of the tablets are written in a new script, quite unknown before. This script is already alphabetic, as it uses only twenty-six signs. M. Virolleaud, the well-known specialist, set to work immediately to decipher these precious documents, which up to the present have still kept their secret. . . .

These documents enabled us to identify Ras Shamra with the seaport conjecturally located there by M. René Dussaud, Member of the French Institute and Keeper of Oriental Antiquities at the Louvre. Enriched by the copper trade with the neighbouring island of Cyprus, and the export of Asiatic products to the Aegean islands and the Greek mainland, Ras Shamra in the second millennium B.C. had attained a position of exceptional importance. Encouraged by the results of the first excavation, the Academy of Inscriptions and Belles Lettres, in association with the Louvre Museum, entrusted me in 1930 with a new mission, to which the Alaouite State contributed a subsidy. My assistant was again M. Georges Chenet, the excellent archaeologist from the Argonne. The Mission excavated from March to June this year [1930] continuously, with a staff of 150 workmen.

Our principal programme at Minet el Beida was to explore the immediate surroundings of the great royal tombs discovered last year. We brought to light some curious houses which seemed to have been intended for the dead princes reposing in the adjacent tombs. In the chambers and passages, and near the stairways and well-holes, were found votive deposits including painted pottery, bronze knives and daggers, pins of bronze, silver and

gold, and lamps of bronze and terra-cotta. The well-holes provided with channels for water had been intentionally filled with
fine earth, in which were mingled some very fine vases. The
entrance was closed with stone slabs, sometimes pierced or
sealed with layers of concrete. In one of the rooms were thirteen
jars, recalling the store-rooms in the Palace of Minos at Knossos.

The chief efforts of the 1930 expedition were directed to the
excavation of the mound at Ras Shamra. The great structure with
thick walls, which we had begun to uncover last year, was revealed as an important temple consisting of two courts placed
side by side on a raised level and formerly paved. The northern
court contained a block of stonework, forming a kind of altar-
platform, on which had doubtless stood large granite statues
(found in fragments at the foot of the altar) representing divinities, in the fine Egyptian style of the New Empire period (18th
to 19th Dynasties). Here lay also a votive *stela*, dedicated to
Baal of Sapouna by a certain "Mami, royal scribe and overseer
of the treasury." It is possible that Sapouna was the ancient
name of the town hitherto known by the Arab name of Ras
Shamra.

Outside the sanctuary, whose equipment shows strong Egyptian
influence, we found several chambers which appear to have been
reserved for local divinities, of whom we have so far found two
images, in the form of *stelae* (pillars). One, a male figure in
relief, fortunately intact, represents a curious god wearing a
head-dress like the Egyptian crown with ostrich feathers, at the
base of which protrudes a large horn. The god holds in one hand
a long spear, and in the other the Egyptian sceptre called a *hiq*.
He is dressed in a *pagne* (short breeches), and in the girdle
round his waist he carries a dagger with a large pommel. His
feet are shod in sandals, with the points turned back after the
Hittite fashion.

Some time before the building of the great temple, the site
had been used as a place of burial. This cemetery dates from a
much older period (16th to 18th centuries B.C.). The dead had
been buried partly in an extended attitude and partly in a
crouching posture. Others, again, had been stripped of flesh and
buried in pieces; the trunk, from shoulders to pelvis, being

placed in a large vase, while the rest of the body—the legs and the skull—was interred beside it. Several of the graves had been overturned by the builders of the temple, who, however, left evidence of great respect for the dead, as the bones from disturbed tombs had been reburied and protected with stones or fragments of large vases.

But the most important discovery made this year on the mound of Ras Shamra has been that of a library and a veritable school of scribes, at a point south of the temple, where we found the first tablets last year. Here we have now brought to light a building of large dimensions and very fine construction in freestone, with a wide entrance and an interior court, provided with wells and a conduit for rain-water. Around this court were ranged paved chambers, with a staircase leading to an upper storey. Scattered among these ruins we found a quantity of large tablets covered with cuneiform texts, sometimes in three and four columns. Others contained lists of words or even actual bilingual dictionaries—a great rarity. One of these dictionaries reveals a second language, hitherto entirely unknown. The study of this bilingual tablet was entrusted to M. Thureau-Dangin, Member of the Institute. Certain fragments of a scribe's exercises show us that we have to do here with an actual school, dependent on the adjacent temple, where young priests learned the difficult craft of the scribe and the various languages in use at Ras Shamra. They had at their disposal lexicons compiled by their masters, one of whom has put his signature on the margin of one of our tablets as follows: "By the hand of Rabana, son of Sumejana, priest of the goddess Nisaba."

What greatly complicated the scribe's task was the fact that no fewer than six languages were known at Ras Shamra—Babylonian, for dealings with neighbouring states (as attested by diplomatic documents found by us); Sumerian, restricted to priests and scholars, like Latin in our own time; Hittite, a language introduced by invaders from Asia Minor, who must have put an end to Egyptian domination at Ras Shamra; Egyptian, of which we found several examples in hieroglyphic inscriptions at the great temple; a language still enigmatic, revealed by the bilingual tablet discovered this year; and, lastly, Phoenician, written in the famous alphabetic script, previously unknown, of which we found the first specimens last year. They were published at the beginning of this year, following our report, by M. Charles Virolleaud, Professor at the Sorbonne, who added a commentary on the meaning of certain symbols. Some time later, M. H. Bauer, Professor at the University of Halle, recognised in the script a Phoenician dialect, and made the first attempt to decipher it. To his translation certain additions were also made by a member of the Biblical School at Jerusalem. The full decipherment of the unknown script was accomplished by M. Virolleaud, after the discovery, this spring, of the new tablets, which added over 800 complete lines. He succeeded in determining twenty-seven out of the twenty-eight letters in the Ras Shamra alphabet.

In a communication to the Academy of Inscriptions and Belles Lettres, M. Virolleaud has just given some explanatory notes on these famous texts, the most important that have been discovered since the finding of the library at El Amarna in Egypt. The language of most of these documents is Phoenician, with very clear traces of Aramaic influence. It was already known, from rare and brief inscriptions, that close affinities existed between Phoenician and Hebrew, but the new texts enable us to push the comparison much further than was hitherto possible. The tablets comprise commercial accounts, various lists, letters, and religious rituals. But the document of prime importance is a kind of epic poem containing, in its present state, nearly 800 lines. The chief character is named Taphon. In the first rank of deities we find the goddess Anat and the god Alein, son of Baal; but there are more than twenty others—among them Asharat, Ashtart, Dagon, El-Hokmot, the "god of wisdom," and Din-El.

To judge from the archaeological evidence obtained from the same level, the tablets of Ras Shamra date from the last centuries of the second millennium B.C., and are contemporary, no doubt, with the Rameses period in Egypt. Moreover, this is the same epoch in which, according to ancient tradition, lived the Phoenician poet, Sanchoniathon, of whose work only a few lines have been preserved for us in a Greek translation dating from the beginnings of the Christian era. Our discovery is therefore one of the greatest importance for the history of Oriental religions, and for Semitic philology. Further, it introduces a new element into the origins of the alphabet.

14. NELSON GLUECK

Dramatic finds in recent years have denied the view that Palestine would always prove an unrewarding field for archaeological exploration. No longer can it be maintained that only in the surrounding areas, particularly in Mesopotamia and Egypt, could significant clues be found to Hebrew origins, Israelite history, and Biblical questions in general. But throughout the nineteenth and into the twentieth century the new light thrown on early Hebrew religion and history by archaeological investigation came almost entirely from non-Palestinian sources. The tablets from Kuyunjik, Tell el-Amarna, and Ras Shamra, for instance, radically redirected Old Testament studies. No wonder surveys of Biblical archaeology still devote much of their discussion to the inscriptions and other testimonies found in Assyria, Babylonia, Syria, and Egypt.

Palestinian archaeology gained momentum after World War I, though it may be said to have begun with Flinders Petrie's stratigraphic researches in 1890. The first spectacular discoveries were made in the 1920s and 30s at Megiddo—ancient Armageddon—and Lachish. Since then there has been a phenomenal progress, thanks to the pioneering work of such men as C. S. Fisher, P. L. O. Guy, L. L. Starkey, William F. Albright, and the latter's pupil, Nelson Glueck. Glueck has been surveying and excavating in Palestine and the land across the River Jordan for about thirty years. It is his deep conviction that the Bible can be used as an "almost infallible divining rod, revealing to the expert the whereabouts and characteristics of lost cities and civilizations."

Adopting the methods of surface exploration by means of pottery fragments so successfully perfected in Palestine by Albright, Glueck has investigated some one thousand ancient sites east of the Jordan. In 1932, on the strength of Biblical references to a valley of smiths, a city of copper, and a land with iron stones and with hills from which copper could be dug, he was directed, after some ingenious philological sleuthing, to the Wadi Araba in the inhospitable southern Negev. This is where part of the geological fault of the Rift Valley joins the Dead Sea depression with the Red Sea and continues into Central Africa. Along the valley's entire length, he encountered forgotten iron and copper deposits, now put to work again by the Israelis, and extensive mining and refining installations of Solomon's time. The Bible had indeed served the archaeologist well.

The Wadi Araba was intensively explored in 1934 under the auspices of the American School of Oriental Research in Jerusalem, the Hebrew Union College in Cincinnati, and the Transjordan Department of Antiquities. Clues found then pointed to the site of Ezion-geber, King Solomon's port on the Gulf of Aqaba at the head of the Red Sea. (It was from Ezion-geber that, in partnership with the Phoenician king, Hiram of Tyre, Solomon sent out a fleet to Ophir.) The Wadi Araba discoveries and the subsequently firmly established site of Ezion-geber (modern Tell el-Kheleifeh) have provided concrete evidence of the surprisingly advanced material and technological Israelite civilization in the tenth century B.C., about which the Bible has so little to say. This evidence has added substantially to our understanding of the age of Solomon and his enterprises. The latter reveal him as a shipping magnate and copper king, a kind of ancient Leopold II.

Nelson Glueck—a reform rabbi with a doctorate from the University of Jena—is now president of Hebrew Union College-Jewish Institute of Religion. For several terms director of the American School of Oriental Research both in Jerusalem and Baghdad, he continued his work in the Negev after Israel became independent. He carried out consecutive campaigns during the three summer months of annual academic recess and discovered 450 sites in the Negev going back as far as the fourth millennium B.C., showing that human resolution and energy in Judaean and Nabataean times enabled agriculture and cities to flourish in the Negev although it was as arid 10,000 years ago as it is now.

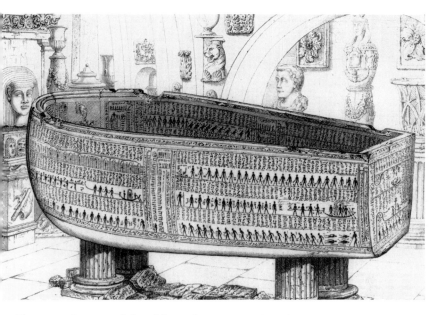

The sarcophagus, exhibited by Belzoni in London, from the tomb of Seti I.

The Serapeum near Memphis as it appeared to Mariette's contemporaries.

The mummy of Ramses II, one of the finds at Deir el-Bahari for which Maspero was responsible.

A tablet found at Tell el-Amarna and acquired by Budge for the British Museum. Photograph courtesy the Trustees of the British Museum.

The step pyramid at Medûm that Petrie investigated. Photograph from Ludwig Borchardt, *Die Entstehung der Pyramide*, J. Springer, Berlin, 1928.

A papyrus, containing the Sayings of Jesus, discovered at Oxyrhynchus by Grenfell and Hunt. Photograph courtesy the Bodleian Library.

The scene that met Carter's eyes in the antechamber of Tutankhamen's tomb. Photograph by Harry Burton, The Metropolitan Museum of Art.

Layard's workmen uncovering
the gigantic head at Nimrud.

The cliff at Behistun which Rawlinson climbed to take casts of the inscriptions of Darius the Great. Photograph courtesy the
Trustees of the British Museum.

The tablet identified by Smith as containing an Assyrian account of the Deluge. Photograph courtesy the Trustees of the British Museum.

A headdress and ornaments found by Woolley at Ur, on a model of the head of a Sumerian lady. Photograph courtesy the Trustees of the British Museum.

The Ur-Nammu law code that Kramer deciphered. Photograph courtesy The University Museum, Philadelphia.

The first alphabetical tablet discovered by Schaeffer at Ras Shamra. Photograph courtesy The British Academy.

A panoramic view of Glueck's excavation of Ezion-Geber

Pottery jars in which Dead Sea Scrolls were found. Photograph
courtesy Arab Information Center.

("King Solomon's Pittsburgh"). Photograph courtesy Dr. Nelson Glueck.

One of the Dead Sea Scrolls (the Manual of Discipline). Photograph
courtesy Israel Office of Information.

The walls of the monastery at Khirbet Qumran in the foreground and, just beyond in the hills overlooking the Dead Sea, caves in which scrolls were found. Photograph courtesy Arab Information Center.

Caves, within sight of the monastery at Khirbet Qumran, in which some of the Dead Sea Scrolls were found. Photograph courtesy Arab Information Center.

Schliemann's excavation at Troy.

The ruins of the royal archives at Boghazköy, where Winckler found the tablets that enabled him to identify the site as the capital of the Hittites. Photograph from Puchstein-Kohl-Krencker, *Boghazköi, Die Bauwerke*, Leipzig, J. C. Hinrichs Verlag, 1912.

Hogarth's excavation at Ephesus. Photograph courtesy
Macmillan & Co., Ltd., London.

A view of Evans' excavation of the Palace of Minos, showing a restored portico. Photograph courtesy British Information Services.

A clay tablet from Knossos written in the Linear Script B first deciphered by Ventris. (BELOW) A drawing of the same tablet, which lists: "9 women, 1 larger girl, 1 smaller girl, 1 larger boy, 1 (?) smaller boy." The first word, in big letters, is probably a feminine adjective describing where the women come from.

Photograph and drawing courtesy Oxford University Press.

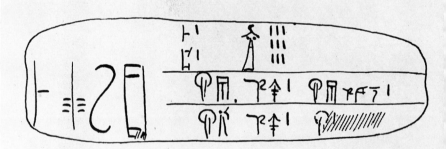

King Solomon's Pittsburgh

NELSON GLUECK

King Solomon made a fleet of ships in Ezion-geber, which is beside Eloth on the shore of the Red Sea in the land of Edom. . . . Once in three years the fleet came in bringing gold, silver, ivory, apes, peacocks . . . a very great amount of red sandalwood and precious stones.   I KINGS 9:26; 10:22, 11.

EZION-GEBER has always been a romantic name to students of ancient history, but little more. It figured in Biblical accounts before the time of Solomon as a resting place of the Israelites for a short time during the years of their wanderings in the wilderness. It is mentioned also as being the seaport of one of his successors, Jehoshaphat, whose newly built fleet foundered on the rocks before it could undertake its first voyage. For almost three thousand years, however, all memory of its location had disappeared from the minds of men, as if it had been little more than a candle-flame that had flickered fitfully in the night and then been blown out.

The Biblical description of the location of Ezion-geber is sufficient to give an approximate idea of its whereabouts. In one passage we are told that the Israelites left Ezion-geber behind when they trekked through the Arabah on their way to Moab and to the promised land (Deuteronomy 2,8). The Wadi Arabah, we may repeat, is the great rift which extends between the southern end of the Dead Sea and the Gulf of Aqabah, and has retained its ancient name down to this very day. The Gulf of Aqabah is the modern name of the northeastern tongue of the Red Sea, or

From Glueck's *The Other Side of the Jordan* (1940). Copyright 1940 by the American Schools of Oriental Research. Reprinted by permission of the author and the American Schools of Oriental Research.

the Yam Suf as it is called in the Hebrew Bible. Somewhere, then, near the southern end of the Wadi Arabah, facing the Gulf of Aqabah, was located the port of Ezion-geber, which subsequently became known as Elath.

There were many different theories as to the exact spot of the original site. Commonly accepted was the notion that the Red Sea had retreated, during the course of three thousand years, for a distance varying between twenty-five and thirty-five kilometers, and therefore that Ezion-geber was to be found nowhere near the present seashore. Scholars paid serious attention to the story of an imaginative guide who was determined to furnish his charges with an interesting account upon which they could buttress their preconceived notions, failing factual information. Thus, on most of the maps of ancient Palestine, it will be seen that Ezion-geber is located at the head of a supposedly dried-up section of the Gulf of Aqabah, at a distance which is more than an ordinary day's camel ride from the present shore-line.

The story was told that the Gulf of Aqabah once extended as far north as a place called Mene'iyeh, which is about thirty-three kilometers from the present shore-line. At Mene'iyeh, so the tale ran, was an ancient seaport, whose inhabitants possessed many ships. Unfortunately, they offended Allah, who caused a long torrential downpour of rain to descend upon the city, with the result that it was completely flooded and destroyed. Furthermore, great quantities of earth and huge boulders were washed down from the neighboring hills, so choking up the bed of the Gulf that its waters were forced to retreat to their present position. This fairy story found favor in the eyes of its hearers, and, on the basis of it, maps were marked with an impossible location for Ezion-geber, situated high and dry in the Wadi Arabah, and far from the harbor where once Solomon's ships were actually anchored. There is some truth to the story that the Gulf of Aqabah has retreated from the ancient shore-line during the course of three thousand years, but the retreat measures some five hundred meters, and not twenty-five thousand or more.

As a result of the discovery of the extensive mining and smelting sites in the Wadi Arabah dating to the time of Solomon, it was possible several years ago to designate Solomon as a great copper king, and by far the most famous of them all. It was known then too that the site of Ezion-geber must be sought somewhere on or very near the present shore-line of the Gulf of Aqabah, because, first of all . . . one of the mining sites belonging to the period of Solomon had been discovered directly overlooking the Gulf. Secondly, the presence nearby of the ancient site of the originally Nabataean city of Aila, which was occupied practically continuously from the 3rd century B.C. down to the mediaeval Arabic period, and which is located near the northeast shore of the head of the Gulf of Aqabah, precluded the possibility that the north shore-line of the Gulf had been radically changed either between the 6th and 3rd centuries B.C. or in the centuries intervening between the mediaeval Arabic period and our day. It remained for a German explorer, named Fritz Frank, to discover an insignificant looking mound, Tell Kheleifeh, which is situated above five hundred meters from the shore and is about half way between the eastern and western ends of the head of the Gulf. He found large quantities of pottery fragments on the surface of the mound, which he judged to be old. When the expedition of the American School of Oriental Research at Jerusalem was able to examine the pottery on the site, it was seen immediately that it was the same as the pottery at the mining sites in the rest of the Wadi Arabah to the north, and that the main period of occupation of Tell Kheleifeh must be assigned to and after the time of King Solomon. The American School expedition was thus able to concur in the suggestion of Frank that Tell Kheleifeh should be identified with Ezion-geber.

At last the long-sought-for site had been found, approximately near the location where one would logically imagine it to have been. Soundings were undertaken to determine the approximate outer depth of the debris and the extent of the ruins of the buried city. We learned that the shifting sands blown out of the Wadi Arabah had covered much of the area of the ruined port, and that extensive excavations would have to be undertaken before it could be uncovered and some of its secrets revealed. The American School, with the assistance of a grant from the American Philosophical Society, undertook the excavations there in March, 1938, and finished its first campaign in May of that year. During April and May, 1939, a second season's excavations were carried out, again financed largely by a generous grant from the American Philosophical Society.

The location of Ezion-geber was conditioned by a number of factors. At first glance, one wonders what induced the original builders to choose the particular site they did, because it is about the most uninviting one along the entire shore of the northern end of the Gulf of Aqabah. Situated in the bottom of a curve banked on the east side by the hills of Edom, which continue into Arabia, and on the west side by the hills of Palestine, which continue into Sinai, it is open to the full fury of the winds and sandstorms from the north that blow along the center of the Wadi Arabah as if forced through a wind tunnel.

It is not difficult to understand why the port could not have been built farther to the west. From Mrashrash, at the northwestern end of the Gulf, to the site of Ezion-geber, there is no sweet water obtainable for drinking purposes in a distance of some three and a half kilometers. The police stationed at Mrashrash send all the way to Aqabah, at the northeastern end of the Gulf, about seven kilometers for their drinking water. The point where the sweet-water wells begin is marked almost exactly by the location of the ruins of Ezion-geber. From there eastwards there is a continuous line of such wells, increasing in number the closer one gets to Aqabah, and marked by a correspondingly increasing number of date-palm trees between the two points.

While one realizes, then, why the early builders of Ezion-geber could not very well have built farther to the west, one wonders at first why they did not build farther to the east, nearer to the site of the modern mud-brick village of Aqabah. There is more water and more protection there from the winds and the sandstorms of Wadi Arabah. The actual excavations were to reveal that the founders of the city had acted wisely. The sandstorms frequently made our work impossible, and at times blotted out vision of the Gulf at a distance of a hundred meters. By the simple process of walking less than a kilometer to the east or west of the site, it was possible to escape the sandstorms; and, looking back, one could see great clouds of sand hovering over the mound and moving directly in front of it towards the sea, calling to mind the Biblical description of the pillar of cloud by day and the pillar of fire by night. The strong winds which blow steadily from the north were evidently a feature so desirable to the architects of Ezion-geber that they built the city directly in their path.

The excavations were begun at the northwest end of the mound for various reasons, not the least of them being consideration for the direction of the winds. It was found that all the houses were made of mud-brick. A large building with ten rooms, which occupied the entire northwest corner of the mound, was opened up. It soon became evident that this was not an ordinary large building or palace, but a completely novel type of structure, the like of which had not previously been discovered in the entire ancient Near East. The walls of the rooms were pierced with two rows of flues, and the main walls were interconnected by a system of air-channels inside the walls, into which the upper rows of flues opened. The lower rows completely pierced the thickness of the walls between the rooms. The originally unfired yellowish mud-bricks had been baked, by the heat of the fires in the rooms, to the consistency of kiln-fired bricks. Masses of hard baked clay-debris, on which pottery crucibles had been placed, completed the picture. It became evident that the building was an elaborate smelter or refinery, where previously "roasted" ores were worked up into ingots of purer metal. It was obvious, both from the sulphuric discoloration of the walls and from the fragments of raw ore and numerous finished articles discovered, that the refinery at Ezion-geber was devoted mainly to copper, of which, as we have seen, great quantities abound in the immediate vicinity and along most of the length of the Wadi Arabah, and in adjacent Sinai. Iron also was treated in this plant.

During the second season of excavations we discovered that the smelter at the northwest corner of the site was not unique at Ezion-geber, but was merely a unit in an elaborate complex of industrial plants of similar nature. They were all devoted to the smelting and refining of copper and iron and the manufacturing of metal articles for home and foreign markets. The entire town, in its first and second periods, was a phenomenal industrial site. A forced draft system for the furnaces was employed, and later abandoned and forgotten, to be re-discovered only in modern times. Ezion-geber was the Pittsburgh of Palestine, in addition to being its most important port. Its rooms were, so to speak, air-conditioned for heat.

The reason, then, why the original builders of Ezion-geber chose the inclement site they did for the location of their city was that they wanted the strong winds blowing from a known direction to furnish the draft for the furnace rooms in the re-fineries, and enable them to dispense with an expensive and burdensome bellows system. It was a matter of harnessing the elements for industrial purposes. More important to them than much water for the palm groves, and protection from sandstorms on a location farther to the east, were strong and continuous winds which would enable them to operate the refineries with their intricate system of flues and air-channels.

In addition to the fact that the entire first town of Ezion-geber, which for convenience we shall call Ezion-geber I, represented a carefully integrated industrial complex, the excavations have shown that it was built completely anew on virgin soil, and that it experienced no gradual growth and development but was built at one time, within the space of a year or two, from a precon-ceived and carefully worked-out plan. Surveyors, architects, and engineers had evidently looked over the north shore of the Gulf of Aqabah in advance with a view to the particular requirements they had in mind. They were industrial scouts, sent out to spy out the land, and they chose a town site which no builders would have selected in the normal course of events for the founding of a settlement. They needed, as we have seen, strong and con-tinuous winds, coming from a known direction to provide drafts for furnaces; they needed also sweet water to drink, a central point commanding strategic commercial and military cross-roads, and access to the sea. Great quantities of copper and iron were present in the Wadi Arabah, and provided the most important impetus for the building of the first town on the site known today as Tell Kheleifeh.

The town site chosen, intricate plans for the establishing of a very complicated factory complex must have been drawn up. A great deal of specialized technical skill was necessary. Thick and high walls of sun-dried bricks had to be erected, with flues and air-channels in them, and with allowances made for the weight of the wall above them. The angle of the buildings had carefully to be chosen to get the full benefit of the winds from the north. Bricks had to be made by the thousands, and laid by expert brick-layers. In no period in the history of the subsequent towns, each built on top of the ruins of the previous one, were bricks as excellently made and skillfully laid as during the first period. Certainly not in the poor little town of Aqabah several miles to the east, which in modern times has superseded Ezion-geber. All the bricks were laid in complicated systems of headers and stretchers, with the corners of the walls well bonded together. One reads today of new towns, planned in advance, and springing up as if by magic on previously bare soil with the aid of modern transportation facilities and mechanical equipment. Ezion-geber, however, still remote from civilized points today, was a long and difficult journey from them in ancient times. It took the writer thirteen days on camel back, several years ago, to travel from the south end of the Dead Sea, which is already comparatively far from Jerusalem, to the north shore of the Gulf of Aqabah. It took a great deal of business ability, as well as architectural, engineering, and metallurgical skill to construct the factory town and seaport of Ezion-geber, and to keep the production-line going.

One can easily visualize the conditions existing about three millennia ago, when the idea of building this place was first conceived and then brilliantly translated into reality. Thousands of laborers had to be assembled, housed, fed, and protected at the chosen building site. As a matter of fact, most of them were probably slaves, who had to be guarded and goaded to work. Skilled technicians of all kinds had to be recruited. Great caravans had to be collected to transport materials and food. An effective business organization had to be called into existence to regulate the profitable flow of raw materials and finished or semi-finished products. There was, so far as we know, only one man who possessed the strength, wealth, and wisdom capable of initiating and carrying out such a highly complex and specialized undertaking. He was King Solomon. He alone in his day had the ability, the vision, and the power to establish an important industrial center and sea-port such a comparatively long distance from the capital city of Jerusalem.

The wise ruler of Israel was a copper king, a shipping magnate, a merchant prince, and a great builder. Through his manifold activities, he became at once the blessing and the curse of his country. With increased power and wealth came a centralization of authority and a ruthless dictatorship which ignored the democratic traditions of his own people. There resulted a counter-development of forces of reaction and revolt, which were immediately after Solomon's death to rend his kingdom asunder. During his lifetime, however, Solomon reigned supreme. The evil he did lived after him. His far-flung net of activities extended from Egypt to Phoenicia, and from Arabia to Syria. Ezion-geber represents one of his greatest, if indeed up to the present time his least known accomplishments. . . .

The likelihood, therefore, that there was no one besides King Solomon in greater Palestine during the latter part of the 10th century B.C., who possessed the energy and the ability and power and wealth to build such a site as Ezion-geber I, seems to become a certainty through the clear archaeological evidence at our disposal. We find it significant that at the very end of the account in I Kings 9 of Solomon's manifold building activities throughout Palestine, there is narrated in some detail the story of the construction of a fleet of ships for him at Ezion-geber, which, manned by Phoenician sailors, sailed to Ophir for gold. For some reason or other, the author of this account failed to mention the fact that Solomon exported ingots of copper and iron and finished metal objects on these ships for the gold and other products obtainable in Ophir; and also failed to state that in all probability at the same time as the ships were being constructed, the port-city and industrial town of Ezion-geber I was also being built.

Inasmuch as the Ezion-geber of Solomon was found to rest on virgin soil, with no traces whatsoever of earlier remains, it becomes necessary to conclude that this is not the Ezion-geber which the Israelites saw when they emerged from the Wilderness of Sinai after the sojourn there lasting forty years. They saw probably a tiny, straggling settlement, with a few mud-brick huts and scraggly palms, farther to the east, where the drinking water is less saline and the sandstorms do not occur. All traces of this earlier site have disappeared, only its name surviving in the bustling town of Ezion-geber I, whose finer residential suburb must also, however, have been farther east, near the site of the modern village of Aqabah.

After the destruction by fire of Ezion-geber I, it was rebuilt in the subsequent period and functioned again as an industrial town of much the same nature as its predecessor. Changes were made in the outer fortifications. A secondary wall was placed outside the former main wall of the previous city, and the gateway was altered. The main changes in the gateway, in addition to the fact that the floor-level was raised, are that the entrances to the two pairs of guard-rooms were blocked up, creating thus four small, squarish rooms behind the passageway, and an additional mud-brick pillar was put on each side of the third gateway, narrowing the passageway. In other words, the general scheme of the gateway of Ezion-geber I with three doors was adhered to, but the guard-rooms were transformed into casemates.

The Solomonic city of Megiddo was destroyed by the Egyptian king Shishak (954-924 B.C.). It does not necessarily follow that Ezion-geber I was destroyed at the same time as Stratum IV at Megiddo, although the possibility must be considered. Professor Albright has called the writer's attention to the fact that in Shishak's list of conquered Asiatic cities, found at Karnak in Egypt, a large section of the names must be Edomite, as pointed out independently by himself and Noth. The general industrial, commercial, and strategic importance of the Wadi Arabah, with its rich mines, and of Ezion-geber, made them a fine prize for invaders. It is interesting in this connection that Albright proposes to explain *ngb* in the Shishak list as Hebrew *nqb*, "tunnel, shaft, mine." Noth also has marshalled considerable evidence indicating that Shishak's campaign extended rather far east of the south side of Palestine, and may in this area have been directed toward the Wadi Arabah. In view of these considerations, and of general and specific archaeological data which cannot be further detailed here, we think it likely that Ezion-geber I was destroyed by Shishak's forces during the same campaign which resulted in the destruction of many towns in Palestine, including Megiddo, shortly after Solomon's death.

When fire radically destroyed the second settlement, there was built over it a third one. In its later history, the site of Ezion-geber was called Elath or Eloth. The third city, in which two periods can be distinguished, was constructed on entirely new lines without regard for the walls or foundations of the preceding settlements, and it is, on the whole, the best preserved one. Many of its walls still stand almost to their original height, and in a number of instances the houses could be completely reconstructed on paper. In a report on the excavations at Hureidha in the Hadhramaut in South Arabia, Miss Caton-Thompson has described one of the homesteads unearthed there. The excavations disclosed a mud-brick building, formerly white-washed, fitted with mud-brick benches. Logs of wood reinforced the door-treads. The ceiling had been constructed, in the fashion still practical in the region, of twigs laid in parallel bundles across the rafters and over-daubed with mud. This description fits almost exactly the houses in Ezion-geber : Elath at an earlier date, and modern Arabic mud-brick houses near there today.

During the first season of excavations we discovered on the level of the third city the fragments of a large jar, on two of whose pieces were incised the first ancient South Arabic letters ever discovered in a controlled excavation. These letters belong to the Minaean script. The Minaeans are reported by Pliny to be the oldest known commercial people in South Arabia, controlling the Incense Route, and monopolizing the trade in myrrh and frankincense. It has been possible since the discovery of these fragments to put them together, and thus to restore most of the shape of the jar, which may well have been the container of precious products from as far away as South Arabia. It was perhaps in similar jars that the Queen of Sheba brought some of her valuable presents to King Solomon. It may have belonged to a Minaean trade representative living in Elath.

In an article on Arabia Miss Caton-Thompson wrote: "And so the Ezion-geber sherd—dating from a century or two after Solomon—with its lettered hall-mark of South Arabian origin, may be a rarity which not all the excavations to come will convert into a commonplace of finds." During the second season of excavations at Tell Kheleifeh, yet another ancient Arabic inscription was found on a large jar, in the same level as the one previously discovered. It may be an owner's mark. The discovery of this additional inscription emphasizes again the intimate commercial relationship between Ezion-geber : Elath and Arabia, and underlines anew the importance of the former as a trade-center and seaport, as well as an important industrial site. Miss Caton-Thompson and her colleagues have recently discovered South Arabian inscriptions during the excavations of the temple at Hureidha, apparently first built in the 4th century B.C. They are similar in type to the Minaean characters found incised on the jar at Tell Kheleifeh. The Hureidha inscriptions thus again furnish an approximate date, less definite to be sure than that obtained from the excavations at Tell Kheleifeh, upon which the history of the South Arabian type of ancient Arabian writing can be pegged. The distance between Ezion-geber and Hureidha is approximately 1200 miles, and about four centuries intervene between the South Arabian inscriptions found at the two sites. It begins to appear, however, that both places were set in one cultural pattern, and that Arabia continued into what is today called Transjordan, and thus in ancient times almost literally abutted the territory of Israel. To this day, for instance, the "skyscraper" houses of southern Arabia described in recent books such as Freya Stark's *Southern Gates of Arabia,* linger on in ruined form as far north as Ma'an in southern Transjordan. The site at the southern end of the great Spice Route, definitely contemporary with Ezion-geber : Elath, is bound sooner or later to be found.

In addition to the trade by sea and land with Arabia, much evidence was discovered of trade with Egypt and Sinai. There were found, particularly in the third town built on the site, counting from the bottom up, such varied objects coming from Sinai and Egypt as carnelian, agate, amethyst, and crystal beads, cartouche-like seal impressions, a tiny faïence amulet head of the god Bes, a small Egyptian amulet of a cat, fragments of alabaster cups and plates and buttons, and a part of a scaraboid bead. The cat amulet was characteristic of the cult of the goddess Bast, whose temple was at Bubastis in Egypt, which was also the seat of the XXIInd dynasty. The founder of that dynasty was Sheshonk I (Shishak), mentioned above.

Stamped impressions were found on pottery, revealing both Syrian and Arabian influence. Various designs were found incised on some of the pottery fragments, one of which looked like a "Byzantine" cross, another of which resembled the "Star of David," and a third one which was like a swastika—in this instance a "non-Aryan" swastika. Stamped jar handles were discovered bearing the legend in ancient Edomite-Phoenician-Hebrew characters *belonging to Qws'nl the servant of the king.* A small jug was found with a late Edomite inscription which may perhaps be read as *belonging to Am(zrn).*

Of much interest were numerous large copper and iron nails (the copper ones being a mixture of iron and copper), found in the third and fourth town. These nails, spikes really, are usually about six inches long. It seems reasonable to believe that they were used in the construction of boats, an important activity of the industrial life of each of the towns built on the site. Pitch was found, used probably, at least partially, for caulking the boats. Furthermore, in several rooms of the two uppermost towns were found numerous fragments of ropes of all sizes, some of them so large and thick that they could only have been used for ship ropes. Some of the smaller ropes were made of twisted palm branches, much as they are in Aqabah today. The larger three-coil ropes were made of hundreds of fibre threads taken from the bark of the palm tree, twisted into large cords and coils and then twisted into a thick, heavy rope. The art of making this type of rope is no longer known in the modern village of Aqabah. Oak planks from timber cut in the forests of the hills of Edom furnished the basic material for the building of the boats, even as these forests furnished the fuel, converted into charcoal, for firing the smelting furnaces in the Wadi Arabah and at Ezion-geber, as we have pointed out. Phoenician craftsmen constructed the boats in all probability, and Phoenician sailors manned them. They gave them the name by which the boats sailing from Phoenicia to Tarshish were known, namely, Tarshish boats. Besides copper and iron nails, other metal objects were found, including fish-hooks, lance- and spear-heads, daggers, fragments of copper dishes, and fibulae, the safety pin of the Iron Age. Pottery, much of it peculiar to this site, beads, cloth, and baskets were also manufactured.

When the third town, which had two periods of occupation, was destroyed by fire, a fourth town was built above it. The foundations of the walls of this fourth town were now between 3.50 and 4 meters above the foundations of the walls of the first town. Whether or not this town was surrounded by an outer fortification wall is impossible to say at present. The likelihood seems to be, to judge from the first two towns, that both of the latter ones were also surrounded by outer fortification walls. There is but little of the fourth town left, because it has been weathered away except on the highest part of the mound. Enough of it was unearthed, however, to show that it was a town of a size comparable with that of the preceding one. A new type of brick was used during its construction. This fourth town was also ultimately destroyed by fire. Whatever buildings, if any, may have been constructed subsequently above its ruins, have completely disappeared.

A few centimeters, on the average, below the topmost surface of the mound at its highest level, were found a number of imported Greek sherds, which belong probably to the latest phase of the fourth town. These sherds were pieces of imported red-figured and degenerate black-figured Attic ware, which may be dated to about the middle of the 5th century B.C. They were probably brought from Greece to Gaza or Ascalon, and then taken by the trade-route which led from Ascalon and Gaza to Qurnub, then to Ain Hosb, and thence through the Wadi Arabah directly to Elath, or via Petra to various sites in Transjordan. This is the trade-route which assumed great importance particularly during the Nabataean period, and continued in use through the Byzantine period. These Attic sherds had travelled a long distance from the shores of Greece to the northern shores of the Gulf of Aqabah, and furnish indisputable evidence of the presence of a settlement on Tell Kheleifeh during the first half of the 5th century B.C. It was probably a trading community,

whose existence depended in all likelihood upon the great incense and spice traffic, which continued as of old to flow along
the route from Arabia to Elath, whence it diverged to Transjordan, Syria, Persia, Palestine, and the Mediterranean countries.
It would seem likely now that Attic pottery of the 5th century
B.C. should be discovered also in Arabia, because the wares found
at Tell Kheleifeh were in all probability transshipped farther
south, either because of their own intrinsic value or because they
may have been containers of products, such as wines, for instance, which were exchanged for the spices of Arabia. There
are no indications of extensive mining and smelting of copper
and iron deposits in the Wadi Arabah during the 5th century B.C.,
which would have yielded the export commodities similar to those
available in great quantities to Solomon in exchange for the
precious products obtainable from South Arabia.

Belonging to the same period as the Attic sherds, and also
found near the top surface of the mound, were several small,
broken, Aramaic ostraca. Some of them were written with the
same characters as found on the Elephantine papyri and ostraca
found in Egypt, and may, like them, be assigned to the 5th century B.C. and later. One was a wine receipt. They are part of the
same picture of occupation that is furnished by the Attic sherds.
They also lend a definite basis for the suggestion made above,
that products of various kinds, including wine, perhaps even
Greek wines, were imported to Elath and then exported to Arabia
in exchange for its incense and spices.

With this last settlement the history of Ezion-geber : Elath was
concluded. It extended from the 10th to the 5th century B.C., and
perhaps even a century later. When the Nabataeans subsequently
rose to great power, they also built a trade-center and port on
the north shore of the Gulf of Aqabah, but moved it about three
kilometers farther to the east, where in Roman times it was
known as Aila. The hey-day of Ezion-geber, later to be known
as Elath, was during the time of Solomon in the 10th century B.C.

15. MILLAR BURROWS

The discovery of the Dead Sea Scrolls was completely unantici-
pated, and their exciting contents came as a shock. In some cases
enthusiasm over the scrolls and conviction of their unique importance have outrun the more hesitant and sober judgments of
scholarship. However, it has gradually been realized by Christian
and Jewish scholars alike that the findings necessitate thorough
and perhaps disturbing re-examination of accepted views.

The value of the scrolls to Old Testament studies has been
generally accepted, but initially some New Testament scholars
showed considerable reluctance to acknowledge their significance.
If their estimated date of origin was correct—and there is no
longer any reason to doubt that they were written during the
first and second centuries B.C.—here were Hebrew Old Testament
manuscripts (and much else besides) about one thousand years
older than texts on which modern Biblical translations are based.
Theologians, philologists, and historians were stimulated by this
evidence from the first and second centuries B.C., for it could add
enormously to knowledge of the Hebrew religion at a vital stage
of its development, just prior to the rise of Christianity.

In time, most New Testament scholars agreed that the ancient
Hebrew (and Aramaic) texts would contribute as much to the
understanding of the Gospels as to Judaism. Renowned scholars
like A. Dupont-Sommer and W. F. Albright were bold enough to
see in the new material evidence that would revolutionize our views
concerning Christian beginnings. Increasingly, even their more
cautious colleagues have found proof in the scrolls of a much
closer connection between certain Jewish sects and the religion
of Jesus than had previously been suspected. For the scrolls revealed the deep-rooted Jewish background of the ethos, practices, and rites of the Christian faith. As described in the "Manual
of Discipline," the name given to one of the scrolls by Millar

Burrows, the Qumran sect had affinities with Christianity, not only in its monastic characteristics, but in certain rituals like ablution and communal eating (the baptism and breaking of the bread of the early Christians) as well as in organization. Also the Qumran sect looked forward to a new covenant and the appearance of a savior. Extremists went so far as to see the life, mission, and martyrdom of Jesus anticipated in the "teacher of righteousness" who is referred to in the Habakkuk Scroll. According to Dupont-Sommer, "the teacher of righteousness was believed to be an incarnate divine being who was put to death by his enemies and was expected by his followers to rise from the dead."

As for the importance of the Qumran texts to Judaism, the knowledge that the latter was far more diversified in its scriptural heritage before it came to be fixed in the Talmudic age, was amply and concretely confirmed. Light is thus thrown on the richness of Judaism in the period of the scrolls, highlighting a non-orthodox deviant, which in previous sources had been dealt with with little sympathy. Professor Burrows summed up judiciously the significance of the scrolls: "Everything that is important for Judaism in the last two or three centuries before Christ and in the first century A.D. is important also for Christianity. By enriching our understanding of Judaism in the period in which Christianity arose, the Dead Sea Scrolls have given us material for a better understanding of the New Testament and early Christianity. It has been said that the discoveries will revolutionize New Testament scholarship. This may perhaps cause some alarm. There is no danger, however, that our understanding of the New Testament will be so revolutionized by the Dead Sea Scrolls as to require a revision of any basic article of Christian faith. All scholars who have worked on the texts will agree that this has not happened and will not happen."

Where beliefs and sentiments are involved, controversies are bound to occur and scholars soon found themselves in disagreement as to the various aspects and implications of the scrolls. Heated discussions ensued, which have been called the battle of the scrolls. Some feared a threat to Christian revelation. Divisions arose, first of all, over the actual genuineness of the scrolls and then over their dating. Still more heat was generated over matters of interpretation. And what was the sect of the scrolls and what was its relationship to Christian origins, the early Church, and the New Testament? Was the sect that had copied and written the scrolls identical with the Essenes, known from famous descriptions in Josephus, Philo Judaeus, and Pliny the Elder? What, in the light of the new evidence, was the role of John the Baptist, who almost certainly had contact with the Essenes and very likely was one of them?

Such debates are still going on. In a sense, it is a token of the immense value of the scrolls that they continue to raise crucial and pertinent questions. The range of debate has also been greatly extended by the additional discoveries that have been made after the 1947 find. The first cave, now usually referred to as Qumran Cave 1 (Q1) was scientifically excavated in 1949 by Father Roland de Vaux, Director of the École Biblique of Jerusalem, and G. Lankester Harding, Director of the Department of Antiquities of Jordan. By then it had been badly ransacked by treasure-seeking Bedouins. Nevertheless, a few valuable fragments were found and the cave was clearly established as a hiding-place for an ancient library. All the time, illegal search by the Bedouins continued, promoted by the high prices paid for manuscripts. The Palestine Archaeological Museum, meanwhile, became a repository for hundreds of fragments of manuscripts and scrolls. More significant Bedouin finds in 1952 led to an organized campaign in the Qumran area under Father de Vaux and William L. Reed. In thirty-nine caves clay vessels were found that were similar to those in Cave 1, and two of the vessels contained manuscripts; in one cave were two copper rolls that proved difficult to unroll but which were deciphered in 1956 in England. Another Bedouin exploit, in late 1952, was the discovery of what has since been called Cave 4. This proved even richer than Cave 1, yielding thousands of fragments and a number of larger texts. About 330 had been identified by 1956 and found to comprise not only parts of all the Old Testament books except Esther but also numerous apocryphal books, some of them of an apocalyptic nature. Much of the contents of Cave 4 were acquired by McGill and Manchester universities.

Further search outside the Qumran area opened up large caves at adjacent Wadi Murabba'at and Khirbet Mird. At both new sites manuscripts of more recent origin than those from the Qumran caves have been encountered; a rare exception was a Hebrew papyrus of the sixth century B.C. In addition to Biblical fragments, these more recent manuscripts were mainly business documents written in Greek and Aramaic. Probably the outstanding finds from Wadi Murabba'at are Hebrew letters written at the time of the revolt against the Romans in 132-35 A.D., perhaps by the rebel leader Simeon ben Kosiba (Bar Kochba) himself.

Although it is little known, the Dead Sea Scrolls found in the 1940s and 1950s were not the first Hebrew manuscript material to come from the Judaean desert. Indeed, once they were persuaded of the authenticity of the Dead Sea Scrolls, scholars remembered a letter written in the ninth century A.D. in which the Nestorian Patriarch Timotheus I mentions discoveries in a cave near Jericho made by a shepherd searching for a lost sheep. Among the discoveries were Old Testament books as well as non-canonical works, and it is possible that these writings came from the Qumran Cave 1. Another earlier Hebrew manuscript discovery is the celebrated Nash Papyrus, found in Egypt in 1902. It closely resembles the script of the Dead Sea Scrolls and, according to Albright, also dates from the first or second century B.C. And although the "Damascus Document" that turned up in Cairo early in this century is a tenth-century copy, it is very likely that its source had come from the caves near the Dead Sea.

At the time of the discovery of the Dead Sea Scrolls, Professor Millar Burrows was director of the American School of Oriental Research in Jerusalem, and he has had firsthand acquaintance with the finding, acquisition, and examination of the scrolls. Internationally known for his studies in Old and New Testament theology and in Semitic languages and for his excavations in Bible lands, he was particularly well prepared for dealing with the scrolls when they turned up during his tenure in Jerusalem.

Professor Burrows has taught since 1934 at the Yale University Divinity School. In 1950 he was appointed chairman of Near

Eastern Languages and Literature of the graduate school at
Yale. He is the author of many articles and books. He has also
been active in relief work for the displaced Palestinian Arabs;
since 1954, he has been president of the American Middle East
Relief, Incorporated.

The Dead Sea Scrolls

MILLAR BURROWS

IF WE HAD ONLY KNOWN it when we went down to the shore
of the Dead Sea on October 25, 1947, we could have walked to
the cave where an extraordinary discovery of manuscripts had
been made some seven or eight months earlier. Conducting field
trips to study the archeology and historical geography of Palestine was one of my duties as Director of the American School of
Oriental Research at Jerusalem that year. This particular excursion, however, was not so much a scientific expedition as a
pleasure trip and pilgrimage combined. At Kallia, near the north-
western corner of the Dead Sea, some of our party took a swim
in the thick brine before we proceeded to the traditional site
of the baptism of Jesus and then back to Jerusalem by way of
Jericho. In the party were two young scholars who will have a
prominent part in this narrative, Dr. John C. Trever and Dr.
William H. Brownlee, who were both students at our school
that year on fellowships. At the time of our excursion the manuscripts, which were later to become famous, were already at
Jerusalem in the possession of the Syrian Monastery of St. Mark
and of the Hebrew University, but we at the American School
of Oriental Research did not learn of their existence for another
four months.

Because these manuscripts were found in a cave near the

Dead Sea, they are commonly called the Dead Sea Scrolls. Father de Vaux of Jerusalem, whose name will appear often in our story, protests that the scrolls did not come out of the Dead Sea. The name is convenient, however, and will be used here. A more exact designation is the Wadi Qumran Manuscripts, but this does not cover the manuscript fragments found later at other places in the region.

Exactly when and how the first cave and its contents were discovered can hardly be determined now, though the discoverer, a fifteen-year-old boy of the Taamirah tribe of Bedouins, was identified and questioned about two years later. His name was Muhammad adh-Dhib (more exactly *al-di 'b,* i.e., "the wolf," pronounced *adh-dheeb,* the *dh* representing the sound of a soft *th* in English, as in *the*). It was probably in February or March 1947 that he found the scrolls. The Syrian Orthodox archbishop who sought some of them says that he first heard of them in the month of Nisan, which corresponds roughly to our month of April; and Father van der Ploeg of Nijmegen saw them at the Syrian Orthodox monastery late in July. According to one form of the story, Muhammad adh-Dhib was herding goats or looking for a lost sheep when he found the cave; according to another, he and one or two companions were taking goods, perhaps smuggled across the Jordan to Bethlehem. One story has it that they took refuge from a thunderstorm in the cave. Another story is that a runaway goat jumped into the cave, Muhammad adh-Dhib threw a stone after it, and the sound of breaking pottery aroused curiosity, whereupon he called another lad, and the two crawled into the cave and so found the manuscripts.

The cave is in a cliff about five miles south of the place where we went swimming at the northwest corner of the Dead Sea, and about a mile and a quarter back from the shore, in the foothills of the Judean plateau. It is within a mile of an old ruin named Khirbet Qumran. The name Qumran, as pronounced by the Bedouins, sounds a little like Gomorrah, and some of the early European explorers of Palestine thought that Khirbet Qumran might be the site of that ill-fated city. That is quite impossible. Gomorrah was not in this vicinity at all. Another association with the Old Testament is more pertinent. The track from the Jordan Valley to Bethlehem passes near this spot. When Elimelech and his family went from Bethlehem to Moab, and when Naomi and Ruth went back to Bethlehem, they must have followed approximately this same route.

Whenever and however the discovery came about, the cave, when first entered, contained several jars, most of them broken, with pieces of many others. Protruding from the broken jars were scrolls of leather wrapped in linen cloth. They were very brittle and rather badly decomposed, especially at the ends, but it was possible to see that they were inscribed in a strange writing. Muhammad adh-Dhib and his friends, the story goes, took these scrolls to a Muslim sheikh at their market town, Bethlehem. Seeing that the script was not in Arabic and supposing that it was Syriac, the sheikh sent them to a merchant who was a member of the Syrian Orthodox (Jacobite) community at Bethlehem, Khalil Eskander, who informed another merchant belonging to their church at Jerusalem, George Isaiah; and he in turn informed their Metropolitan-Archbishop, Athanasius Yeshue Samuel. In the meantime, if the late Professor Sukenik of the Hebrew University at Jerusalem was correctly informed, the great manuscript of the book of Isaiah, the largest and oldest of all the scrolls, had been offered to a Muslim antiquities dealer at Bethlehem for twenty pounds, but he, not believing that it was ancient, had refused to pay that much for it.

In the heart of the Old City of Jerusalem, just south of what the British and Americans call David Street, there is an interesting little monastery with a fine library of old Syriac manuscripts. This is the Syrian Orthodox Monastery of St. Mark. There is a tradition that it stands on the site of the house of Mark's mother, where the disciples were gathered for prayer when Peter came to them after his miraculous deliverance from prison (Acts 12:12-17). A few years ago a Syriac inscription recording this tradition was found in the monastery. Here Khalil Eskander and George Isaiah brought one of the scrolls and showed it to Archbishop Samuel.

The archbishop recognized that the writing was not Syriac but Hebrew. After breaking off a little piece and burning it, he perceived by the odor that the material was leather or parchment. He told the merchants that he would buy the scrolls. Several weeks went by, however, before they could again get in touch with the Bedouins, who came to Bethlehem only for the weekly market on Saturday. It was not until the first Saturday of the month of Tammuz, which corresponds to July, that the Metropolitan received a telephone call from Khalil Eskander, the merchant in Bethlehem, saying that three Bedouins were there with the scrolls.

Even the archbishop did not see the Bedouins. Instead of coming with them, Eskander apparently sent them to George Isaiah, the Jerusalem merchant. He took them to the monastery but was refused admission, because the priest who met them at the door thought that their dirty, dilapidated manuscripts were of no interest. When the archbishop learned what had happened he telephoned in considerable perturbation to Eskander, who said that two of the Bedouins had returned and consented to leave their scrolls with him, but the third had decided to look elsewhere for a buyer and had taken his share of the scrolls to the Muslim sheikh at Bethlehem. It was presumably this portion that Professor Sukenik acquired in November for the Hebrew University.

Khalil Eskander told Archbishop Samuel further that when George Isaiah and the Bedouins were sent away from the monastery they proceeded to the square just inside the Jaffa Gate. Here they encountered a Jewish merchant who offered to buy the scrolls for a good price and asked the Bedouins to come to his office for the money. George Isaiah, however, persuaded them to refuse this offer.

Two weeks later the two Bedouins who had left their scrolls with Eskander at Bethlehem came back to his shop, and both he and George Isaiah went with them to St. Mark's Monastery. This time they succeeded in seeing the archbishop, and he bought the manuscripts still in their possession—five scrolls. Two of the five scrolls turned out to be successive portions of one manuscript, which had come apart. This was what I named later the "Manual of Discipline." The other three scrolls were the great manuscript of Isaiah already mentioned, a commentary on the book of Habakkuk, and a badly decomposed Aramaic scroll which at this writing has still not been unrolled. For some time we called this simply "the fourth scroll" (counting the two parts of the Manual of Discipline as one). After our return to America, Dr. Trever detached one column, and on the basis of its text identified the document tentatively as the lost book of Lamech; from then on we called it the Lamech Scroll.

At the suggestion of the archbishop, George Isaiah persuaded the Bedouins to take him to the cave, where he saw one whole jar and fragments of others, a mysterious piece of wood lying on a stone, and many fragments of manuscripts, as well as bits of cloth in which the scrolls had been wrapped. In August the archbishop sent one of his priests, Father Yusef, to examine the cave again. The idea of removing the whole jar still in the cave was considered but abandoned, because the jar was too heavy to carry in the intense summer heat of that region, more than a thousand feet below sea level.

During the course of the summer Archbishop Samuel consulted several scholars and showed his scrolls to a number of visitors at the monastery, hoping to gain accurate information concerning the contents, age, and value of the manuscripts. The first person consulted seems to have been a member of the Syrian Orthodox Church, the late Stephan Hannah Stephan, a well-known Orientalist, who was then working with the Department of Antiquities of Palestine. He confidently pronounced the scrolls worthless. Since his special competence was in the field of Arab history rather than in Hebrew archeology or paleography, his judgment in this case can only be attributed to general skepticism.

Archbishop Samuel also mentioned the scrolls to one of the scholars of the French Dominican School of Archeology, Father A. S. Marmadji, another Arabist. It happened that an eminent biblical scholar from Holland, Father J. P. M. van der Ploeg, was then staying at the Dominican Monastery of St. Stephen, with which the School of Archeology is connected. Father Marmadji therefore brought him to see the scrolls and the other manuscripts at the Syrian monastery. Father van der Ploeg at once identified the largest scroll as the book of Isaiah, being perhaps the first to make this identification.

Early in September, Archbishop Samuel took his scrolls to Syria and showed them to the Patriarch of his church at Homs. He tried also to consult the professor of Hebrew at the American University of Beirut, but found that he had not yet returned from his vacation. After returning to Jerusalem, the archbishop tried again to get information from Stephan Hannah Stephan, who at his request brought him some books about the Hebrew alphabet, but these did not give him much help. Still skeptical, Stephan offered to bring a Jewish scholar of his acquaintance, who, he said, was a specialist in such matters. Apparently this was Toviah Wechsler, who later took a prominent part in the public controversy concerning the scrolls.

Wechsler agreed with Stephan that the scrolls were not ancient. Archbishop Samuel quotes him as pointing to a table and saying, "If that table were a box and you filled it full of pound notes, you couldn't even then measure the value of these scrolls if they are two thousand years old as you say!" Later Wechsler decided that he had been misled by some marginal corrections in one of the manuscripts, which were written in ink still so black that he thought it could not be ancient.

Early in October, Archbishop Samuel showed his scrolls to Dr. Maurice Brown, a Jewish physician who had called at the monastery in connection with the use of a building owned by the Syrian Orthodox community. Dr. Brown informed President Judah L. Magnes of the Hebrew University, at whose request two men were sent to the monastery from the university library. After seeing the manuscripts, however, they suggested that someone from the university more competent than they were should be invited to examine the scrolls. Meanwhile Dr. Brown spoke to a Jewish dealer in antiquities named Sassun, who came and looked at the scrolls and suggested that pieces of them be sent to antiquities dealers in Europe and America, but this the Metropolitan was unwilling to do.

The late Dr. E. L. Sukenik, Professor of Archeology at the Hebrew University, had been in America while all this was going on and did not hear of the manuscripts immediately when he returned to Palestine. On November 25 he was shown a fragment of a scroll by an antiquities dealer, who told him about the discovery of the cave and asked whether he would like to buy the scrolls. Although he naturally suspected forgery, Sukenik answered in the affirmative. Four days later he met the dealer again and bought from him some bundles of leather, together with two pottery jars in which the Bedouins claimed to have found the manuscripts.

On the very day that this purchase took place the General Assembly of the United Nations passed the fateful resolution recommending the partition of Palestine. Welcomed by the Jews but bitterly resented by the Arabs, this led to a rapid deterioration in the relations between Jews and Arabs, so that peaceful communication between them soon became impossible. Before this point was reached, however, Sukenik managed to bring his two jars from Bethlehem to the Jewish part of Jerusalem and to buy a few more portions of manuscripts. In this he was encouraged and assisted by President Magnes, who provided money for the purpose.

Up to this time Sukenik had not been informed of the scrolls acquired by the Archbishop Samuel. Early in December he learned about them from one of the men in the university library who had visited the monastery during the summer. Rightly supposing that these manuscripts probably belonged to the same collection as those he had purchased, Sukenik endeavored to visit the monastery, but found that this was no longer possible. There the matter rested until the latter half of January, when he received a letter from a member of the Syrian Orthodox Church named Anton Kiraz, in whose property south of Jerusalem he had previously excavated an ancient tomb. Kiraz wrote that he had some old manuscripts which he would like to show to Sukenik.

Since by this time there was no going back and forth between the Arab and Jewish quarters, the meeting took place at the YMCA, located in what was then Military Zone B, to which passes could be secured for entry from other parts of the city. On seeing the scrolls, Sukenik recognized at once that they and the portions of manuscripts in his possession were indeed parts of the same collection. Kiraz admitted that they had been found in a cave near the Dead Sea, and said he had been to the cave.

He offered to sell the scrolls to the Hebrew University and proposed a conference with the archbishop to discuss terms. Archbishop Samuel, however, says that all this was done without his consent or knowledge.

Kiraz allowed Sukenik to borrow three scrolls for two days, and Sukenik took this opportunity to copy several columns, which he later published, from the Isaiah manuscript. On February 6, according to his account, he returned the scrolls to Kiraz and was shown two others, one or both of which belonged to the Manual of Discipline. It was agreed that there should be another meeting, and that President Magnes and Archbishop Samuel should be present, in order that negotiations for the purchase of the scrolls might be concluded. This meeting never took place.

Meanwhile Archbishop Samuel was making his own arrangements. One of the monks of St. Mark's Monastery, the late Butrus Sowmy, suggested that a trustworthy judgment concerning the scrolls might be obtained from the American School of Oriental Research. To this end he telephoned on February 17 to Bishop Stewart at the Collegiate Church of St. George and asked for the name of some person at the American School whom he might consult. I was absent from Jerusalem at the time, having left on the preceding Sunday for a visit to Iraq. It happened, however, that one of my students, Dr. William H. Brownlee, who was taking Arabic lessons at the Newman School of Missions, had found it necessary to obtain from a resident clergyman a statement certifying that he was a Christian, so that the Arab guards at the roadblocks would allow him to pass back and forth between our school and the Newman School of Missions. He had obtained this certificate from Bishop Stewart, who therefore thought of him at once and gave Sowmy his name, mentioning the fact that I had just left for Baghdad.

Accordingly on Wednesday, February 18, 1948, Butrus Sowmy telephoned to the American School of Oriental Research and asked for Brownlee. Shortly before the call came Brownlee had gone out to buy some wrapping paper for shipping his personal effects to America. The servant who answered the telephone told Sowmy, therefore, that Dr. Brownlee was not in the building, and that I was out of the city, but that Dr. John C. Trever was the Acting Director of the school in my absence. Trever was therefore called to the telephone and invited Sowmy to bring the manuscripts to the school the next day.

At two-thirty Thursday afternoon, as agreed, Butrus Sowmy and his brother Ibrahim came to the school with the scrolls. This time Brownlee had gone to the post office and had again been delayed through roadblocks, so that he missed this opportunity to meet the Syrians. Trever received them and looked at the scrolls, and with Sowmy's permission copied two lines from the largest scroll. Puzzled by the form of the Hebrew alphabet used in the manuscript, he compared it with the script of several old Hebrew manuscripts, as illustrated in a collection of Kodachrome slides which he had prepared. The manuscript whose writing seemed most like that of the scrolls was the Nash Papyrus, a fragment variously dated by different scholars from the second century B.C. to the third century A.D.

When Brownlee returned, Trever showed him the passage he had copied, which he had soon found to be the first verse of the sixty-fifth chapter of Isaiah. Others, as we have seen, had already identified this scroll as the book of Isaiah; one of the Syrians, indeed, said that he thought one of the scrolls was Isaiah, but Trever did not take the statement seriously because the Syrians could not read Hebrew, and he did not know then that other scholars had seen the manuscript.

The following morning Trever managed to get into the Old City and visit St. Mark's Monastery, where Butrus Sowmy introduced him to the Archbishop Samuel. He was given permission to photograph the scrolls, and the archbishop and Sowmy agreed to bring them to the American School for that purpose. They also brought out the Isaiah manuscript, in order that Trever might see how much of the book of Isaiah it contained. Unrolling it with difficulty, he copied what seemed to be the beginning of the first column, which turned out to be the first verse of the first chapter of Isaiah.

The scrolls were brought to the school on Saturday, February 21, and the two young scholars began the difficult task of photographing them. The following Tuesday afternoon, having completed the first stage of their task, Brownlee and Trever took the scrolls back to the monastery of the Old City. During the rest of the week the development of the negatives was completed, and prints were made from them. A few of the first prints made were sent to Professor William F. Albright of Johns Hopkins University, to get his judgment on the nature and age of the manuscripts. Prints of the Isaiah scroll and the two scrolls later identified as parts of the Manual of Discipline were made first. On Friday, February 27, prints of another scroll were completed, which Brownlee discovered to be a commentary on the first two chapters of the book of Habakkuk. The contents of the other two scrolls were not determined until after I returned from Baghdad.

A complete set of the photographs was given to Archbishop Samuel. According to his account, it was after he received these that Kiraz asked his permission to show the scrolls to Sukenik at the YMCA. The Archbishop suggested, he tells us, that Kiraz take the photographs, but Kiraz protested that they were not large enough. This does not agree with Sukenik's statement that, after copying some of the Isaiah manuscript, he returned the scrolls to Kiraz on the sixth of February, three weeks before Trever's photographs were finished. How the discrepancy is to be resolved I do not know. In any case, Archbishop Samuel decided to retain possession of the scrolls and entrust their publication to the American School of Oriental Research, while Kiraz assured Sukenik that the Hebrew University would be given priority whenever the scrolls should be offered for sale.

Late Saturday afternoon, February 28, our party returned to Jerusalem. To my relief I learned that there had been no trouble at the school during our absence, though there had been a frightful bomb explosion in the city, causing more than fifty deaths. My diary says: "Everything OK at the school, but John and Bill all excited over manuscripts at the Syrian Convent in script John thinks older than the Nash Papyrus, including the whole book of Isaiah, a text of Habakkuk with midrashic material in verse (so Bill says), and an unidentified composition resembling Wisdom Literature." The unidentified composition was, of course, the Manual of Discipline.

Monday morning, March 1, I went with Trever to the monastery, after securing from the Arab Higher Committee a pass into the Old City, now carefully guarded at every entrance. At the monastery I met Archbishop Samuel and saw the scrolls. In a small fragment of the badly damaged fourth scroll which had come loose, my eye caught the word *'ar'ā,* and I remember exclaiming in surprise, "This is Aramaic!"

That afternoon we had our first class session on the Habakkuk Commentary. One of the courses I was giving was in epigraphy, and we agreed to devote the rest of our time in this course to the study of the scrolls.

The first photographs of the Isaiah scroll proved unsatisfactory because the limited amount of film at hand compelled Trever to photograph two columns on each sheet, and so the photographs were too small for adequate enlargement. It was therefore necessary to photograph the scroll again, but finding suitable film of the right size proved very difficult. The best that could be found was some outdated portrait film.

Under such circumstances it was remarkable that the photographs came out as well as they did. The plates in our subsequent publication of the Dead Sea Scrolls were made from these photographs. Critics of the publication who do not consider the reproductions satisfactory have not seen the manuscript itself. Some have said that the manuscripts should have been rephotographed after they were brought to the United States, but they were not then in our possession, and Archbishop Samuel was unwilling to have them photographed again.

Still the Aramaic scroll had not been unrolled. On Wednesday, March 3, the archbishop gave Trever permission to attempt to open it; Butrus Sowmy, however, with some justification, was opposed to the undertaking, and it was postponed in the hope that it might be carried out later with better facilities in Europe or the United States.

On the morning of Thursday, March 4, Mr. R. W. Hamilton, the Director of the Department of Antiquities, came to see me at the school. As I looked back on our conversation later, it seemed strange that the subject of the scrolls had not come up at all. Both Mr. Hamilton and I were just then much more concerned about other matters. The purpose of his call was to discuss plans for the administration of the Palestine Museum after the impending termination of the British Mandate.

The department, however, was not uninformed about the scrolls. It will be remembered that one of the first persons to see the manuscripts at St. Mark's Monastery was a member of the Department of Antiquities, Stephan H. Stephan. Mistakenly regarding them as useless, he apparently did not think it worth while to make any report to the department concerning them. Two years later Hamilton wrote to me that Stephan had never even mentioned the scrolls to him.

He was told about them by Trever, but at the time of their first conversation Trever did not yet know that the scrolls had been discovered within the past year. Archbishop Samuel and Sowmy, with characteristic caution, had talked vaguely at first about the manuscripts as being in the library of their monastery, leaving the impression that they had been there for about forty years, and Trever was still under the impression when he first discussed the scrolls with Hamilton. Not until March 5 was he told that the scrolls had been found in a cave only about a year earlier.

Soon thereafter this information was passed on to Mr. Hamilton. On March 20 Trever wrote to his wife: "I have already talked with Hamilton at the Museum about the proper procedure. He has given me permission to visit the place to gather up any loose materials left." On February 27, the day before my return from Baghdad, Trever had spoken about the antiquities laws with the archbishop, who consequently relinquished a plan to visit the cave and assured Trever that he "would cooperate in every way possible with the American School of Oriental Research and the Department of Antiquities in carrying out the excavation of the cave."

My diary mentions a visit of Archbishop Samuel and Butrus Sowmy at the school on Monday, March 8, after which I drove them back to the Allenby Square in the school's station wagon. My note continues, "Three or four cars, especially station wagons, have been stolen lately in broad daylight at the point of guns, though most politely, so we aren't eager to take ours out." Three days later the building of the Jewish Agency was damaged by explosives believed to have been brought in by an Arab using a car that belonged to the American Consulate.

Most of the entries in my diary during these weeks record shootings, explosions, and casualties in Jerusalem and in other parts of the country, with many rumors, like the one we heard on March 15 that our water supply had been poisoned. That same day, however, Trever received a reply from Professor Albright, confirming his judgment as to the age of the manuscripts and pronouncing the find "the greatest manuscript discovery of modern times."

On March 18 the archbishop called on me at the school, and Trever and I discussed with him several matters concerning the manuscripts. I expressed to him my conviction that the Isaiah scroll was the oldest known manuscript of any book of the Bible, and he was duly impressed. I also submitted for his approval a news release I had prepared. Having learned by this time that the manuscripts have been discovered in a cave near the Dead Sea, I felt that it would materially help us in establishing their age if we could visit the cave and find any remains of the jars in which they had been found. We therefore discussed with the archbishop the possibility of a trip to the cave. We talked also about plans for the publication of the manuscripts by the American Schools of Oriental Research.

My diary for March 19 says: "John saw the bishop again today and learned that Dr. Magnes was taking an interest in the manuscripts!" This was our first intimation of the negotiations between the Hebrew University and St. Mark's Monastery. We still knew nothing of the scrolls and fragments Professor Sukenik had acquired.

During the morning of the twentieth we went with guards sent by a good friend to the Haram, the sacred enclosure containing the Dome of the Rock. Here we met a man from the shrine of Nebi Musa, near the Jericho road, who said he could arrange for us a trip to the cave. We were to drive to Nebi Musa and proceed on foot to the cave, with a local Bedouin as guide. To our great disappointment, when the appointed day came the man who was to come for us did not put in an appearance. We were later told that the trip was considered too dangerous because Jewish troops were in training on the plain north and west of the Dead Sea. Who was really responsible for the frustration of our plan we shall probably never know, though we have our suspicions. We could not go by ourselves, and could not have found the cave if we had attempted it.

On March 25, Archbishop Samuel told Trever that Sowmy was on his way with the manuscripts to a place outside Palestine. I myself had suggested that they were not safe in the monastery in the Old City, and Trever had mentioned the possibility of removing them to another Syrian Orthodox monastery down by the Jordan River. The soundness of these suggestions was demonstrated when St. Mark's Monastery was damaged by shellfire and Butrus Sowmy himself was killed not many weeks later. The removal of the scrolls from the country, however, without an export license from the Department of Antiquities, was illegal. How fully the archbishop realized this I cannot say; I know only that we tried to tell him. He had already, of course, taken the scrolls to Syria and back.

In all fairness it should be remembered that for many centuries Palestine had not had an independent government of its own, but had been ruled by one foreign power after another. Under such circumstances it was not unnatural that there was sometimes, even in high places, an attitude toward law which is not entirely unknown in the Western democracies. It should be said also, not as extenuating but as partly explaining what happened, that in March 1947 there was no longer any effective government in the country, and no perceptible prospect of any. The Department of Antiquities was still carrying on as best it could, but its major anxiety was to protect its treasures in the face of impending chaos. What the future would bring, both to Jerusalem and to the Dead Sea Scrolls, could not then be foreseen.

During the rest of the month of March we spent many hours in making arrangements for our trip home. Conditions were growing steadily worse. Facilities for transportation, communication, banking, and other needed services had reached a point where the word "facility" was no longer appropriate. On March 27 we held our last class, completing the first reading of the Habakkuk Commentary.

The next day, Easter Sunday, was one of the saddest days I can remember. An effort had been made to obtain a truce for the day, but it broke down completely. On Tuesday, March 30, Brownlee departed for America. My wife and I left Jerusalem on April 2 but could not get away from Haifa for another two weeks. Trever, after a final conference with Archbishop Samuel and Butrus Sowmy on April 3, went down to Lydda on the fifth and took a plane to Beirut.

On April 11, while my wife and I were still in Haifa waiting impatiently for our ship to come into the harbor, the statement I had sent from Jerusalem was released to the newspapers in America. Unfortunately a mistake had somehow been introduced into the version given to the press. I had written, "The scrolls were acquired by the Syrian Orthodox Monastery of St. Mark." As released to the press in America the statement said that the scrolls had been "preserved for many centuries in the library of the Syrian Orthodox Monastery of St. Mark in Jerusalem." Who inserted this I do not know. Professor Sukenik, on reading the published account, issued a statement to set the matter right, pointing out that the scrolls had been found in a cave near the Dead Sea within the previous year. From this statement, which I read in the *Rome Daily American* of April 28, 1948, when our ship stopped at Genoa, I first learned that the discovery included manuscripts other than those bought by Archbishop Samuel.

During the leisurely, restful voyage home in a small Norwegian freighter I had time to "collate" the whole text of the Isaiah manuscript with the Masoretic or traditional Hebrew text, having brought with me a set of Trever's photographs as well as a standard edition of the Hebrew Old Testament. This collation was the basis of articles published during the ensuing year.

The first trickle of published statements concerning the scrolls soon swelled into a veritable flood. The American Friends of the Hebrew University issued a special news bulletin on July 16. A further statement appeared in their November bulletin. The September number of the *Biblical Archaeologist* carried an article by Trever on the discovery of the scrolls and one by me on their contents and significance.

The same month saw the publication of Sukenik's first volume on the manuscripts, entitled *Megilloth Genuzoth* (Hidden Scrolls). In this he gave an account of his acquisition of the manuscripts in his possession, with a summary of their contents as far as they had been ascertained at that time, and the text of selected passages, together with notes and some excellent photographs. The text of Chapters 42 and 43 of the book of Isaiah, as copied by him when he had Archbishop Samuel's scrolls in his possession, was included in this volume, side by side with the Masoretic text.

The October number of the *Bulletin of the American Schools of Oriental Research* carried an article by Trever entitled "Preliminary Observations on the Jerusalem Scrolls," and the first part of an article by me on variant readings in the Isaiah manuscript. The December and February numbers contained a translation of the Habakkuk Commentary by Brownlee, an article by H. L. Ginsberg on Sukenik's scrolls, the remainder of my article on the variant readings in Isaiah, an article on the paleography of the scrolls by Trever, and one on the date of the Isaiah scroll by Solomon A. Birnbaum. Interested scholars were therefore fairly well informed on the general nature and contents of the scrolls within a year after we first learned of their existence. At the meetings of the Society of Biblical Literature and Exegesis and the American Schools of Oriental Research at New York in December 1948, Brownlee presented two papers on the Habakkuk Commentary, anticipating some ideas that were later published independently by other scholars.

Further discoveries were to follow, but already the first gun in what soon came to be called "the battle of the scrolls" had been fired. Suspicions and charges—with few, if any, retreats—followed thick and fast. The smoke of battle has not even yet been quite cleared away by the wholesome breezes of unimpassioned investigation and discussion. . . .

Six distinct compositions are represented by the eleven scrolls, or parts of scrolls, first discovered and removed from the cave by the Bedouins in 1947. These are: (1) the Old Testament book of the prophet *Isaiah,* contained in its entirety in the largest and oldest of the scrolls, and also in part in one of those acquired by the Hebrew University; (2) the *Commentary on Habakkuk;* (3) the *Manual of Discipline,* which had come apart, so that when discovered it was in two separate scrolls; (4) the Aramaic manuscript, now tentatively called the *Lamech Scroll,* which has not been unrolled; (5) the *War of the Sons of Light with the Sons of Darkness;* and (6) the *Thanksgiving Psalms* contained in four of the pieces bought by Professor Sukenik. Many fragments of other books were found later when the cave and other caves in the vicinity were explored. Others were bought from Bedouins who had found them. No text discovered since 1947, however, is comparable in extent to the first scrolls found then by the Bedouins. . . .

The first question that occurs to one who hears for the first time of such an extraordinary discovery as that of the Dead Sea Scrolls is, "Can they be genuine?" The forgery of antiquities is a prosperous occupation in countries where archeologists have been at work for many years and have found statues, coins, inscriptions, and other objects for which museums and collectors pay good prices. Skillful craftsmen can make imitations of such antiquities which the best experts are hardly able to detect. Forgeries of inscriptions and manuscripts have not been unknown in Palestine also, though they have not hitherto been very common, because Palestinian excavations do not yield many objects that lend themselves to nefarious purpose.

When I first saw Trever's photographs of Archbishop Samuel's manuscripts, I naturally asked myself, "Are these not forgeries?" I confess, however, that I could never really bring myself to take this question seriously, especially after I had seen the manuscripts themselves. The fact that they looked old, of course, proved nothing, and the writing was amazingly clear. What impressed me most from the beginning, however, was the fact that the forms of the letters represented a period in the history of the alphabet for which we had relatively few specimens, and most of these had become known fairly recently.

For somewhat earlier and somewhat later periods we have many more inscriptions, and also papyri. As I have already related, Dr. Trever noted immediately the resemblance between the scrolls and the Nash Papyrus. He saw also, however that the two types of script were not quite contemporary, and he judged that the Nash Papyrus was somewhat later than the scrolls. I agreed with him, and our judgment was supported by the letter which Trever soon received from Professor Albright.

Paleography, the comparative study of the script, was at first our only means of dating the scrolls. It remains one of the most important criteria. Scientific analyses of the leather, the ink, and the linen wrappings of the scrolls would later contribute somewhat to the solution of the problem, but such techniques were not available to us in Jerusalem in the troubled circumstances of that time.

All these criteria, of course, apply to the age of the manuscripts themselves and the time when they were made. Archeological evidence later served to fix the time they were left in the cave, but that too was beyond our reach in the spring of 1948 because of our inability to visit the cave. Since the scrolls were presumably copies, not original manuscripts, the time, when the books they contained were composed could not be determined by paleography, by analysis of the leather and ink, or by archeological context. Only the internal evidence of the texts themselves could help us here. . . .

The discussion entered a new phase when the cave where the manuscripts had been found was rediscovered and excavated. Much of the controversy and doubt might have been obviated if the cave could have been immediately excavated or even inspected by competent archeologists when the first scrolls were found. Not only was that impossible; the cave was visited several times by unauthorized and incompetent persons before any archeologist knew of the discovery. In November or early December 1948, before order had been established in the country after the fighting of that year, unscrupulous individuals interested in nothing but plunder and gain cut a second opening into the cave, lower than the natural opening. They dug up the floor of the cave and threw some rubbish outside. An accurate description of the cave's condition and contents as first found by the Bedouins was thus rendered forever impossible.

16. LANKESTER HARDING

On a barren, sunny terrace above the Dead Sea, about half a mile south-southwest of the cave in which the first scrolls were found, lie the ruins of Khirbet Qumran, which had been commonly believed to be an abandoned Roman fortress. Adjacent to it is a large cemetery with more than a thousand graves that defied identification and seemed unlikely to have been connected with a military outpost. Since they face north and south, the graves could not be of Moslem origin. The site, though never previously excavated, had drawn the attention of various travelers and explorers. A French Orientalist C. Clermont-Ganneau, who investigated the area in 1873, believed the graves went back to a pre-Islamic age, but, apart from Roman artifacts, no other evidence was found. When the Dead Sea Scrolls came to light, interest in the site was revived. Several scholars suggested that there might be a connection between the caves and the nearby ruins, for although the scrolls had been stored in the caves, they obviously had been written elsewhere. Could it have been as far away as Jericho or Jerusalem?

In 1949, when Father Roland de Vaux and G. Lankester Harding systematically excavated the first Qumran cave, they also dug trial trenches at Khirbet Qumran. A link between the Roman ware found in the caves and the contemporary occupation of the site seemed indicated, but they failed to come up with conclusive results. The call for further and intensive excavation was renewed, particularly by the German scholar P. Kahle, who suggested that the ruins were not Roman at all but were directly related to the contents of the caves. And so de Vaux and Harding returned to Khirbet Qumran in 1951 for the first of several systematic campaigns. Their findings rank with the cave documents in revealing a largely unknown chapter of religious history. The cave manuscripts had pointed to a holy community, abiding by monastic rules, which had copied and composed the various texts. Now, with the finds made at Khirbet Qumran, it was possible to determine when the scrolls had been deposited in the caves and under what circumstances. As is so often the case, coins proved the most reliable evidence, and radiocarbon techniques later confirmed the dating.

As Kahle had predicted, the principal buildings that were laid free turned out not to be Roman. Nor were they part of an ordinary Palestinian village; a monastic structure was clearly revealed. And with the discovery of a jar of exactly the same design and material as those used in the cave for storing the manuscripts, the testimony of the cave writings was borne out. The findings at the caves and the monastery elucidated and explained each other. Since Khirbet Qumran was excavated later than Cave Q1, the archaeologists could use the scrolls as a guide. Among them, the "Manual of Discipline," a description of the community life at Khirbet Qumran, was invaluable.

G. W. Lankester Harding has been a Biblical archaeologist for more than thirty years. He started excavating as a young man of twenty-five under Flinders Petrie near Gaza and later was an assistant director under James Leslie Starkey of the archaeological expedition at Lachish (Tell el-Duweir) that in the mid-thirties uncovered a dozen remarkable Hebrew letters on potsherds from the time of Jeremiah. From 1936 to 1956 Harding served as Director of the Department of Antiquities in Jordan and he has taken a leading part in all phases of the scroll discoveries in the Jordan valley. The various excavations he has carried out jointly with Father de Vaux have added considerably to the value of "the most important finds ever made in Biblical archaeology."

Where Christ May Have Studied

LANKESTER HARDING

In an account of the discovery of these documents, then known as the Dead Sea Scrolls, which appeared in *The Illustrated London News* of October 1, 1949, I wrote as follows: "About a kilometre to the south of the cave is a small ancient site called Khirbet Qumran. It seemed at first possible that the cave deposit might have some relation to this site, but a trial excavation showed that it dates to the third or fourth century A.D., much later than the cache."

The trial excavation referred to was carried out in the cemetery of the site, and the following year, still feeling there should be some connection between the two places, we cleared three rooms of the actual building. Buried in the floor of one of the rooms was a jar identical with those found in the cave, and beside it a coin of about A.D. 10. A clear connection thus being established, the site has been systematically excavated over the past four years, and has resulted in a wealth of material and information as surprising as it is unusual.

The site was in the nature of a self-contained monastery, complete with potters' quarter, flour mills, ovens, storage bins, and an elaborate system of water conservation in twelve large cisterns. More than 400 coins give us the maximum and minimum dates for the history of the building, which can be briefly summarised as beginning about 125 B.C., destroyed by earthquake in 31 B.C., rebuilt about 5 B.C., and finally destroyed by the Tenth Roman Legion in A.D. 68. A few squatters occupied part of the place during the Second Jewish Revolt, A.D. 122-135 after which it was abandoned.

From Harding's article in *The Illustrated London News*, September 3, 1955.

From this it is apparent that the manuscripts cannot be later than A.D. 68, a date about a century later than that to which we originally assigned them on the basis of the pottery found with them. The reason for this error is that while the Roman period is very well known from the historic point of view, archaeologically, i.e., so far as pottery is concerned, it is still rather vague, for under the Pax Romana the pottery types maintained the same forms throughout the whole period. . . .

The settlement as now completely excavated consists of a main building some 37 ms. (121 ft.) square, with a strong tower at the north-west corner. To the south and west of this building lie the domestic and industrial quarters, and most of the cisterns. It is not possible to assign definite uses to most of the rooms, but there is one, the largest, which is clearly the general assembly room; another is a dining-room or perhaps a room for special meetings; a cistern within the main building with divided upper steps, which might be the baptistery; a pottery storeroom, etc.

The cistern just referred to gives the most dramatic evidence of the severity of the earthquake, for it is cracked diagonally across its length and the eastern side has sunk some 50 cms. (1 ft. 7 ins.). The tower was also apparently badly damaged, for it was subsequently strengthened by a sloping revetment all round.

In one of the inner rooms was found a quantity of broken plaster moulded on mud bricks: when assembled, this turned out to be a long table-like structure with a low bench behind it. It had clearly fallen from an upper storey. During the process of disengaging it, ink-pots were found in the débris, of pottery and of bronze, so it is suggested that this may have been the *scriptorium* where many of the scrolls were written. A projecting ledge of plaster with two depressions may have held water for washing the scribe's hand before writing the holy name of God.

Another curious and interesting discovery was of a number of pots, of various kinds, containing animal bones, goats and sheep chiefly, which had been carefully set down in various places outside the building. There are clearly the remains of food, but we have no clue as to the reason for such careful preservation of the bones, even if one assumes they are the remains of ritual feasts.

The coins begin with John Hyrcanus, 135-104 B.C., maintaining a good quantity up to Antigonus Mattathias, 40-37 B.C.: only one coin of Herod the Great has been found, and then there is a gap to Herod Archaelus, 4 B.C. to A.D. 6. The last to be found in quantity are of Caesarea under Nero, A.D. 67-68. The place was then destroyed by burning, and on top of this fill some rooms were constructed in which were found coins of the Tenth Legion: the latest is one of Agrippa II, about A.D. 86. This year a hoard of 563 silver coins, in three small pots, was found in the floor of a room on the west, just inside the door. These are of two types only, of Antiochus VII, beginning at 135 B.C., and Tyre autonomous, of which the latest is 9 B.C. They may be someone's secret hoard, hidden there while the building was still a ruin: the position is an unlikely one for anyone living in the place to have chosen.

In addition to excavation of the site, a thorough search of the scarp of the Wadi to the south was made last year, to try and establish whether there were any more caves there. (Cave IV was found in this scarp.) The débris covering the face of the scarp was scraped down to the natural deposit by workers suspended over the side, in many cases on ropes. As a result of this work the eroded remains of six more caves were found, in two of which were small fragments of inscribed leather and papyrus, suggesting that they also had once contained scrolls. Two of the caves had staircases leading down to them.

It would seem that the inhabitants of the monastery had warning of the approach of the Roman Legion to attack them in A.D. 68 and concealed their most valuable possessions, the great library, in various caves round about. No doubt they intended to return later and retrieve these scrolls, but apparently the Romans were too thorough in their methods of destruction.

Study of the scrolls themselves has made it fairly certain that the sect who inhabited the monastery were the Essenes, so well described by Flavius Josephus and Pliny the Elder. The latter's description of their settlement and its position tallies very closely indeed with our remains. John the Baptist was almost certainly an Essene, and must have studied and worked in this building:

he undoubtedly derived the idea of ritual immersion, or baptism, from them. Many authorities consider that Christ himself also studied with them for some time. If that be so, then we have in this little building something unique indeed, for alone of all the ancient remains in Jordan, this has remained unchanged—indeed, unseen and unknown, to this day. These, then, are the very walls He looked upon, the corridors and rooms through which He wandered and in which He sat, brought to light once again after nearly 1900 years.

Anatolia, Crete,
and Greece

17. HEINRICH SCHLIEMANN

Homer's two great epics have been called the Bible of the Greeks. The Homeric poems furnished the classical dramatists and sculptors with themes and gave all Hellenic people ideals on which to model their lives. Through Homer the Greeks gained a sense of common excellence and destiny that, despite political differences, united them into one people sharing the same essential cultural attitudes. Homer also helped to efface the many bewildering local cults of conflicting Mediterranean and Indo-European origins by furnishing the Greeks with a pantheon of heroes and gods whom they could look up to as paragons of divine strength and enlarged humanity. Aeschylus referred to his own plays as "crumbs from the banquet of Homer." Plato called Homer "the schoolmaster of the Greeks." The *Iliad* and the *Odyssey* remained a precious European heritage long after ancient classical civilization had vanished and, nearly three thousand years after their composition, inspired Heinrich Schliemann, whose search for the Troy of the Achaean conquerors was itself an epic of Homeric proportions.

Every profession has its hero, the man of genius whose struggles and accomplishments seem to personify the highest aspirations of his chosen field and who captures the imagination of the general public. In archaeology that unique hero has long been Heinrich Schliemann. He comes closer than anyone else to representing the spirit of archaeological romance in the public eye. His fabulous life and persistent dream of unearthing Troy, crowned by astonishing successes, has never lost interest. Indeed, to many it is hardly conceivable that archaeology existed before Schliemann appeared on the scene. Schliemann's legendary reputation is secure, even though his stature and achievements may have been oversimplified. Despite what Schliemann himself thought of Homer, an epic romance is not all authentic history.

Schliemann, a poor clergyman's son, was raised in a provincial town of northern Germany. His father's death forced him to leave school at the age of fourteen and become a grocer's apprentice. But after a series of hair-raising adventures, setbacks, and lucky breaks, he became a shrewd merchant prince and millionaire in St. Petersburg. He traveled widely, mastered a dozen modern and ancient languages, and made several fortunes, one as a banker in the California gold rush (he became an American citizen in 1848). In all those years he never lost sight of his one great goal, aroused in boyhood, of finding Troy. Nothing deterred him from his absolute conviction that Homer's *Iliad* had an historical basis. "Thank God," he writes in his autobiography, "my firm belief in the existence of that Troy has never forsaken me amid all the vicissitudes of my eventful career."

Such a childlike belief, rooted in the fervent imaginings of an impressionable, untutored boy found little encouragement from the world of learning of his day. It was the age of scientific history, of Higher and Lower Criticism in the study of the Bible, and of the so-called "Homeric question." The answer to the latter, many of Schliemann's scholarly contemporaries held, was that the Homeric poems had simply evolved through the ages; they virtually denied the existence of the poet Homer. The episodes in Homer's epics, like those in the Bible, were considered little more than figments of poetic imagination, perhaps some kind of folk poetry that expressed sublimely the collective spirit of a nation rather than actual happenings of the remote past. Thus, the Anglo-German Orientalist Max Müller declared: "I am convinced that the Trojan War is not to be distinguished from the wars of the Mahabharata and the Shahnama, or from that of the Nibelungen." In discussing the Trojan War, George Grote in his *History of Greece* said: "Though literally believed, reverentially cherished, and numbered among the gigantic phenomena of the past, by the Grecian public, it is in the eyes of modern enquiry essentially a legend and nothing more."

It required the enthusiasm and inspired dilettantism of a man whose self-confidence had been steeled in the Darwinian struggles of the import-export business to assert his views against those of the leading experts. No wonder he aroused the suspicions of the classical scholars and philologists from the very beginning, particularly among his German countrymen. However, Schliemann's lack of formal education has been exaggerated. He devoted years to the study of Greek literature and history and to archaeology before embarking on his own campaigns. He even acquired, quite legitimately, a doctorate from a German University with a work written in ancient Greek. Schliemann's business stratagems, which were not always beyond reproach, also served him in good stead when organizing his digs, acquiring concessions, hiring workers, safeguarding the results of his labors, and effectively recording his campaigns in meticulous detail.

At the age of 46, after having amassed a fortune and mastered ancient and modern Greek, he decided to retire from business. Though he had to return intermittently to his business affairs, he now began his new career in earnest, with travels to Scandinavia, Germany, Italy, Egypt, Syria, Asia Minor, and, finally, Greece. In 1866 he settled down to intensive studies of archaeology in Paris and two years later set forth "to realize the dream of my life." First, he began his excavations at Hissarlik in Asia Minor, which he identified as ancient Troy and where, after several seasons of strenuous work, he came upon what he announced to be the "Scaean Gate" and "Priam's Palace." In 1873 his enthusiasm knew no bounds when he dug up a cache of rich ornaments. His success at Hissarlik, where he continued to dig throughout his remaining years, encouraged him to launch, from 1871 to 1890, excavations at Mycenae, Tiryns, Orchomenos, and a number of lesser Mediterranean sites. But none of his other finds equaled his triumph at Mycenae. There, guided by the second-century A.D. Greek travel writer Pausanias, he uncovered five royal shaft graves, which contained a stunning wealth of golden cups, inlaid swords, brooches, diadems, and masks. All were executed with a degree of artistry and refinement that dazzled its discoverer and the world at large.

Years before, a small amount of digging in Ithaca at the alleged "Castle of Odysseus" had raised Schliemann's dreams to the point where he was certain he had come across the mortal remains of Ulysses himself. At Hissarlik he hastened to call the

jewelry he found "Priam's treasure," and had his young Greek
wife wear the gaudy gear of Hecuba. Now at Mycenae he was
supremely confident he had unearthed nothing less than the
shaft graves of Agamemnon and Clytemnestra. Elated, he dis-
patched telegrams to the King of Greece, who soon appeared on
the scene, to the Emperor of Brazil, and to his fellow Homeric
scholar, Gladstone. The London *Times* printed his almost daily
bulletins. The announcements of these great discoveries were
sensational and made Schliemann an international celebrity.
Never before had archaeological conquests so aroused public
interest.

Schliemann's Trojan and Mycenaean finds, nevertheless, had
their detractors. Some stooped to ridicule; others showed considerable insight. One of Germany's leading archaeologists, A.
Conze, ascribed the treasures and artifacts at Troy to a Greek
colony. No less illustrious, E. Curtius, the excavator of Olympia,
held the gold masks from Mycenae to be of Byzantine origin,
and the mask Schliemann thought represented Agamemnon he
declared to be a portrait of Christ. Still others maintained the
Mycenaean finds to be Celtic, Gothic, or Oriental. However,
some insisted that the Mycenaean civilization, dogmatically
identified by Schliemann as the Homeric Age, belonged to a still
earlier civilization.

Schliemann, as we know, was mistaken, but most of the greatest professional scholars of his day were even farther from the
mark than Schliemann. Both in Greece and in Asia Minor, he had
uncovered remains of an ancient Aegean age. The royal shaft
graves of Mycenae antedated Agamemnon by several hundred
years and the city at the second or third Hissarlik level had
thrived about one thousand years before the Trojan War.

Nothing is easier than to criticize past achievements from the
vantage point of present-day knowledge. It cannot be denied
that Schliemann's enthusiasm for Homer verged on blind obses-
sion and lacked the disinterested, critical spirit of scientific investigation. And at least before he enlisted the help of Virchow
and Burnouf and above all that of W. Dörpfeld, whom Arthur
Evans has called "Schliemann's greatest discovery," his methods
of excavation were, on the whole, crude by modern and even

some contemporary standards. In his haste to get to Priam's city, he destroyed buildings of a period in which he was not interested, without first thoroughly recording and photographing them. In contemporary etchings the wide trench he cut through the Hissarlik mound looks as if he had embarked on a project to divert the waters of the Dardanelles. Only gradually did the concept of stratigraphy, of chronologically successive layers, dawn upon him; at Troy he recognized seven levels, which were later amended by his assistant Dörpfeld to nine (Dörpfeld also proposed the sixth level as that of Homeric Troy; it is now widely believed to be found at level 7A).

If Schliemann's faults were numerous, they are more than outweighed by his accomplishments. Not only did his sensational discoveries, announced with considerable showmanship and delight in publicity, enhance the prestige of archaeology, but his actual contributions were considerable. Despite isolated previous finds, his excavations really created the study of Aegean prehistory, ranging from the third-millennium Anatolian civilization of Troy II to the magnificent second-millennium Mycenaean age of the Greek mainland. The Homeric associations that fired Schliemann's mind and inspired his entire archaeological career are of only secondary value to us. But, because of Schliemann, a splendid lost Bronze Age civilization in the eastern Mediterranean and Greece was recovered and put on a solid archaeological basis. His discoveries opened up new vistas, new concepts, and a host of new problems that would keep scholars busy for several generations.

As for Schliemann's methods, it should be acknowledged that he was among the first to pay full attention to everyday, nonprecious articles and to reproduce or photograph them fully, also indicating their position on discovery. He has frequently been commended for his extensive, businesslike recording of archaeological operations and prompt publishing of his results.

Unearthing Troy

HEINRICH SCHLIEMANN

AT LAST I was able to realize the dream of my life, and to visit at my leisure the scene of those events which had always had such an intense interest for me, and the country of the heroes whose adventures had delighted and comforted my childhood. I started therefore, in April 1868, by way of Rome and Naples, for Corfu, Cephalonia, and Ithaca. This famous island I investigated carefully; but the only excavations I made there were in the so-called Castle of Ulysses, on the top of Mount Aëtos. I found the local character of Ithaca to agree perfectly with the indications of the *Odyssey*. . . .

I afterwards visited the Peloponnesus, and particularly examined the ruins of Mycenae, where it appeared to me that the passage in Pausanias in which the Royal Sepulchres are mentioned, and which has now become so famous, had been wrongly interpreted; and that, contrary to the general belief, those tombs were not at all understood by that writer to be in the lower town, but in the Acropolis itself. I visited Athens, and started from the Piraeus for the Dardanelles, whence I went to the village of Bounarbashi, at the southern extremity of the Plain of Troy. Bounarbashi, together with the rocky heights behind it, called the Bali Dagh, had until then, *in recent times,* been almost universally considered to be the site of the Homeric Ilium; the springs at the foot of that village having been regarded as the two springs mentioned by Homer, one of which sent forth warm, the other cold water. But, instead of only two springs, I found thirty-four, and probably there are forty, the site of them being called by the Turks Kirk-Giös,—that is to say, "forty eyes," moreover, I found in all the springs a uniform temperature of 17°

From Schliemann's *Ilios. The City and Country of The Trojans* (1880).

centigrade, equal to 62.6° Fahrenheit. In addition to this, the distance of Bounarbashi from the Hellespont is, in a straight line, eight miles, whilst all the indications of the *Iliad* seem to prove that the distance between Ilium and the Hellespont was but very short, hardly exceeding three miles. Nor would it have been possible for Achilles to have pursued Hector in the plain round the walls of Troy, had Troy stood on the summit of Bounarbashi. I was therefore at once convinced that the Homeric city could not possibly have been here. Nevertheless, I wished to investigate so important a matter by actual excavations, and took a number of workmen to sink pits in hundreds of different places, between the forty springs and the extremity of the heights. But at the springs, as well as in Bounarbashi and everywhere else, I found only pure virgin soil, and struck the rock at a very small depth. At the southern end of the heights alone there are some ruins belonging to a very small fortified place, which I hold with the learned archaeologist, my friend Mr. Frank Calvert, United States Vice-Consul at the Dardanelles, to be identical with the ancient city of Gergis. Here the late Austrian Consul, G. von Hahn, made some excavations, in May 1864, in company with the astronomer Schmidt, of Athens. The average depth of the *débris* was found not to exceed a foot and a half; and Von Hahn, as well as myself, discovered there only fragments of inferior Hellenic pottery of the Macedonian time, and not a single relic of archaic pottery. The walls too of this little citadel, in which so many great luminaries of archæology have recognized the walls of Priam's Pergamus, have been erroneously called Cyclopean.

Bounarbashi having thus given negative results, I next carefully examined all the heights to the right and left of the Trojan Plain, but my researches bore no fruits until I came to the site of the city called by Strabo New Ilium, which is at a distance of only three miles from the Hellespont, and perfectly answers in this, as well as in all other respects, to the topographical requirements of the *Iliad*. My particular attention was attracted to the spot by the imposing position and natural fortifications of the hill called Hissarlik, which formed the north-western corner of Novum Ilium, and seemed to me to mark the site of its Acropolis as well as of the Pergamus of Priam. According to the measurement of my friend M. Émile Burnouf, honorary director of the French School at Athens, the elevation of this hill is 49.43 metres or 162 ft. above the level of the sea.

In a hole dug here at random by two villagers, some twenty-five years ago, on the brink of the northern slope, in a part of the hill which belonged to two Turks of Koum-Kaleh, there was found a small treasure of about 1200 silver staters of Antiochus III.

The first recent writer who asserted the identity of Hissarlik with the Homeric Troy was Maclaren. He showed by the most convincing arguments that Troy could never have been on the heights of Bounarbashi, and that, if it ever existed, Hissarlik must mark its site. But already before him, Dr. Edw. Dan. Clarke had declared himself against Bounarbashi, and thought that the Homeric city had been at the village of Chiblak, a theory afterwards adopted by P. Barker Webb. Such weighty authorities as George Grote, Julius Braun, and Gustav von Eckenbrecher, have also declared in favour of Hissarlik. Mr. Frank Calvert further, who began by upholding the theory which placed Troy at Bounarbashi, became, through the arguments of the above writers, and particularly, it appears, through those of Maclaren and Barker Webb, a convert to the Troy-Hissarlik theory and a valiant champion of it. He owns nearly one-half of Hissarlik, and in two small ditches he had dug on his property he had brought to light before my visit some remains of the Macedonian and Roman periods; as well as part of the wall of Hellenic masonry, which, according to Plutarch (in his Life of Alexander), was built by Lysimachus. I at once decided to commence excavations here, and announced this intention in the work *Ithaque, le Péloponnèse et Troie*, which I published at the end of 1868. Having sent a copy of this work, together with a dissertation in ancient Greek, to the University of Rostock, that learned body honoured me with the diploma of Doctor of Philosophy. With unremitting zeal I have ever since endeavoured to show myself worthy of the dignity conferred on me.

In the book referred to I mentioned (p. 97) that, according to my interpretation of the passage of Pausanias (ii. 16, § 4) in which he speaks of the Sepulchres at Mycenae, the Royal Tombs must be looked for in the Acropolis itself, and not in the lower town. As this interpretation of mine was in opposition to that of all other scholars, it was at the time refused a hearing; now, however, that in 1876 I have actually found these sepulchres, with their immense treasures, on the very site indicated by me, it would seem that my critics were in the wrong and not myself.

Circumstances obliged me to remain nearly the whole of the year 1869 in the United States, and it was therefore only in April 1870 that I was able to return to Hissarlik and make a preliminary excavation, in order to test the depth to which the artificial soil extended. I made it at the north-western corner, in a place where the hill had increased considerably in size, and where, consequently, the accumulation of *débris* of the Hellenic period was very great. Hence it was only after digging 16 ft. below the surface, that I laid bare a wall of huge stones, 6½ ft. thick, which, as my later excavations have shown, belonged to a tower of the Macedonian epoch.

In order to carry on more extensive excavations I needed a firman from the Sublime Porte, which I only obtained in September 1871, through the kind offices of my friends the United States Minister Resident at Constantinople, Mr. Wyne McVeagh, and the late dragoman of the United States Legation, Mr. John P. Brown.

At length, on the 27th of September, I made my way to the Dardanelles, together with my wife, Sophia Schliemann, who is a native of Athens and a warm admirer of Homer, and who, with glad enthusiasm, joined me in executing the great work which, nearly half a century ago, my childish simplicity had agreed upon with my father and planned with Minna. But we met with ever-recurring difficulties on the part of the Turkish authorities, and it was not until the 11th of October that we could fairly commence our work. There being no other shelter, we were obliged to live in the neighbouring Turkish village of Chiblak, a mile and a quarter from Hissarlik. After working with an average number of eighty labourers up to the 24th of November, we were compelled to cease the excavations for the winter. But during that interval we had been able to make a large trench

on the face of the steep northern slope, and to dig down to a
depth of 33 ft. below the surface of the hill.

We first found there the remains of the later Aeolic Ilium,
which, on an average, reached to a depth of 6½ ft. Unfortunately
we were obliged to destroy the foundations of a building, 59 ft.
long and 43 ft. broad, of large wrought stones, which, by the inscriptions found in or close to it, which will be given in the
chapter on the Greek Ilium, seems to have been the Boulenterion
or Senate House. Below these Hellenic ruins, and to a depth of
about 13 ft., the *débris* contained a few stones, and some very
coarse hand-made pottery. Below this stratum I came to a large
number of house-walls, of unwrought stones cemented with earth,
and, for the first time, met with immense quantities of stone
implements and saddle-querns, together with more coarse hand-
made pottery. From about 20 ft. to 30 ft. below the surface,
nothing was found but calcined *débris*, immense masses of sun-
dried or slightly-baked bricks and house-walls of the same, numbers of saddle-querns, but fewer stone implements of other kinds,
and much better hand-made pottery. At a depth of 30 ft. and
33 ft. we discovered fragments of house-walls of large stones,
many of them rudely hewn; we also came upon a great many
very large blocks. The stones of these house-walls appeared as if
they had been separated from one another by a violent earthquake. My instruments for excavating were very imperfect: I had
to work with only pickaxes, wooden shovels, baskets, and eight
wheelbarrows.

I returned to Hissarlik with my wife at the end of March 1872,
and resumed the excavations with 100 workmen. But I was soon
able to increase the number of my labourers to 130, and had
often even 150 men at work. I was now well prepared for the
work, having been provided by my honoured friends, Messrs.
John Henry Schröder & Co. of London, with the very best English wheelbarrows, pickaxes, and spades, and having also procured three overseers and an engineer, Mr. A. Laurent, to make
the maps and plans. The last received monthly £20, the overseers £6 each, and my servant £7 4s.; whilst the daily wages of
my common labourers were 1 fr. 80 c., or about 18 pence sterling.

I now built on the top of Hissarlik a wooden house, with three rooms and a magazine, kitchen, &c., and covered the buildings with waterproof felt to protect them from the rain.

On the steep northern slope of Hissarlik, which rises at an angle of 45°, and at a perpendicular depth of 46½ ft. below the surface, I dug out a platform 233 ft. wide, and found there an immense number of poisonous snakes; among them remarkably numerous specimens of the small brown adder called *antelion* (ἀντήλιον), which is hardly thicker than an earthworm, and gets its name from the vulgar belief, that the person bitten by it only survives till sunset.

I first struck the rock at a depth of about 53 ft. below the surface of the hill, and found the lowest stratum of artificial soil to consist of very compact *débris* of houses, as hard as stone, and house-walls of small pieces of unwrought or very rudely cut limestone, put together so that the joint between two of the stones in a lower layer is always covered by a single stone in the course above it. This lowest stratum was succeeded by house-walls built of large limestone blocks, generally unwrought, but often rudely cut into something resembling a quadrangular shape. Sometimes I came upon large masses of such massive blocks lying close upon one another, and having all the appearance of being the broken walls of some large building. There is no trace of a general conflagration, either in this stratum of buildings built with large stones or in the lowest layer of *débris;* indeed, the multitudinous shells found in these two lowest strata are uninjured, which sufficiently proves that they have not been exposed to a great heat. I found in these two lowest strata the same stone implements as before, but the pottery is different. The pottery differs also from that in the upper strata.

As the cutting of the great platform on the north side of Hissarlik advanced but slowly, I began on the 1st of May a second large trench from the south side; but the slope being there but slight, I was forced to give it a dip of 14°. I here brought to light, near the surface, a pretty bastion, composed of large blocks of limestone, which may date from the time of Lysimachus. The southern part of Hissarlik has been formed principally by the *débris* of the later or Novum Ilium, and for this reason Greek antiquities are found here at a much greater depth than on the top of the hill.

As it was my object to excavate Troy, which I expected to find in one of the lower cities, I was forced to demolish many interesting ruins in the upper strata; as, for example, at a depth of 20 ft. below the surface, the ruins of a pre-historic building 10 ft. high, the walls of which consisted of hewn blocks of limestone perfectly smooth and cemented with clay. The building evidently belonged to the fourth of the enormous strata of *débris* in succession from the virgin soil; and if, as cannot be doubted, each stratum represents the ruins of a distinct city, it belonged to the fourth city. It rested on the calcined bricks and other *débris* of the third city, the latter being apparently marked by the ruins of four different houses, which had succeeded each other on the site, and of which the lowest had been founded on remnants of walls or loose stones of the second city. I was also forced to destroy a small channel made of green sandstone, 8 in. broad and 7 in. deep, which I found at a depth of about 36 ft. below the surface, and which probably served as the gutter of a house.

With the consent of Mr. Frank Calvert, I also began on the 20th of June, with the help of seventy labourers, to excavate in his field on the north side of Hissarlik, where, close to my large platform and at a perpendicular depth of 40 ft. below the plateau of the hill, I dug out of its slope another platform, about 109 ft. broad, with an upper terrace and side galleries, in order to facilitate the removal of the *débris*. No sooner had I commenced the work than I struck against a marble triglyph with a splendid metope, representing Phoebus Apollo and the four horses of the Sun. This triglyph, as well as a number of drums of Doric columns which I found there, can leave no doubt that a temple of Apollo of the Doric order once existed on the spot, which had, however, been so completely destroyed that I did not discover even a stone of its foundation *in situ*.

When I had dug this platform for a distance of 82 feet into the hill, I found that I had commenced it at least 16½ ft. too high, and I therefore abandoned it, contenting myself with cutting into its centre a trench 26 ft. wide at the top and 13 ft. wide at the bottom. At a distance of 131 ft. from the slope of the hill, I came upon a great wall, 10 ft. high and 6½ ft. thick, the top of which is just 34 ft. below the surface. It is built in the so-called Cyclopean manner, of large blocks joined together with small ones: it had at one time been much higher, as the quantity of stones lying beside it seemed to prove. It evidently belonged to the city built with large stones, the second in succession from the virgin soil. At a depth of 6 ft. below this wall I found a retaining wall of smaller stones, rising at an angle of 45°. This latter wall must of course be much older than the former: it evidently served to support the slope of the hill, and it proves beyond any doubt that, since its erection, the hill had increased 131 ft. in breadth and 34 ft. in height. As my friend Professor A. H. Sayce was the first to point out, this wall is built in exactly the same style as the house-walls of the first and lowest city, the joint between two of the stones in the lower layer being always covered by a third in the upper layer. Accordingly, in agreement with him, I do not hesitate to attribute this wall to the first city. The *débris* of the lower stratum being as hard as stone, I had very great difficulty in excavating it in the ordinary way, and I found it easier to undermine it by cutting it vertically, and with the help of windlasses and enormous iron levers, nearly 10 in. in length and 6 in. in circumference, to loosen and so break it down in fragments 16 ft. high, 16 ft. broad, and 10 ft. thick. But I found this manner of excavating very dangerous, two workmen having been buried alive under a mass of *débris* of 2560 cubic feet, and having been saved as by a miracle. In consequence of this accident I gave up the idea of running the great platform 233 ft. broad through the whole length of the hill, and decided on first digging a trench, 98 ft. wide at the top and 65 ft. at the bottom.

As the great extent of my excavations rendered it necessary for me to work with no less than from 120 to 150 labourers, I was obliged, on the 1st of June, on account of the harvest season, to increase the daily wages to 2 francs. But even this would not have enabled me to collect the requisite number of men, had not the late Mr. Max Müller, German Consul at Gallipoli, sent me 40 workmen from that place. After the 1st of July, however, I easily procured a constant supply of 150 workmen. Through the kindness of Mr. Charles Cookson, English Consul at Constantinople, I secured 10 hand-carts, which are drawn by two men and pushed by a third. I thus had 10 hand-carts and 88 wheelbarrows to work with, in addition to which I kept 6 horse-carts, each of which cost 5 francs or 4s. a day, so that the total cost of my excavations amounted to more than 400 francs (£16) a day. Besides screw-jacks, chains and windlasses, my implements consisted of 24 large iron levers, 108 spades, and 103 pick-axes, all of the best English manufacture. I had three capital foremen, and my wife and myself were present at the work from sunrise to sunset; but our difficulties increased continually with the daily augmenting distance to which we had to remove the *débris*. Besides this, the constant strong gale from the north, which drove a blinding dust into our eyes, was exceedingly troublesome.

On the south side of the hill, where on account of the slight natural slope I had to make my great trench with an inclination of 76°, I discovered, at a distance of 197 ft. from its entrance, a great mass of masonry, consisting of two distinct walls, each about 15 ft. broad, built close together, and founded on the rock at a depth of 46½ ft. below the surface. Both are 20 ft. high; the outer wall slopes on the south side at an angle of 15°, and is vertical on the north side. The inner wall falls off at an angle of 45° on its south side, which is opposite to the north side of the outer wall. There is thus a deep hollow between the two walls. The outer wall is built of smaller stones cemented with clay, but it does not consist of solid masonry. The inner wall is built of large unwrought blocks of limestone; it has on the north side solid masonry to a depth of only 4 ft., and leans here against a sort of rampart 65½ ft. broad and 16½ ft. high, partly composed of the limestone which had to be removed in order to level the rock for building the walls upon it. These two walls are perfectly flat on the top, and have never been higher; they are 140 ft. long, their aggregate breadth being 40 ft. on the east and 30 ft. at the west end. The remnants of brick walls and masses of broken bricks, pottery, whorls, stone implements, saddlequern-stones, &c., with which they were covered, appear to indicate that they were used by the inhabitants of the third or burnt city, as the substructions of a great tower; and I shall therefore, to avoid misunderstanding, call these walls, throughout the present work, "the Great Tower," though they may originally have been intended by their builders for a different purpose. . . .

Up to the beginning of May 1873, I had believed that the hill of Hissarlik, where I was excavating, marked the site of the Trojan citadel only; and it certainly is the fact that Hissarlik was the Acropolis of Novum Ilium. I therefore imagined that Troy was larger than the latter town, or at least as large; but I thought it important to discover the precise limits of the Homeric city, and accordingly I sank twenty shafts as far down as the rock, on the west, south-west, south-south-west, and east of Hissarlik, directly at its foot or at some distance from it, on the plateau of the Ilium of the Greek colony. As I found in these shafts no trace of fragments either of pre-historic pottery or of pre-historic house-wall, and nothing but fragments of Hellenic pottery and Hellenic house-walls; and as, moreover, the hill of Hissarlik has a very steep slope towards the north, the north-east, and the north-west, facing the Hellespont, and is also very steep on the west side towards the Plain, the city could not possibly have extended in any one of those directions beyond the hill itself. It therefore appears certain that the ancient city cannot have extended on any side beyond the primeval plateau of Hissarlik, the circumference of which is indicated on the south and south-west by the Great Tower and the double gate; and on the north-west, north east, and east, by the great boundary wall. . . .

Each of these three tombs [which Schliemann came upon in three of the shafts] was cut out of the rock and covered with flat slabs: each contained a corpse; but the corpses were all so much damaged, that the skulls crumbled to dust when exposed to the air. The tombs evidently belonged to persons of small means and of a late date, since what little pottery was found in them was of a very inferior description and evidently of the Roman period. But the fact that in three out of the twenty shafts, which I sank at random on the site of Novum Ilium, tombs were discovered, seems to denote with great probability that the inhabitants of that city buried their dead, or at least a large portion of them, within the precincts of the town. Cremation however was also in use with them, since in the first trench I opened, in April 1870,

I struck upon an urn of the Roman period, filled with ashes of animal matter intermixed with remnants of calcined bones, which are evidently those of a human body. I did not find any other burnt bodies in the strata of Novum Ilium, but it must be remembered that I only excavated in Hissarlik, which does not cover a twenty-fifth part of the later city. Hissarlik moreover was the Acropolis of Novum Ilium and contained the principal temples, in consequence of which it is likely that it was considered sacred ground, in which no burials were allowed. Hence it is very probable that, if systematic excavations were made in the lower city, many sepulchres and funeral urns would be found.

The inhabitants of the five pre-historic cities of Hissarlik seem generally to have burnt the dead, as I found in 1872 two tripod-urns with calcined human remains on the virgin soil in the first city; and in 1871, 1872, and 1873, a vast number of large funeral urns, containing human ashes, in the third and fourth cities. I found no bones however except a single tooth, and on one occasion among the ashes a human skull, which is well preserved, with the exception of the lower jaw, which is missing: as I found a brooch of bronze along with it, I suppose it may have belonged to a woman. . . .

It is true that nearly all the pottery found in the pre-historic ruins of Hissarlik is broken, and that there is hardly one large vessel out of twenty which is not in fragments; nay, in the first two cities the pottery has all been shattered by the weight and pressure of the stones with which the second city was built. But still, even if all the funeral urns with human ashes ever deposited in Hissarlik had been well preserved, yet, judging from the fragments of them—in spite of the abundance of these fragments—I can hardly think that I could have found even a thousand entire urns. It is, therefore, evident that the inhabitants of the five pre-historic cities of Hissarlik buried only a small part of their funeral urns in the city itself, and that we must look for their principal necropolis elsewhere.

Whilst these important excavations were going on, I neglected the trenches on the north side, and only worked there when I had workmen to spare. But I brought to light here the prolongation of the great wall which I agree with Prof. Sayce in attributing to the second stone city.

Wishing to investigate the fortifications on the west and north-west sides of the ancient city, in the beginning of May 1873 I also commenced making a trench, 33 ft. broad and 141 ft. long, on the north-west side of the hill, at the very point where I had made the first trench in April 1870. I broke first through an Hellenic circuit-wall, probably that which, according to Plutarch in his Life of Alexander, was built by Lysimachus, and found it to be 13 ft. high and 10 ft. thick, and to consist of large hewn blocks of limestone. Afterwards I broke through an older wall, 8¾ ft. high and 6 ft. thick, composed of large blocks cemented with earth. This second wall is attached to the large wall which I brought to light in April 1870, and the two form two sides of a quadrangular Hellenic tower, a third wall of which I had to break through later on.

This part of the hill was evidently much lower in ancient times, as seems to be proved not only by the wall of Lysimachus, which must at one time have risen to a considerable height above the surface of the hill, whereas it is now covered by 16½ ft. of rubbish, but also by the remains of the Hellenic period, which are here found to a great depth. It appears, in fact, as if the rubbish and *débris* of habitations had been thrown down on this side for centuries, in order to increase the height of the place.

In order to hasten the excavations on the north-west side of the hill, I cut a deep trench from the west side also, in which, unfortunately, I struck obliquely the circuit-wall of Lysimachus, here 13 ft. high and 10 ft. thick, and was consequently compelled to remove a double quantity of stones to force a way through it. But I again came upon the ruins of large buildings of the Hellenic and pre-Hellenic periods, so that this excavation could only proceed slowly. Here at a distance of 69 ft. from the declivity of the hill, at a depth of 20 ft., I struck an ancient enclosure-wall, 5 ft. high, with a projecting battlement, which, on account of its comparatively modern structure and small height, must belong to a post-Trojan period. Behind it I found a level place, paved partly with large flags of stone, partly with stones more or less hewn; and after this a wall of fortification, 20 ft. high and 5 ft.

thick, built of large stones and earth, which ran below my wooden house, but 6½ ft. above the Trojan circuit-wall, which starts from the Gate.

While following up this circuit-wall, and bringing more and more of it to light, close to the ancient building and north-west of the Gate, I struck upon a large copper article of the most remarkable form, which attracted my attention all the more, as I thought I saw gold behind it. On the top of it was a layer of red and calcined ruins, from 4¾ to 5¼ ft. thick, as hard as stone, and above this again the above-mentioned wall of fortification (5 ft. broad and 20 ft. high), built of large stones and earth, which must have been erected shortly after the destruction of Troy. In order to secure the treasure from my workmen and save it for archaeology, it was necessary to lose no time; so, although it was not yet the hour for breakfast, I immediately had *païdos* called. This is a word of uncertain derivation, which has passed over into Turkish, and is here employed in place of ἀνάπαυσις, or time for rest. While the men were eating and resting, I cut out the Treasure with a large knife. This required great exertion and involved great risk, since the wall of fortification, beneath which I had to dig, threatened every moment to fall down upon me. But the sight of so many objects, every one of which is of inestimable value to archaeology, made me reckless, and I never thought of any danger. It would, however, have been impossible for me to have removed the treasure without the help of my dear wife, who stood at my side, ready to pack the things I cut out in her shawl, and to carry them away. . . .

As I found all these articles together, in the form of a rectangular mass, or packed into one another, it seems certain that they were placed on the city wall in a wooden chest. This supposition seems to be corroborated by the fact that close by the side of these articles I found a copper key. It is therefore possible that some one packed the treasure in the chest, and carried it off, without having had time to pull out the key; when he reached the wall, however, the hand of an enemy, or the fire, overtook him, and he was obliged to abandon the chest, which was immediately covered, to a height of 5 ft., with the ashes and stones of the adjoining house.

Perhaps the articles found a few days previously in a room of the chief's house, close to the place where the Treasure was discovered, belong to this unfortunate person. These articles consisted of a helmet and a silver vase, with a cup of electrum, which will be described in the chapter on this Third City.

On the thick layer of *débris* which covered the Treasure, the builders of the new city erected a fortification-wall aeready mentioned, composed of large hewn and unhewn stones and earth. This wall extended to within 3¼ ft. of the surface of the hill.

That the Treasure was packed together at a moment of supreme peril appears to be proved, among other things, by the contents of the largest silver vase, consisting of nearly 9000 objects of gold. . . . The person who endeavoured to save the Treasure had, fortunately, the presence of mind to place the silver vase, with the valuable articles inside it, upright in the chest, so that nothing could fall out, and everything has been preserved uninjured.

18. HUGO WINCKLER

Schliemann's search for his beloved Homeric world unwittingly revealed among the successive strata of the Hissarlik mound the prehistoric dawn of Asia Minor. Because he equated the second and third levels with Homeric Troy, he hit upon far more important settlements than the one he actually sought. The lower cities going back to the second half of the third millennium B.C. may lack romantic connotations, but they represent vital phases in eastern Mediterranean developments and have offered clues to the metallurgical evolution in Europe. Another chapter was added to the prehistory of Asia Minor with the unearthing of the lost Hittite empire, an archaeological achievement which parallels the rediscovery of the Sumerians.

Unlike the Sumerians, the name of the Hittites had not been entirely lost, but their identity as a great nation had faded completely from human memory. Only a few centuries after their eclipse, the Ionian Greeks in the territory of the once powerful empire never even mentioned them, and Herodotus, a native of the coast of Asia Minor and a man of unlimited curiosity about Oriental history, believed that great Hittite monuments above Smyrna represented Niobe of Greek mythology and the Pharaoh Sesostris. Although the Old Testament frequently refers to a people called the Hittites, it reveals little of their origin or political importance in the Near Eastern world of the second millennium; they appear simply one of the host of nations and tribes that the invading Hebrews encountered in Palestine. Thus, for a long time the Hittites were considered just one of the numerous aboriginal peoples of Syria-Palestine. Yet, there is some evidence in the Old Testament that should have put scholars on their toes. Solomon takes foreign Hittite wives and, according to 2 Chronicles 1:17, he bought horses from Egypt "for all the kings of the Hittites, and for the kings of Syria . . .", a clear indication that the Hittites were not just a local tribe subdued by the Hebrews but an independent people ruled by a king and ranking with the Syrians. More suggestive is a passage in 2 Kings 7:6-7 that reports the fears of Syrian soldiers: "Lo, the king of Israel hath hired against us the kings of the Hittites and the kings of the Egyptians . . . wherefore they arose and fled in the twilight . . ." Obviously, a king classed with an Egyptian ruler and commanding an army that aroused so much fear could not be the potentate of a minor tribe.

Despite these Biblical hints, to which little attention was paid, the rehabilitation of the Hittites was effected from other sources. It took several generations of archaeologists and Orientalists working with widely scattered pieces to solve the puzzle. A powerful second-millennium B.C. empire emerged that was on a par with the great powers of Egypt and Mesopotamia, and occasionally even got the better of them. The Hittite empire was centered in the Anatolian highlands of Asia Minor, although splinter groups and smaller subsidiary kingdoms in Syria survived the decline of the empire. The archaeological unfolding of Hittite history was largely completed by the unlocking of the Hittite hieroglyphs after a Phoenician-Hittite bilingual was discovered at Karatepe in 1945.

Their strange pictographs first drew attention to the Hittites. In 1812 the Anglo-Swiss explorer John Burckhardt, the discoverer of Petra, noticed at Hamath in north Syria inscriptions on "a stone with a number of small figures and signs which appear to be a kind of hieroglyphic writing, though it does not resemble that of Egypt." In 1870, several more such stones were found at Hamath by two American diplomats, and similar inscriptions were also discovered at Aleppo in the wall of a mosque, and farther away at Ivriz in the Taurus Mountains on a rock-carving. Meanwhile, travelers in Asia Minor had encountered enormous inland fortified cities and rock-carvings, some of which also bore hieroglyphic symbols. Among the earliest of those travelers was Charles-Félix-Marie Texier who in 1839 visited the gigantic ruins near the Turkish village of Boghazköy some hundred miles east of Ankara. He was hoping to find Tavium, a Celtic settlement of Roman days, but "the grandeur and peculiar nature of the ruins" soon compelled him to abandon a Celtic identification; Sir William Hamilton, however, who visited Boghazköy in 1842, persisted in the opinion that the ruins were indeed Celtic. Further visits by European travelers increased interest in Anatolian antiquities, and new evidence was furnished by unknown art forms, buildings, inscriptions, seals, and fortified cities. George Smith, on his last ill-fated trip to Mesopotamia, identified correctly a huge mound on the upper Euphrates as Carchemish. Excavated before and after World War I by British archaeologists D. G. Hogarth, R. Campbell Thompson, C. Leonard Woolley, and T. E. Lawrence, Carchemish was to become one of the most thoroughly investigated Hittite cities.

Credit for the rehabilitation of the Hittites goes to the Reverend Archibald Henry Sayce, a professor of comparative philology and of Assyriology at Oxford, whom Gladstone called "high priest of the Hittites." A flash of intuition led Sayce to pool all the varied testimony from northern Syria and throughout Asia Minor and to reach a valid generalization. Having already previously ascribed the Hamathite inscriptions to the Hittites, he now realized that similar characteristics were present in the monuments and inscriptions at Carchemish and Ivriz, and near Smyrna and Boghazköy. From the wide geographic range of these similarities he inferred the great extent and power of the Hittite Empire. In his *Reminiscences* Sayce describes his discovery, which came to him during a visit to his friend Isaac Taylor, who was writing a book on the alphabet:

> One morning I was with him in his library when the question of the so-called Hamathite inscriptions turned up. These were inscriptions in a new form of hieroglyphic script which had first been detected on certain stones at Hamath. . . . While I was talking to Taylor, a sudden inspiration came to me. I asked him for a copy of Rawlinson's Herodotus, and then pointed out to him that a picture in it of a monument in the pass of Karabel near Smyrna, which Herodotus believed to have been a memorial of the Egyptian Pharaoh Sesostris, presented us with a figure in precisely the same style of art as that of the monuments of Ivriz and Carchemish, and accompanied by badly copied hieroglyphs which would probably turn out to be those I called Hittite. The "Pseudo-Sesostris" had already been recognized as belonging to

the same school of art as certain figures cut on the rocks of an
ancient sanctuary near Boghaz Keui in Cappadocia, the age and
artistic relations of which were unknown, and about which various fantastic theories were current. Photographs of them had been
taken by the French explorer and scholar Perrot. These Taylor
hunted up, and we saw that not only was the art the same at
Boghaz Keui, at Karabel, at Ivriz and at Carchemish, but that
the figures of Boghaz Keui were accompanied by hieroglyphs
similar to those of Ivriz. It was clear that in pre-Hellenic days a
powerful empire must have existed in Asia Minor which extended
from the Aegean to the Halys and southward into Syria, to
Carchemish and Hamath, and possessed its own special artistic
culture and its own special script. And so the story of the Hittite
empire was introduced into the world. . . . *

Sayce's thesis was not accepted immediately. But he de-
fended his theories vigorously in several papers, addresses, and
books, submitting more corroborative evidence from the Bible
and identifying the Hittites with the Kheta or Khatti of Egyptian
records. Meanwhile the search for the Hittite capital continued.
Further inscriptions were found at different sites and were published in 1900 by the German scholar, L. Messerschmidt. But the
most dramatic confirmation of Sayce's views came with the discovery in 1887 of the Tell el-Amarna archives, in which Syrian
and Palestinian rulers complained frequently of Hittite incursions. Among the letters was one from the Hittite king, Sup-
piluliumas, and also two mysterious cuneiform letters in an
unknown language mistakenly termed "Arzawan," that a Norwegian philologist in 1902 declared to be Indo-European in character. Already in 1893 a French explorer, E. Chantre, had found
near Boghazköy a few fragments of cuneiform tablets in the
same language. It was deciphered during World War I by the
Czech F. Hrozny and was indeed Indo-European; it is sometimes called Kanesian.

By this time Boghazköy seemed the most likely capital of the
Hittite Empire, and several archaeologists eyed the site. A. H.
Sayce was anxious for the British to start excavating there and
interested Professor Garstang and the Committee of the Archaeo-

*From Sayce's *Reminiscences* (1923). Reprinted by permission of Macmillan
& Co., Ltd., London.

logical Institute at Liverpool in the project. But as Sayce reports: "Unfortunately the Germans were on the same track, and they had managed to interest the Emperor in the project. The German ambassador was now all-powerful in Constantinople; the English ambassador cared for none of these things." There was no longer a Layard as the influential British plenipotentiary at the Porte. The Germans were granted a concession and the Assyriologist Dr. Hugo Winckler undertook a preliminary expedition to Boghazköy in 1905. He carried out major excavations from 1906 to 1908 with the assistance of his Turkish friend Mackridy Bey, whom he had met previously during excavations in Syria and Lebanon. Mackridy continued, mostly alone, until 1912.

The preparatory work done by various scholars before the actual excavations near Boghazköy began was so extensive and had been guided to such an extent by sound research and reasoning that the stage was fully set for major discoveries. Little was left to chance. Still, the returns from the digs were spectacular. The royal archives soon came to light and more than 10,000 cuneiform tablets, written predominantly in the same "Arzawa" language of the two Tell el-Amarna letters. Others were in international Akkadian and in a number of unknown idioms. Altogether the Swiss philologist Emil Forrer later counted eight different languages (among them Hurrian and even Sumerian), perhaps a reflection of the multi-national character of the Hittite Empire. The archives were indeed, as Magoffin says, a "philological Eldorado."

By internal evidence, Winckler was able to show that the Boghazköy ruins had been the Hittite capital. Though a majority of the texts could not be read at the time, he was able, nevertheless, to reveal a great deal about the Hittites and Near-Eastern affairs of their era. A trained cuneiform scholar and editor of the Orientalist journal *Ex Oriente Lux,* Winckler brilliantly reconstructed from the tablets lists of kings and a rough chronological outline of Hittite history. Considerable attention was given his publication of a treaty between the Hittites and the Mitanni in which the gods of the two countries are invoked, among them Mithra, Varuna, and Indra—Indo-Europeon divinities also known to the ancient Persians and the Aryans of India. Undoubtedly, the

Boghazköy archives must rank with the Kuyunjik libraries and Tell el-Amarna tablets in contributing to the reconstruction of pre-Hellenic Near-Eastern history.

Few archaeologists today are able to marshal any enthusiasm when reviewing Winckler's excavating work at Boghazköy. They generally agree that even Schliemann thirty years earlier had had a greater grasp of basic methods than this querulous and ailing German philologist. Sayce complained that no proper archaeologist, only an architect, was attached to the expedition. And "had it not been for the accidental visit of Garstang to the place while excavations were going on we should never have known even the little we do about its archaeological history. Even the sequence of pottery is uncertain." The German classical scholar Ludwig Curtius, who had joined the Boghazköy operations in 1907, was shocked by Winckler's procedures, which consisted of staying in his workroom all day to study the cuneiform tablets brought to him by Mackridy, who in turn obtained basket loads of them from a Kurdish overseer. When following the latter, Curtius saw him heading with basket and pickax for the Hittite temple in the plain below. Entering the interior, Curtius was surprised to find "well-preserved clay tablets in tilted, orderly rows, placed one above the other," but to his dismay the Kurd "hastily snatched away as many pieces as would fill his basket like a peasant woman digging potatoes from her little acre."

The Capital of the Hittites

HUGO WINCKLER

EARLY IN THE MORNING of July 17 [1906] we rode back to Zia-bey's residence where (with pleasant memories of former baksheesh) we were received as old acquaintances. As the de-

From Winckler's "Nach Boghasköi! Ein Fragment," *Der Alte Orient*, XIV, No. 3 (1913). Translated from the German by Willard R. Trask.

scendant of an ancient princely family, the Bey still enjoys great respect, and his influence is a factor to be reckoned with by anyone who wants to work in this region without running into difficulties. Of course, no one will put any open hindrances in the way of a project sponsored by the Government; but there are others, not less difficult to cope with. In such cases the European is always at a disadvantage, for he has not the inexhaustible reserves of time that the Oriental enjoys. And time is precisely the most important ammunition in this kind of warfare! We maintained friendly relations with the Bey—he made many requests, from a good bottle of cognac to being extricated from momentary financial embarrassment—and so in turn he did us services too. A strike on the part of our workmen was instantly settled by his mere word—little favors to friends are well repaid in the East!

We expected the work to take about eight weeks, and since it was already midsummer, we wanted to spend them in the shade of tents or branch shelters. I could not but recall the pleasures of summer in the Lebanon! But though here in Asia Minor too it is customary to go up the mountains to get a little summer coolness into one's tent—Zia-bey was doing just that!—I had a bitter disappointment awaiting me so far as my need for warmth was concerned. We were able to set up our tent directly at the foot of the Büyük-kale massif, where an adequate spring rises. It is the same spot on which, the next year, our house was built. Under the torrid rays of the day's sun, the modest tent which had to suffice for the two of us provided a temperature that one finds not unpleasant in a Turkish bath, but that is not particularly refreshing for a noonday nap. Soon after sundown the air becomes suddenly cooler, and a strong evening wind whistles from the summits, as prelude to a night during which only the most urgent occasions can persuade one to leave the warmth of one's bed. So of an evening we sat in the howling wind in front of our tent, gulping down our supper, while our cloaks billowed out around us. After that we were usually cooled off enough to crawl into the tent without any lingering ceremony. There was just room in it for two men, completely wrapped up in their work and between whom this enforced close companionship never gave rise to an angry word or even an impatient thought, despite the fact that both of them had to put up with considerable physical hardship during this time.

The kitchen had been set up in a sort of arbor, and there a cook of Bulgarian extraction did his work as best (or as worst) he could. My experienced friend had taken him on because the fellow knew a little German, which would make life easier for me; he had once been allowed to practice his art on the patients in a German hospital. I took his antics in stride, for in my travels I always had the idea that if one is out for pleasure, one had better not go too far afield. But my poor Macridy swallowed the annoyance for the two of us—enough for three—and he could not find solace in clay tablets! A second arbor had to provide the shade for my clay-tablet studies, and it could soon be put to abundant use. The whole camp site was surrounded by a high fence of woven boughs, which at the same time provided a modicum of shelter from the wind. A little distance away and somewhat lower down, a larger arbor had been set up, providing shelter for five creatures that never had been so well off since they were born—our horses. They earned their living almost exclusively by doing nothing, while everyone else was more than busy. Their presence nearby resulted of course in an enormous surplus of flies, which meant that I had the dubious pleasure of copying my clay tablets with my head and neck covered and gloves on my hands, if I did not feel like stopping after every character to ward off the excessive interest these confiding little beasts were taking in my work. Protecting one's rights of priority is a frequent preoccupation in our line of work!

From the camp site (as now from the front of the house that was built in 1907) you can look across the trough of Boghazköy and Jükbas, all the way to the mountain range that blocks it to the west. Behind us we have the elevation of Büyük-kale, which connects with the eastern ascent out of the trough.

So we were quickly settled, and my pencils were sharpened and ready to get the hoped-for documentary treasures down on paper.

The reader must recall what, on the basis of the previously known facts, the expected results were bound to be. The language of the country would be the language of the country of Arzawa (of the el-Amarna letters), and the documents would belong to the el-Amarna period. Hence the next conclusion would be that there might be further information on Arzawa and that its center would be here in Boghazköy. For the very extent of the urban area suggested that the place was of unusual importance and hence the country too.

We did not have too long to wait. On July 21, work at Büyükkale could begin, and right from the start documents were brought to light. At first there were only small fragments. Those picked up previously had been found on the slopes of the fortress hill among fallen debris, within a quite sharply delimited strip. So it was naturally our task to single out for investigation this particular strip within the very extensive slope, and the procedure had to be to remove the debris from below upward. For the workmen it was a rather risky job that could not be taken lightly, for the sudden collapse of the overhanging masses of earth and rock could at times be avoided only through the greatest care. The farther the work progressed up the mountain, the larger were the fragments found. The productive strip became somewhat narrower higher up, and the results proved that Macridy's keen eye had from the first correctly picked out the area where findings could be made. Nothing was recovered either to the right or to the left of this strip, and the following year demonstrated that the edge of the summit had been the original source of the treasure.

The majority of the pieces first found showed the familiar character in the unknown language. They were of various content, but for the time being they were too small to provide an answer to the most important question still unanswered: In what spot of the ancient world are we here? That this must have been a great center was now definitely clear; that these fragments, coming to hand at the rate of one or two hundred a day, could not be the remains of the archives of some insignificant king and state was established too. The inference about Arzawa, based on the language, had to be abandoned after the first few days.

Soon sporadic pieces in Babylonian served to clarify the issue. These were at first small fragments of letters, quite in the ex-

pected manner of el-Amarna—odds and ends of diplomatic ex-
changes between two kings. They were the King of Egypt and
the King of Chatti [a cuneiform variant of *Hittite* that, as Winckler uses it, means the Hittite people, their capital, or their land].
So after the first few days no doubt remained: we were on the
ground where the capital of the Empire of the Chatti had stood,
and we had found the royal archives of the rulers of Chatti during the period of their relations with Egypt. That was the time of
el-Amarna and the period immediately following, that is, from
the fifteenth to the thirteenth centuries B.C. The first pieces did
not yet disclose the names of the kings involved. So too, a rather
well-preserved tablet dealing with some agreement between
Egypt and Chatti did not, contrary to common usage, give the
names of the rulers, so that a more precise identification was not
immediately possible. That one should think, in connection with
negotiations and agreements between Egypt and Chatti, of the
great treaty between Ramses II and "Chetasar," as he was then
called, went without saying. But that we might find something
of immediate bearing on all this is more than I would have
hoped, imbued as I was with the pessimistic teaching of experience—that the facts will never evolve as we calculate they should.

But this once the unhoped-for thing did come true. On August
20, after some 20 days of work, the breach we were driving into
the rubble of the slope had reached a first dividing wall. At its
foot a beautifully preserved tablet was found whose very appearance promised something good. One glance and—all my life's
experiences crumbled into insignificance. Here it was—something
I might in jest have thought of as a fairy's gift. Here it was:
Ramses writing to Chattusil—formerly Chetasar—about their mutual covenant. To be sure, in the course of the last few days, time
and again small fragments had been found in which the compact
between the two states was mentioned. But here now was confirmation that indeed the famous treaty, known from the version
in hieroglyphics on the temple walls of Karnak, was also to be
illuminated by the party of the second part. Ramses, identified
by titles and lineage precisely as in the text of the treaty, writes
to Chattusil, who is similarly defined, and the content of the
communication is identical, word for word, with certain para-

graphs of the treaty. So it is not the actual final version of the treaty itself, but a letter of the kind that was exchanged about it, perhaps the final draft sent out from Egypt, which was then used as the basis for the definitive wording worked out in Chatti. Moreover, we also found a small fragment of another copy of the same document, representing the beginning of this particular tablet. Hence like other important documents, this one too was preserved in the archives in at least two copies.

That I, of all men, should be permitted to contemplate this document could not but evoke unparalleled emotions in me. Eighteen years had passed since I had come to know the Arzawa letter of el-Amarna at what was then the Museum of Bulaq, and the Mitanni language at Berlin. At that time I had suggested, on the basis of the facts that had come to light through the el-Amarna find, that the Ramses treaty too could well have been written originally in cuneiform characters, and now I held in my hands one of the missives exchanged about it—in exquisite cunei-form writing and in excellent Babylonian. Strange indeed, this coming together in one man's life that what my first visit to the Orient had revealed in Egypt should now in the heart of Asia Minor find its confirmation! A coincidence miraculous as a tale of fortune and vicissitude in the Arabian Nights—and yet the following year was to bring me still more astonishing gifts, when all the documents were found in which emerged the series of figures with whom, these eighteen years, I had so often been preoccupied. When the King of Mitanni, Tushratta, appeared in a Chattian light, and when even the Prince of Amuri, Aziru, the opponent of Rib-Addi of Byblos and the big fish in the Phoeni-cian pond, showed up in documents that could not but seem a commentary on his letters from el-Amarna! Verily, a strange con-catenation in one man's life!

Meanwhile too the answer had been found to another ques-tion that had worried me every day, since every day new evi-dence had confirmed that we were indeed excavating the cap-ital of the Chatti. In previously extant relations this capital was not called by name, and actually even the location of the state of the Chatti was itself in many respects quite vague. In the mean-time more than 2000 pieces had gone through my hands, and in

looking them over I had constantly been preoccupied with the
question of the name of the city on whose soil we were standing.
A striking thing was the following usage: The numerous territories mentioned in the most different documents—so far as the
territories were situated within the Chatti empire—were always
referred to as the "land of the city of X," that is, the notion was
strictly adhered to that a "land" or a "territory" is more or less
what we might call a "district," a geographic area with only one
town or capital at the center, its core of defense, where the population seeks protection in case of danger, while the open country with its villages is abandoned. The city is the seat of the god
of the region. His presence makes the strength of the place. And
hence here is the natural seat of the ruler who is, after all, the
representative of the god. This leads to the supposition that the
name of the capital may have been identical with the name of
the land—that is to say, that it was Chatti. And indeed, we did
find references to the city of Chatti, so that no doubt remained
as to the soundness of the inference. To be sure, it is not a name
like Babylon, Nineveh, Susa, Memphis, which were never completely lost in the history of the ancient Western world. Just like
the history of the people of Chatti, the name, too, was completely
forgotten. And the culture that the name represented cannot, in
originality, compare with that which gave those other names
their luster. Nevertheless, the people of Chatti did play a significant role in the evolution of that ancient world; and if the
name and the name of the people and the names of its dwelling
places were totally lost for so long, their rediscovery now opens
vistas all the more unsurmised.

19. DAVID HOGARTH

Invasion or occupation by the Hittites, Phrygians, Lydians, Assyrians, Cimmerians, Persians, Macedonians, Celts, Romans, Byzantines, and many more, has made Asia Minor, that peninsula between western Asia and southern Europe, something of a compendium of the racial, political, and cultural elements of Mediterranean antiquity. In modern times, since the coming of the Turks, it has been less important, but to the ancients Asia Minor was very much in the center of things. To them it was a blessed, extensive country, productive of human values and material wealth, surpassing "all other lands," as Cicero said, "in the richness of its soil, in the variety of its products, in the extent of its pastures, and the number of its exports." No people who settled there added more to its glory than the Greeks—Achaeans, Aeolians, Ionians, and later Dorians. They probably began to arrive toward the middle of the second millennium B.C. (Hittite records mention the Ahhiyawa, who were very likely Achaeans) and founded what became the most celebrated and prosperous cities of the Mediterranean. Here on Asian soil was the fountainhead of Greek and Western civilization. Homer, Thales, Herodotus, and Sappho were Greeks from the "Ionian" coast of Asia Minor. It was, of course, the Greek miracle which brought Schliemann to the Asia Minor site of "Sacred Ilios," determined to "augment the universal love for the noble study of all of the beautiful Greek classics, and particularly of Homer, that brilliant sun of all literature!"

A man of a quite different type, who perhaps even more successfully helped to recapture what he himself called the "Ionian Springtime of Greece," was David George Hogarth, a descendant of the eighteenth-century artist. A reticent, publicity-shy Oxonian of donnish eccentricity, Hogarth cast himself in the self-effacing role of wandering scholar or digger in the Levant.

In the 1880s and 90s Hogarth undertook strenuous archaeological field trips up and down Asia Minor. He began as a kind of apprentice to William Martin Ramsay, a noted epigraphist, and mainly copied Hittite inscriptions. After his scholarly peregrinations across Anatolia, Hogarth went to Cyprus for one season and then to Egypt, where he learned to dig scientifically under Petrie. Toward the end of the century, he searched for papyri with Grenfell and Hunt, two fellow Oxonians; but Hogarth clung, as he confessed, to his "old love Asia," and left the field to them. In 1899, he joined Arthur Evans in his first exploration of Knossos.

Hogarth started work at Ephesus in 1904. This great Ionian city had remained a busy seaport into Roman days until its harbor silted up and was famous for its temple to Artemis (Diana). The Artemisium, one of the seven wonders of the ancient world, had been located by an earlier excavator. However, he had discontinued his work in 1874, and Hogarth found the area "as hopeless as an ancient site can look." After working for two months without any significant results, he was about to close the season's labor. Then he realized that the so-called Great Altar was, in fact, the pedestal of the statue of the goddess. Digging there, he was quickly rewarded by a treasure of early Ionian art, more than 3,000 objects of the finest workmanship in precious metals, ivory, bronze, and terra cotta. In addition to these objects Hogarth found old Ionian inscriptions and a cache of primitive Lydian electrum coins that is one of the most valuable numismatic discoveries ever made.

Because of Sayce, Hittitology had almost become an Oxford monopoly, and after the excavation at Ephesus, Hogarth continued the tradition. He raised funds for an archaeological expedition to Carchemish and became its director in 1910. Leonard Woolley and T. E. Lawrence were his assistants on this expedition; Lawrence also served under him during World War I, when Hogarth headed the British-organized Arab Bureau in Cairo.

Dredging for Diana's Treasure

DAVID HOGARTH

THE SEARCH for ancient things below ground appeals to most minds, but especially to those of women, who are moved even more than men by curiosity and the passion of hazard. But few whose interest it excites seem to understand how rare are the high lights of success and how many the low lights of failure in a faithful picture of a digger's life. When I have been presented by a vague hostess as a "digger in the Levant," and we are between fish and flesh, my neighbour, glancing at my hands, will usually ask if my calling is a painful one in those climes. I reply that I dig *per alios,* and (with some shame) that, myself, I could not ply pick or spade anywhere for half a day. Incontinently she protests she could wish for nothing better than to lead such a life as mine. Whereupon, as best I may, I change the subject, not in fear she be as good as her word, but despair of giving her or any other inexpert person in that company and amid dinner table talk an understanding of the real nature of the digger's trade.

Indeed it is of such infinite variety, according to where, when, and why it happens to be followed, that generalities, even hedged about by all the caution of a leisured writer, are vanity: and the best I can do for you, my dinner partner, and for others who have felicitated me on the fascinating holidays which I spend in the Near East, is to describe briefly and, if I can, faithfully, the course of my . . . latest excavations. . . .

Wood, the discoverer of the site of the great Artemisium at Ephesus, achieved the all but impossible in lighting on its pavement, which had been buried under twenty feet of silt, and

From Hogarth's *Accidents of an Antiquary's Life* (1910). Reprinted by permission of Macmillan & Co., Ltd., London.

performed a feat not less to his credit in opening out thereafter an area as large as the floor-space of a great cathedral. But when he left the site in 1874, he had manifestly not found all that remained of the most famous of ancient temples; nor of what he did indeed find would he ever compose a sufficient record. For thirty years doubts remained which the first Museum in the world, owner of the site, could not well refuse to resolve; and to resolve them I was sent to Ephesus in the last days of September, 1904.

The site looked then as hopeless as an ancient site can look— an immense water-logged pit choked with a tangled brake of thorns and reeds; and when axe and billhook and fire had cleared the jungle, it looked, if possible, more hopeless still. The shallow surface waters, however, when no longer sheltered by leafy canopies, dried quickly under the early October sun, and I got to work with little delay on the platform of the temple which King Croesus had helped to build. A hundred men were enrolled, and every local means of carriage was pressed into their service. I got mule-carts and horse-carts, asses with panniers and asses with sacks, barrows and close-woven country baskets to be borne by boys. A central way was cut through the hillocks of marble, and from right and left of it broken stuff was sent up the ramps to dumping-grounds on the plain. But we were only reopening an earlier explorer's clearance, and could hope for little strange or new among his leavings. Not twice in a ten hour day did a scrap of carved or written stone, unseen or unsaved by Wood, reward our painful levering of tumbled blocks and sifting of stony soil. A common ganger with a hundred unskilled navvies could have served science as well as we.

As the polyglot labourers—half a dozen races chattered in the gangs—learned the ways of their taskmaster and became handy with their tools, the daily round grew ever more same, and each hour longer and emptier than the last. The beginning of an ambitious excavation is inspirited by an interest independent of results achieved or hoped. There are the local nature of the soil and the local peculiarities of the ancient remains to be learned: you have new and unhandy human instruments to temper, sharpen, and set: confidence must be gained and community of hope engendered. The days will go briskly for a week, two weeks, three weeks, according to the difficulties to be overcome. Then, if the instinct of the gamester be your mainstay in the digging trade, you will begin to crave winnings or, at least, the fair chance of them. Should there be some well-guarded kernel of the site, some presumed lode of antiquarian ore, you will endure still, performing hopefully the monotonous tasks of the digger's duty, while pick and shovel and knife are cutting onwards or downwards towards the hidden treasure; and if you can make your men comprehend and share your hope, the work will go forward well enough, with a fillip now and again from trifling loot found by the way. But if hope is deferred overlong, yet more if you have never held it confidently or never held it at all, your lot will insensibly become one of the dreariest that can fall to man. The germ of your hopelessness, infecting your labourers, will be developed more virulently in them. Their toil will lack life, and their tasks be scamped and vamped; their eyes will see not or their hands will not spare the evanescent relics of the past, while tired voices of their taskmasters rise and fall over their listless labour.

Many excavations I have seen—most indeed—go forward thus for a longer or a shorter time: and, since sometimes they cannot go forward otherwise, I have almost envied that sort of scientific excavator, generally Teuton, who seems to feel little or nothing of the gamester's goad, and plods on content to all appearance with his maps or his plans or his notes or nothing in particular, that might not be done better in his German study; while his labourers, clearing monuments that could not be missed in the dark by the worst trained observer in the world, shovel earth and stones like machines day in and day out for months together, and send them down a tramway under an overseer's eye. I say I have almost envied his content; but I always remember in time that, in digging, you only find if you care to find, and according to the measure of your caring; or, as a famous and fortunate explorer once put it, you find what you go out to find; and reckoning the momentary joy of success against the slow sorrow of failure, I rate the quality of the first so immeasurably more worth than the quantity of the last, that I am consoled. If lack of luck

vexes the gamester's soul, it is to him that the rare prizes of
hazard most often fall.

October passed away thus, and November was on the wane;
but no prize had appeared to lighten our weary days. Already we
had pierced the platform at several points to meet with nothing
better below it than sand and water. What, in reason, was to be
hoped above it, where diggers from Justinian's day to Wood's
had rummaged and robbed? We cajoled despair with the most
insignificant discoveries—with patches of bare pavements, with
scraps of Roman inscriptions chipped out of masses of Byzantine
concrete, with a few sherds of Greek vases and broken terra-
cottas sifted out of the bedding of the temple-steps built in
Alexander's day. In a world where the absolute is never attained,
the relative, thank heaven! can always please, and Nature, of her
pity, with a little of your contributory good will, will blind you
to relativity.

No other antiquarian work could be done elsewhere to fill the
days. The rest of the site of Ephesus, city, suburbs, and district,
had been conceded to an Austrian Mission which was even then
present in full force, exploring the great market-place and its
southern approach, as well as the famous double Church of Mary
Mother of God. Its distinguished leaders, greatly though they
had desired the Artemisium site for their own, treated me from
the first with all sympathy and courtesy, and the least return I
could make was to respect all their wide preserves. Now and
then I visited their work, which was proceeding almost as un-
eventfully as my own, and rode an aimless round on the Cayster
plain and the dusty hills. Rarely I received visitors who were
politely contemptuous of my sodden pit, and every day I
watched the slow fall of the leaf in the fig orchards of Ayassolúk.

The last days of November came. The platform of Wood's
"earliest temple" was almost cleared, and several shafts had been
sunk fruitlessly through its massive foundations. To go on with
such work in a second season would be to waste time and money,
and it seemed best to make an end in one campaign by keeping
the men through December into January. The gang, which was
clearing the central sanctuary, had reached its midway point and
begun to lay open the meagre remains of a small oblong struc-

ture, which Wood had named the "Great Altar," and left un-disturbed. I noted that it had only an outer skin of marble, and was filled in solid with small limestone slabs. So far we had sunk no pits through the pavement of the sanctuary itself, though many in the peristyle; and where better might we probe than in the heart of this "Altar," where no massive foundations would have to be broken through? Moreover, we might hope to learn whether the structure were indeed a "Great Altar" or not rather the pedestral of the divine image which was set up in the Holy of Holies.

The topmost slabs were lifted easily out of their beds: and not less easily those of a second layer. Gazing dully at their prints on the mud-mortar I noticed some bright specks, and stooping, picked out two or three. They were flakes of leaf-gold, fallen from some gilded object which had perished, whatever it was. But no sooner was the first slab of a third layer raised than some-thing better than a flake of foil shone on its bed, namely a little plate of impure gold, stamped with a geometric Ionian pattern, and pierced at the corners. I thought of the goddess who had stood in effigy on this pedestal, of her plated diadem and gold-encrusted robe, and sent for sieves.

For the rest of that day hours passed as minutes. Every hand-ful of mud-mortar washed through the meshes left treasure be-hind—women's gauds for the most part, earrings of all patterns and weights, beads of sundered necklace-string, pins for the hair, and brooches for the shoulder or throat, some of these last fash-ioned after the likeness of hawks in the finest granular work of Ionian smiths. With them appeared primitive electrum coins, fresh from the mint. I was as puzzled as pleased. How had deli-cate jewels come to lurk there, fresh and unspoiled? When the first specimens appeared, I thought them accidents of ruin—pre-cious trappings of the statue carried down by water through chinks of its pedestal, or, perhaps, contents of some perished cas-ket. But such possibilities became impossible as the jewels con-tinued to be found in each successive bed of mortar. It grew clear that we had chanced on some sort of foundation deposit—on objects hidden with a purpose when the first builders were laying course on course of the pedestal, and that we had the

most desired of treasures, fine work of the Ionian springtime of
Greece. Perhaps also we had solved at last the mystery of Greek
foundation deposits. Under Egyptian temples Petrie has found
many such deposits, whether beneath corner stones or the main
threshold, or in the central axis of a building; but under Greek
shrines the hiding place of foundation records had never yet
been divined. Yet what spot more fitting than the pedestal of the
most sacred statue at the very heart of the sacred plan?

We had dug out only a small part of our vein of treasure when
dark came down with a rising gale, whose fierce squalls brought
up the long expected rains. On and off, at some hour of every
day and night, it would rain for a week and more, sometimes
with lightning and cyclonic winds, sometimes in sodden calm.
The storms which had begun in unnatural warmth continued,
after the third day, in cruel cold, which coated the pools with
ice, and froze the very marrow of the men who had to grope for
jewels waist-deep in water and slime; but we dared not pause
.for even a day. The fame of our find had gone abroad, and
others would have dredged had we not. The blue fingers of the
men cracked and swelled with washing sharp shingle in the
sieves till they could hardly pick out jewels, and I knew what it
was to be wet through and chilled through for a week on end.

During a momentary brightening of the sky we sank pits outside the pedestal, and there too found foundations of walls earlier than our predecessors had found, and fragments of fine Ionian things lying among them. Then down again came the
deluge to flood the pits. For eight days we fought the weather,
replacing the worn-out and sick with eager volunteers. Each
morning the water had risen above its morning level of the day
before, and at last it began to well up faster than we could bale.
The rains of winter had come in earnest, and we must await
spring. The hole which we had made in the pedestal was choked
again with blocks too heavy for furtive marauders to drag out,
so long as water lay deep around, and before the middle of December I had gone to Constantinople carrying more than half a
thousand jewels. Whatsoever of the goddess's treasure might be
buried still was left to the keeping of watchmen and the flood.

The waters guarded their trust. That winter is yet remembered in Anatolia for its rains and the fevers which followed. When I returned to the site near the end of March, I looked out over a lake below whose unruffled surface the pedestal lay drowned too deep for anyone but a diver to rob its core, and its upper stones, said the Ephesians, would not emerge till late summer. What was to be done? The water could not be drained out of that great hollow, which lies many feet below the general level of the plain and hardly higher than the surface of the distant sea, except by the help of a very powerful steam pump. I left a contractor to clear away the upper part of Wood's great rubbish heaps, which still blocked the two ends of the site, and went back to Smyrna.

To make a long story short, an engine and pump were lent by the Ottoman Railway Company and dragged to the edge of our pit three weeks later; and after we had cut a passage seaward for the strong stream which its twelve-inch pipe would disgorge, it was set to work to lower the lake. But we were only at the beginning of difficulties. The upper waters were sucked up in a few hours; but the drainage of the lower levels, which were dammed by deep and massive foundation walls, could not be collected fast enough to keep the great pipe free of air, and unchoked by mud. If the engine stopped, the waters ceased to flow towards it, and in the lapse of a night the pond would rise nearly as high again as at the first. There was nothing for it but to spend many days in cutting a network of channels through the foundations and in deepening the pool below the pipe by hauling out great rubble blocks which had been bedded down by the builders of the latest temple. The men, who had to wade to their middles under a hot sun, fell sick of fevers, and I myself began to feel none too well. On the last day of April I took to my bed, and after fighting my malady for a week, went down to Smyrna in high fever and was put to bed in the Seamen's Hospital for another ten days. Thus it was not till May was half gone that, with drainage channels dug, the central area of the temple fenced against inflow, and a second and smaller pump rigged over the treasure-spot, we could hunt again for jewels.

They appeared one after another in the sieves just as they had done five months before; and when the clean bottom sand had been scraped out of the four corners of the pedestal, we had added nearly five hundred trinkets. But now I cared for none of these things. The fever had left me unstrung, and I longed for nothing but the moment when I might scrape Diana's mud off my feet for the last time. Every evening I hoped against hope that the lode would be exhausted next day. I have never struck such a vein of luck, and never liked my luck less. The site, it must be allowed, was no place for a hardly convalescent man. The end of May approached. Each noon the sun beat more fiercely into our windless hollow, and the flood, which was sucked out by the great pump each morning, left tracts of slowly drying slime and stranded water-beasts withering and stinking among rotten weeds. One could not watch the workmen without wading and mud-larking and groping in that fetid ooze. Every page of my diary breathes utter disgust of it and yearning for a cleaner, sweeter life. For all I cared, Science and Duty might go to the wall; and thither I had sent them and myself as well but for shame of old Gregóri and his cold, unsleeping eye. He had dug a dozen sites with me, and never yet stopped short of the bottom or refused to follow a likely lead. Was I going to tempt him now?

I did not. I held out, even to the dog days. Before the pedestal was exhausted we had begun to probe the mud about it, and there find ruins of three small shrines, one below the other, and many precious broken things in the slimy bottom of the lowest and earliest. These were rarely jewels and articles of personal wear like those that made up the Pedestal Treasure, but chiefly things used in worship, and fragments of votive offerings. These had not been hidden of set purpose where we found them, but were lost and forgotten things, sucked into the bottom ooze, or trodden under foot in some wild hour of ruin or sack. Since the earliest shrine on the site must be supposed founded not later than 700 B.C., it may well be we dredged from its nether slime treasures unseen since the sanctuary was violated by a rude Cimmerian horde in the reign of Ardys II. of Lydia. That these objects belonged to much the same period as the Pedestal Treasure, the artistic character of many bore witness: that, like that Treasure, they were of earlier date than the second of the three primitive shrines was proved by our finding certain of them bedded under its surviving foundations. In one case only did we seem to light on anything buried with intention. This was a little jar, set upright in an angle of the lowest foundations and once sealed with a covering, whose binding-cord still clung to the clay. My men were no longer in their first innocence, and dealers in contraband waited at noon and night to tempt them. He who first sighted this jar, as he was scraping slime into his basket, looked stealthily about him; but I was at his back, poor fellow, ready to lift his prize myself, and I see his sad eyes still as nineteen electrum coins of the earliest mintage of Lydia fell out of his pot.

We got statuettes, whole or broken, by the score, whether in ivory—priceless treasures these of early Ionian art—or in bronze, or in terra-cotta, or even in wood. We got vessels in ivory and vessels in clay. We got much gold and electrum, which had been used for casing or adorning things decayed: we got some silver, and, best prize of all, a plate engraved on both faces, in the oldest Ionic character, with a record of contributions towards a rebuilding of the shrine. We got many another object, broken or imperfect, but not less precious, in crystal and paste and amber and bronze. In sum, when all the ground had been searched, we had recovered from the treasures of the first House of Artemis in the Ephesian plain hard on three thousand objects, one with another and greater with less. I took them all to Constantinople, as in honour bound, for we had subscribed to the Ottoman Law and made no bargain with the Turk. But in return for our good faith, all the objects were suffered to go for a season to England to be ordered and studied. I wanted nothing less than to see them again when I left Stambul, and nothing more than to keep them forever in London, when, a year later, they had to return.

20. ARTHUR EVANS

The interest aroused by Schliemann's discoveries at Mycenae led to the exploration of other sites on the Greek mainland and firmly established the importance and brilliance of the civilization that flourished at Mycenae some eight hundred years before the classical Greek epoch. But like any fruitful advance in human knowledge, the recovery of the Mycenaean age raised at least as many questions as it answered. Was this earliest civilization on European soil Greek? Was it entirely indigenous, or was it related to any of the earlier civilizations outside Europe? And if so, how and when did these influences take effect? Were there perhaps intermediaries or direct antecedents closer to Greece who helped to plant civilization there? Cultural manifestations as vigorous, differentiated, and apparently full-grown from the start as those of the Mycenaeans could not have evolved suddenly and in a vacuum. The problem, then, was not so much to prove Homer right, as Schliemann wished to do, as to trace the origins of this advanced civilization and see whether it could be shown to have had any contacts with the Near East—either directly or through a missing link—which would explain its development.

Inevitably, attention turned to Crete, which is roughly equidistant from the Peloponnesus and Asia Minor. By this time vague traditions and legends were recognized as representing folk memory based on historical facts, no matter how adorned and modified; and so, all kinds of allusions in Greek literature and mythology came to mind. While there is no evidence that the ancient Greeks entertained any strong belief in a brilliant Bronze Age civilization preceding them, references to Crete are not lacking. For instance, Mount Ida in the island's center was considered to be the birthplace of mighty Zeus himself. And then there was fabulous King Minos of Crete, a wise lawgiver

279

and a mighty builder for whom the inventor-engineer Daedalus designed the labyrinth to house the human-bodied, bull-headed Minotaur. The annual dispatch of seven Greek youths and seven maidens to satisfy the anthropophagous appetite of the monster —a form of tribute that ended when the Athenian hero Theseus slew the Minotaur with the guileful aid of Ariadne—seems to imply Cretan hegemony over the mainland, an inference confirmed by Thucydides' discussion of the Cretan maritime empire in the eastern Mediterranean: "Minos is the earliest ruler we know of who possessed a fleet and controlled most of what are now Greek waters. He ruled the Cyclades, and was the first colonizer of most of them, installing his own sons as governors. In all probability, he cleared the sea of pirates, so far as he could, to secure his own revenues." Herodotus reports that Greeks from the mainland and the islands were enlisted by force as rowers on Cretan galleys. And the Iliad mentioned Cretan warriors— undoubtedly of a later date, when Cretans no longer had control over the Aegean islands—who had joined Agamemnon's host in the Achaean siege of Troy. Finally, there was a memorable passage in the Odyssey: "Out in the dark blue sea there lies a land called Crete, a rich and lovely land, washed by the waves on every side, densely peopled and boasting ninety cities. . . . One of the ninety towns is a great city called Knossos, and there, for nine years, King Minos ruled and enjoyed the friendship of almighty Zeus."

So avid an admirer of the Greek epics as Heinrich Schliemann could not afford to bypass Crete on his search for Homeric sites from Sicily to the Bosporus. In 1878 he negotiated for the purchase of a site at Kephala, where a native Cretan, fittingly called Minos Kalokairinos, had sunk some shafts and identified the site as ancient Knossos. But Schliemann's plans came to nothing, because of the excessive demands of the local Moslem landowner. Political disturbances on the island after Schliemann's death, in 1890, delayed systematic excavation until 1898, when Turkish rule ended. In 1899 Arthur Evans succeeded in buying the Kephala site and started his excavations. It has been said that "No archaeologist has ever been granted the opportunity of revealing in its entirety a civilization the very existence of which was hardly suspected before the excavations began . . . no archaeological venture had been so richly rewarded, no enterprise so full of surprises and so generous of results."

To the Homeric-Mycenaean age recovered by Schliemann, Evans now added a richer, more original, and far older phase, which came to an end when Mycenae had just become established and which stood in a virtually parental relationship to the latter. The dawn of European history was pushed back another 1500 years as there rose from the rubble of Crete a civilization that Evans called "Minoan." It was a civilization that dazzled by its artistic refinement, naturalism, vivacity, urbanity, and material comfort. Unlike the somber, forbiddingly monumental buildings of Mesopotamia and Egypt, the architecture of Minos was designed to human dimensions. Apparently this civilization was dedicated not to the glory of rapacious and unfathomable gods or of despotic rulers, but to the joy of living. Here, it was felt, the secular spirit of the West pulsated for the first time. Visitors of the excavated place were struck by the beauty of its architecture and the gayness of its wall decorations. These buildings, with their elaborate drainage systems, were planned for easy living.

Arthur Evans did not go to Crete as a philhellene with Homer as his guide. In fact, classical Greece bored him. But in the course of his frequent visits to the Balkans, he had drifted down to the Mycenaean sites and visited Schliemann, an acquaintance of Evans' father, a wealthy industrialist and prominent student of the European palaeolithic and neolithic ages. Mycenaean civilization excited the younger Evans' interest—he felt that it compared favorably with that of classical Greece—and decided to study it thoroughly. He shrugged off Schliemann's sentimental literary theories and, as might have been expected of a man trained to the scientific study of antiquity from childhood, set about methodically to find out the extent and sources of this splendid European Bronze Age civilization. Particularly, it seemed inconceivable to him that the sophisticated Mycenaeans could have carried on without any writing.

The first clue to writing of the Mycenaean era came in 1889, when Evans, who had been Keeper of the Ashmolean Museum in Oxford since 1884, was sent a curious four-sided, early Greek sealstone engraved with hieroglyphic-like symbols. Evans made his first trip to Crete in search of such seals, for he had found that ultimately they all came from the sites of ancient cities on the island. He traveled all over the island, still without any intention of excavating there. He had now come to believe that Crete was the cultural bridge between the Near East, especially Egypt, and Europe and thought the Cretan hieroglyphic script might be evidence of Egyptian influence. (Earlier he had considered the possibility that the so-called Keftiu, who appeared as alien invaders on Egyptian reliefs, were Aegean people.) His primary interest, however, remained the minute pictographic symbols engraved on seals, and in 1893 he announced his findings to the Hellenic Society. Three years later he wrote a more extensive paper, *Cretan Pictographs and Prae-Phoenician Script.*

Evans was a man of substantial means, and, finally, to solve the riddle of the Cretan script—perhaps to find longer texts and archives, if not the most coveted of all archaeological objects, a bilingual—he bought the Kephala-Knossos site. He began digging in 1899, and from the beginning the excavations were extremely successful. A little below the surface a vast palace was found that had been built by a highly advanced, previously unknown civilization. Many of the objects that Evans uncovered in year-by-year digs—wonderful murals with "bullfight" scenes, statuettes, bronzes, ivories, faïences, jewelry, and vases—were unsurpassed in splendor and wonderfully modern in spirit. Evans also found a considerable number of written records. These he classified according to their types of writing into three different scripts that had apparently succeeded each other: a Cretan hieroglyphic and the cursive Linear A and Linear B. Evans' greatest ambition was to find a key to Minoan writing, but he made comparatively little progress. Of a planned two-volume work, *Scripta Minoa,* he published the first volume in 1909, which surveyed and analyzed the various Cretan inscriptions. The second volume, which, together with additional material, was to include translations of the texts in the first, was not published until 1952. At that time Sir John Myres assembled a second volume from Evans' extensive notes, but there were still no translations.

Evans was more successful in establishing the chronology of the Minoan Age, by crossdating Egyptian artifacts according to Petrie's method. He was able to distinguish three main periods —Early, Middle, and Late Minoan, with three subdivisions for each—and to synchronize them with eras in ancient Egyptian history. With some qualifications and adjustments, Evans' scheme has, on the whole, remained valid. He also proposed a corresponding scale for the mainland (Helladic) and the islands (Cycladic). As for the ethnic background of ancient Crete, Evans held that it had been settled by people of Anatolian stock in the neolithic age; but he was certain that the Minoans' principal cultural impulse had come from northern Egypt, probably around the beginning of dynastic times.

There was great excitement in 1901 when Evans published the gist of his discoveries in an article in *The Monthly Review,* and Evans' scholarship and archaeological competence could not be questioned, as Schliemann's had been. (In later years, however, Evans' reconstruction of Cretan buildings and restoration of frescoes and artifacts, which he paid for out of his own fortune, have been criticized as a "concrete Crete.")

Outstanding work in Cretan archaeology has been carried out by other scientists. For instance, Frederico Halbherr, the Italian excavator of Phaestos and Hagia Triada, appeared on the Cretan scene even earlier than Evans; two Americans, Harriet Boyd-Hawes and Richard B. Seager, unearthed Gournia; the Cretans themselves discovered a palace at Tylissos; and the French made an important contribution at Mallia. But Evans is mainly responsible for the resurrection of Minoan civilization.

He continued his excavations at Knossos for many years, even building a permanent home there, the Villa Ariadne. In Crete and in England he labored on his major work, *The Palace of Minos,* a work of 3,000 pages which he completed in 1935. Evans' mantle fell on J. D. S. Pendlebury, who was killed fighting with the Greek guerrillas against the German invaders in World War II. Sir Arthur himself died in England in 1941, three days after his ninetieth birthday. The Villa Ariadne had fallen into German hands and become their command headquarters.

The Palace of Minos

ARTHUR EVANS

LESS THAN a generation back the origin of Greek civilisation, and with it the sources of all great culture that has ever been, were wrapped in an impenetrable mist. That ancient world was still girt round within its narrow confines by the circling "Stream of Ocean." Was there anything beyond? The fabled kings and heroes of the Homeric Age, with their palaces and strongholds, were they aught, after all, but more or less humanised sun-myths?

One man had faith, accompanied by works, and in Dr. Schlie-mann the science of classical antiquity found its Columbus. Armed with the spade he brought to light from beneath the mounds of ages a real Troy; at Tiryns and Mycenae he laid bare the palace and the tombs and treasures of Homeric Kings. A new world opened to investigation, and the discoveries of its first explorer were followed up successfully by Dr. Tsountas and others on Greek soil. The eyes of observers were opened, and the traces of this prehistoric civilisation began to make their appearance far beyond the limits of Greece itself. From Cyprus and Palestine to Sicily and Southern Italy, and even to the coasts of Spain, the colonial and industrial enterprise of the "Myce-naeans" has left its mark throughout the Mediterranean basin. Professor Petrie's researches in Egypt have conclusively shown that as early at least as the close of the Middle Kingdom, or, approximately speaking, the beginning of the Second Millennium

From Evans' "The Palace of Minos," *The Monthly Review*, II, No. 3 (March 1901). Reprinted by permission of the executors of the estate of Sir Arthur Evans.

B.C., imported Aegean vases were finding their way into the
Nile valley. By the great days of the XVIIIth Dynasty, in the sixteenth and succeeding centuries B.C., this intercourse was of such
a kind that Mycenaean art, now in its full maturity of bloom,
was reacting on that of the contemporary Pharaohs and infusing
a living European element into the old conventional style of
the land of the Pyramids and the Sphinx.

But the picture was still very incomplete. Nay, it might even
be said that its central figure was not yet filled in. In all these
excavations and researches the very land to which ancient tradition unanimously pointed as the cradle of Greek civilisation had
been left out of count. To adapt the words applied by Gelon to
slighted Sicily and Syracuse, "The spring was wanting from the
year" of that earlier Hellas. Yet Crete, the central island—a half-
way house between three Continents—flanked by the great
Libyan promontory and linked by smaller island stepping stones
to the Peloponnese and the mainland of Anatolia, was called
upon by Nature to play a leading part in the development of the
early Aegean culture.

Here, in his royal city of Knossos, ruled Minos, or whatever
historic personage is covered by that name, and founded the
first sea empire of Greece, extending his dominion far and wide
over the Aegean isles and coast-lands. Athens paid to him its
human tribute of youth and maidens. His colonial plantations extended east and west along the Mediterranean basin till Gaza
worshipped the Cretan Zeus and a Minoan city rose in Western
Sicily. But it is as the first lawgiver of Greece that he achieved
his greatest renown, and the Code of Minos became the source
of all later legislation. As the wise ruler and inspired lawgiver
there is something altogether biblical in his legendary character.
He is the Cretan Moses, who every nine years repaired to the
Cave of Zeus, whether on the Cretan Ida or on Dicta, and received from the God of the Mountain the laws for his people.
Like Abraham he is described as the "friend of God." Nay, in
some accounts, the mythical being of Minos has a tendency to
blend with that of his native Zeus.

This Cretan Zeus, the God of the Mountain, whose animal figure was the bull and whose symbol was the double axe had in-

deed himself a human side which distinguishes him from his more ethereal namesake of classical Greece. In the great Cave of Mount Dicta, whose inmost shrine, adorned with natural pillars of gleaming stalactite, leads deep down to the waters of an unnavigated pool, Zeus himself was said to have been born and fed with honey and goat's milk by the nymph Amaltheia. On the conical height immediately above the site of Minos' City—now known as Mount Juktas—and still surrounded by a Cyclopean enclosure, was pointed out his tomb. Classical Greece scoffed at this primitive legend, and for this particular reason, first gave currency to the proverb that "the Cretans are always liars." St. Paul, too, adopted this hard saying, but in Crete itself the new religion, which here, as elsewhere, so eagerly availed itself of what might aid its own propaganda in existing belief, seems to have dealt more gently with the scenes of the lowly birth and Holy Sepulchre of a mortal God. On the height of Juktas, on the peaks of Dicta, which overlooked, one the birth-place, the other the temple of the Cretan Zeus, pious hands have built chapels, the scenes of annual pilgrimage, dedicated to *Avhentés Christos,* "the Lord Christ." In his shrine at Gaza the Minoan Zeus had already in Pagan days received the distinguishing epithet of Marnas, "the Lord" in its Syrian form.

If Minos was the first lawgiver, his craftsman Daedalus was the first traditional founder of what may be called a "school of art." Many were the fabled works wrought by them for King Minos, some gruesome, like the brass man Talos. In Knossos, the royal city, he built the dancing ground, or "Choros," of Ariadne, and the famous Labyrinth. In its inmost maze dwelt the Minotaur, or "Bull of Minos," fed daily with human victims, till such time as Theseus, guided by Ariadne's ball of thread, penetrated to its lair, and, after slaying the monster, rescued the captive youths and maidens. Such, at least, was the Athenian tale. A more prosaic tradition saw in the Labyrinth a building of many passages, the idea of which Daedalus had taken from the great Egyptian mortuary temple on the shores of Lake Moeris, to which the Greeks gave the same name; and recent philological research has derived the name itself from the *labrys,* or double axe, the emblem of the Cretan and Carian Zeus.

Mythological speculation has seen in the Labyrinth, to use the words of a learned German, "a thing of belief and fancy, an image of the starry heaven with its infinitely winding paths, in which, nevertheless, the sun and moon so surely move about." We shall see that the spade has supplied a simpler solution.

When one calls to mind these converging lines of ancient tradition it becomes impossible not to feel that, without Crete, "the spring is taken away" indeed from the Mycenaean world. Great as were the results obtained by exploration on the sites of this ancient culture on the Greek mainland and elsewhere, there was still a sense of incompleteness. In nothing was this more striking than in the absence of any written document. A few signs had, indeed, been found on a vase-handle, but these were set aside as mere ignorant copies of Hittite or Egyptian hieroglyphs. In the volume of his monumental work which deals with Mycenaean art, M. Perrot was reduced to the conclusion that, "as at present advised, we can continue to affirm that, for the whole of this period, neither in Peloponnese nor in Central Greece, no more upon the buildings nor upon the thousand-and-one objects of domestic use and luxury that have come forth from the tombs, has anything been discovered that resembles any form of writing."

But was this, indeed, the last word of scientific exploration? Was it possible that a people so advanced in other respects—standing in such intimate relations with Egypt and the Syrian lands where some form of writing had been an almost immemorial possession—should have been absolutely wanting in this most essential element of civilisation? I could not believe it. Once more one's thoughts turned to the land of Minos, and the question irresistibly suggested itself—was that early heritage of fixed laws compatible with a complete ignorance of the art of writing? An abiding tradition of the Cretans themselves, preserved by Diodorus, shows that they were better informed. The Phoenicians, they said, had not invented letters, they had simply changed their forms—in other words, they had only improved on an existing system.

It is now seven [eleven?] years since a piece of evidence came into my hands which went far to show that long before the days of the introduction of the Phoenician alphabet, as adopted by the later Greeks, the Cretans were, in fact, possessed of a system of writing. While hunting out ancient engraved stones at Athens I came upon some three- and four-sided seals showing on each of their faces groups of hieroglyphic and linear signs distinct from the Egyptian and Hittite, but evidently representing some form of script. On inquiry I learnt that these seals had been found in Crete. A clue was in my hands, and like Theseus, I resolved to follow it, if possible to the inmost recesses of the Labyrinth. That the source and centre of the great Mycenaean civilisation remained to be unearthed on Cretan soil I had never doubted, but the prospect now opened on finally discovering its written records.

From 1894 onwards I undertook a series of campaigns of exploration chiefly in Central and Eastern Crete. In all directions fresh evidence continually came to light, Cyclopean ruins of cities and strongholds, beehive tombs, vases, votive bronzes, exquisitely engraved gems, amply demonstrating that in fact the great days of that "island story" lay far behind the historic period. From the Mycenaean sites of Crete I obtained a whole series of inscribed seals, such as I had first noticed at Athens, showing the existence of an entire system of hieroglyphic or quasi-pictorial writing, with here and there signs of the co-existence of more linear forms. From the great Cave of Mount Dicta—the birth-place of Zeus—the votive deposits of which have now been thoroughly explored by Mr. Hogarth, I procured a stone Libation Table inscribed with a dedication of several characters in the early Cretan script. But for more exhaustive excavation my eyes were fixed on some ruined walls, the great gypsum blocks of which were engraved with curious symbolic characters, that crowned the southern slope of a hill known as Kephala, overlooking the ancient site of Knossos, the City of Minos. They were evidently part of a large prehistoric building. Might one not uncover here the palace of King Minos, perhaps even the mysterious Labyrinth itself?

These blocks had already arrested the attention of Schliemann and others, but the difficulties raised by the native proprietors had defeated all efforts at scientific exploration. In 1895 I succeeded in acquiring a quarter of the site from one of the joint owners. But the obstruction continued, and I was beset by difficulties of a more serious kind. The circumstances of the time were not favourable. The insurrection had broken out, half the villages in Crete were in ashes, and in the neighbouring town of Candia the most fanatical part of the Mahomedan population were collected together from the whole of the island. The faithful Herakles, who was at that time my "guide, philosopher, and muleteer," was seized by the Turks and thrown into a loathsome dungeon, from which he was with difficulty rescued. Soon afterwards the inevitable massacre took place, of which the nominal British "occupants" of Candia were in part themselves the victims. Then at last the sleeping lion was aroused. Under the guns of Admiral Noel the Turkish Commander evacuated the Government buildings at ten minutes' notice and shipped off the Sultan's troops. Crete once more was free.

At the beginning of this year I was at last able to secure the remaining part of the site of Kephala, and with the consent of Prince George's Government at once set about the work of excavation. I received some pecuniary help from the recently started Cretan Exploration Fund, and was fortunate in securing the services of Mr. Duncan Mackenzie, who had done good work for the British School in Melos, to assist me in directing the works. From about eighty to one hundred and fifty men were employed in the excavation which continued till the heat and fevers of June put an end to it for this season.

The result has been to uncover a large part of a vast prehistoric building—a palace with its numerous dependencies, but a palace on a far larger scale than those of Tiryns and Mycenae. About two acres of this has been unearthed, for by an extraordinary piece of good fortune the remains of walls began to appear only a foot or so, often only a few inches, below the surface. This dwelling of prehistoric kings had been overwhelmed by a great catastrophe. Everywhere on the hill-top were traces of a mighty conflagration; burnt beams and charred wooden columns lay within the rooms and corridors. There was here no gradual decay. The civilisation represented on this spot had been cut short in the fulness of its bloom. Nothing later than remains of the good Mycenaean period was found over the whole site. Nothing even so late as the last period illustrated by the remains of Mycenae itself. From the day of destruction to this the site has been left entirely desolate. For three thousand years or more not a tree seems to have been planted here; over a part of the area not even a ploughshare had passed. At the time of the great overthrow, no doubt, the place had been methodically plundered for metal objects, and the fallen *débris* in the rooms and passages turned over and ransacked for precious booty. Here and there a local Bey or peasant had grubbed for stone slabs to supply his yard or threshing-floor. But the party walls of clay and plaster still stood intact, with the fresco painting on them, still in many cases perfectly preserved at a few inches depth from the surface, a clear proof of how severely the site had been let alone for these long centuries.

Who were the destroyers? Perhaps the Dorian invaders who seem to have overrun the island about the eleventh or twelfth century before our era. More probably, still earlier invading swarms from the mainland of Greece. The Palace itself had a long antecedent history and there are frequent traces of re-modelling. Its early elements may go back a thousand years before its final overthrow, since, in the great Eastern Court, was found the lower part of an Egyptian seated figure of diorite, with a triple inscription, showing that it dates back to the close of the XIIth or the beginning of the XIIIth Dynasty of Egypt; in other words approximately to 2000 B.C. But below the foundation of the later building, and covering the whole hill, are the remains of a primitive settlement of still greater antiquity, belonging to the insular Stone Age. In parts this "Neolithic" deposit was over twenty-four feet thick, everywhere full of stone axes, knives of volcanic glass, dark polished and incised pottery, and primitive images such as those found by Schliemann in the lowest strata of Troy.

The outer walls of the Palace were supported on huge gypsum blocks, but there was no sign of an elaborate system of fortification such as at Tiryns and Mycenae. The reason of this is not far to seek. Why is Paris strongly fortified, while London is practically an open town? The city of Minos, it must be remembered, was the centre of a great sea-power, and it was in "wooden walls" that its rulers must have put their trust. The mighty blocks of the Palace show, indeed, that it was not for want of engineering power that the akropolis of Knossos remained unfortified. But in truth Mycenaean might was here at home. At Tiryns and Mycenae itself it felt itself threatened by warlike Continental neighbours. It was not till the mainland foes were masters of the sea that they could have forced an entry into the House of Minos. Then, indeed, it was an easy task. In the Cave of Zeus on Mount Ida was found a large brooch (or *fibula*) belonging to the race of northern invaders, on one side of which a war galley is significantly engraved.

The Palace was entered on the south-west side by a portico and double doorway opening from a spacious paved court. Flanking the portico were remains of a great fresco of a bull, and on the walls of the corridor leading from it were still preserved the lower part of a procession of painted life-size figures, in the centre of which was a female personage, probably a queen, in magnificent apparel. This corridor seems to have led round to a great southern porch or *Propylaeum* with double columns, the walls of which were originally decorated with figures in the same style. Along nearly the whole length of the building ran a spacious paved corridor, lined by a long row of fine stone doorways, giving access to a succession of magazines. On the floor of these magazines huge store jars were still standing, large enough to have contained the "forty thieves". One of these jars, contained in a small separate chamber, was nearly five feet in height.

Here occurred one of the most curious discoveries of the whole excavation. Under the closely compacted pavement of one of these magazines, upon which the huge jars stood, there were built in, between solid piles of masonry, double tiers of stone cists lined with lead. Only a few were opened and they proved to be empty, but there can be little doubt that they were constructed for the deposit of treasure. Whoever destroyed and plundered the Palace had failed to discover these receptacles, so that when more come to be explored there is some real hope of finding buried hoards.

On the east side of the Palace opened a still larger paved

court, approached by broad steps from another principal entrance to the North. From this court access was given by an ante-room to what was certainly the most interesting chamber of the whole building, almost as perfectly preserved—though some twelve centuries older—as anything found beneath the volcanic ash of Pompeii or the lava of Herculaneum. Already a few inches below the surface freshly preserved fresco began to appear. Walls were shortly uncovered decorated with flowering plants and running water, while on each side of the doorway of a small inner room stood guardian griffins with peacocks' plumes in the same flowery landscape. Round the walls ran low stone benches, and between these on the north side, separated by a small interval and raised on a stone base, rose a gypsum throne with a high back, and originally coloured with decorative designs. Its lower part was adorned with a curiously carved arch, with crocketed mouldings, showing an extraordinary anticipation of some most characteristic features of Gothic architecture. Opposite the throne was a finely wrought tank of gypsum slabs —a feature borrowed perhaps from an Egyptian palace—approached by a descending flight of steps, and originally surmounted by cyprus-wood columns supporting a kind of *impluvium*. Here truly was the council chamber of a Mycenaean King or Sovereign Lady. It may be said to-day that the youngest of European rulers has in his dominions the oldest throne in Europe.

The frescoes discovered on the Palace site constitute a new epoch in the history of painting. Little, indeed, of the kind even of classical Greek antiquity has been hitherto known earlier at least than the Pompeian series. The first find of this kind marks a red-letter day in the story of the excavation. In carefully uncovering the earth and *débris* in a passage at the back of the southern Propylaeum there came to light two large fragments of what proved to be the upper part of a youth bearing a gold-mounted silver cup. The robe is decorated with a beautiful quatre-foil pattern; a silver ornament appears in front of the ear, and silver rings on the arms and neck. What is specially interesting among the ornaments is an agate gem on the left wrist, thus illustrating the manner of wearing the beautifully engraved signets of which many clay impressions were found in the Palace.

The colours were almost as brilliant as when laid down over three thousand years before. For the first time the true portraiture of a man of this mysterious Mycenaean race rises before us. The flesh tint, following perhaps an Egyptian precedent, is of a deep reddish-brown. The limbs are finely moulded, though the waist, as usual in Mycenaean fashions, is tightly drawn in by a silver-mounted girdle, giving great relief to the hips. The profile of the face is pure and almost classically Greek. This, with the dark curly hair and high brachycephalic head, recalls an indigenous type well represented still in the glens of Ida and the White Mountains—a type which brings with it many reminiscences from the Albanian highlands and the neighbouring regions of Montenegro and Herzegovina. The lips are somewhat full, but the physiognomy has certainly no Semitic cast. The profile rendering of the eye shows an advance in human portraiture foreign to Egyptian art, and only achieved by the artists of classical Greece in the early fine-art period of the fifth century B.C.—after some eight centuries, that is, of barbaric decadence and slow revival.

There was something very impressive in this vision of brilliant youth and of male beauty, recalled after so long an interval to our upper air from what had been till yesterday a forgotten world. Even our untutored Cretan workmen felt the spell and fascination. They, indeed, regarded the discovery of such a painting in the bosom of the earth as nothing less than miraculous, and saw in it the "icon" of a Saint! The removal of the fresco required a delicate and laborious process of underplastering, which necessitated its being watched at night, and old Manolis, one of the most trustworthy of our gang, was told off for the purpose. Somehow or other he fell asleep, but the wrathful Saint appeared to him in a dream. Waking with a start, he was conscious of a mysterious presence; the animals round began to low and neigh, and "there were visions about"; "φαντάζει," he said, in summing up his experiences next morning, "the whole place spooks!"

To the north of the Palace, in some rooms that seem to have

belonged to the women's quarter, frescoes were found in an entirely novel miniature style. Here were ladies with white complexions—due, we may fancy, to the seclusion of harem life—*décolletées*, but with fashionable puffed sleeves and flounced gowns, and their hair as elaborately curled and *frisé* as if they were fresh from a *coiffeur's* hands. "Mais," exclaimed a French savant who honoured me with a visit, "ce sont des Parisiennes!"

They were seated in groups, engaged in animated conversation, in the courts and gardens and on the balconies of a palatial building, while in the walled spaces beyond were large crowds of men and boys, some of them hurling javelins. In some cases both sexes were intermingled. These alternating scenes of Peace and War recall the subjects of Achilles' shield, and we have here at the same time a contemporary illustration of that populousness of the Cretan cities in the Homeric age which struck the imagination of the bard. Certain fragments of fresco belong to the still earlier period of Aegean art, which precedes the Mycenaean, well illustrated in another field by the elegant painted vases found by Mr. Hogarth in some private houses on this site. A good idea of the refinement already reached in these earlier days of the Palace is given by the subject of one fresco fragment in this "pre-Mycenaean" style—a boy, namely, in a field of white crocuses, some of which he has gathered and is placing in an ornamental vase.

Very valuable architectural details were supplied by the walls and buildings of some of the miniature frescoes above described. In one place rose the façade of a small temple, with triple cells containing sacred pillars, and representing in a more advanced form the arrangement of the small golden shrines, with doves perched upon them, found by Schliemann in the shaft graves at Mycenae. This temple fresco has a peculiar interest, as showing the character of a good deal of the upper structure of the Palace itself, which has now perished. It must largely have consisted of clay and rubble walls, artfully concealed under brilliantly painted plaster, and contained and supported by a woodwork framing. The base of the small temple rests on the huge gypsum blocks which form so conspicuous a feature in the existing remains, and below the central opening is inserted a frieze, recalling the alabaster reliefs of the palace hall of Tiryns, with triglyphs, the prototypes of the Doric, and the half-rosettes of the "metopes" inlaid with blue enamel, the Kyanos of Homer.

A transition from painting to sculpture was supplied by a great relief of a bull in hard plaster, coloured with the natural tints, large parts of which, including the head, were found near the northern gate. It is unquestionably the finest plastic work of the time that has come down to us, stronger and truer to life than any classical sculpture of the kind.

Somewhat more conventional, but still showing great naturalistic power, is the marble head of a lioness, made for the spout of a fountain. It too had been originally tinted, and the eyes and nostrils inlaid with brightly coloured enamels. A part of a stone frieze, with finely undercut rosettes, recalled similar fragments from Tiryns and Mycenae, but far surpasses them in execution.

Vases of marble and other stones abounded, some exquisitely carved. Among these was one cut out of alabaster in the shape of a great Triton shell, every coil and fold of which was accurately reproduced. A porphyry lamp, supported on a quatre-foil pillar, with a beautiful lotus capital, well illustrates the influence of an Egyptian model. But the model was here surpassed.

Among the more curious arts, practised in prehistoric Knossos, was that of miniature painting on the back of plaques of crystal. A galloping bull thus delineated on an azure background is a little masterpiece in its way. A small relief on a banded agate, representing a dagger in an ornamental sheath resting on an artistically folded belt, to a certain extent anticipates by many centuries the art of cameo carving. A series of clay seals was also discovered, exhibiting impressions of intaglios in the fine bold Mycenaean style; one of these, with two bulls, larger than any known signet gem of the kind, may well have been a royal seal. The subjects of some of these intaglios show the development of a surprisingly picturesque style of art. We see fish naturalistically grouped in a rocky pool, a hart beside a water-brook in a mountain glen, and a grotto, above which some small monkey-like creatures are seen climbing the overhanging crags.

But manifold as were the objects of interest found within the palace of Knossos, the crowning discovery—or, rather series of discoveries—remains to be told. On the last day of March, not far below the surface of the ground, a little to the right of the southern portico, there turned up a clay tablet of elongated shape, bearing on it incised characters in a linear script, accompanied by numeral signs. My hopes now ran high of finding entire deposits of clay archives, and they were speedily realised. Not far from the scene of the first discovery there came to light a clay receptacle containing a hoard of tablets. In other chambers occurred similar deposits, which had originally been stored in coffers of wood, clay, or gypsum. The tablets themselves are of various forms, some flat, elongated bars, from about 2 to 7½ inches in length, with wedge-like ends; others, larger and squarer, ranging in size to small octavo. In one particular magazine tablets of a different kind were found—perforated bars, crescent and scallop-like "labels," with writing in the same hieroglyphic style as that on the seals found in Eastern Crete. But the great mass, amounting to over a thousand inscriptions, belonged to another and more advanced system with linear characters. It was, in short, a highly developed form of script, with regular divisions between the words, and for elegance hardly surpassed by any later form of writing.

A clue to the meaning of these clay records is in many cases supplied by the addition of pictorial illustrations representing the objects concerned. Thus we find human figures, perhaps slaves; chariots and horses; arms or implements and armour, such as axes and cuirasses; houses or barns; ears of barley or other cereal; swine; various kinds of trees; and a long-stamened flower, evidently the saffron crocus, used for dyes. On some tablets appear ingots, probably of bronze, followed by a balance (the Greek τάλαντον), and figures which probably indicate their value in Mycenaean gold talents. The numerals attached to many of these objects show that we have to do with accounts referring to the royal stores and arsenals.

Some tablets relate to ceramic vessels of various forms, many of them containing marks indicative of their contents. Others, still more interesting, show vases of metallic forms, and obviously relate to the royal treasures. It is a highly significant fact that the most characteristic of these, such as a beaker like the famous gold cups found in the Vapheio tomb near Sparta, a high-spouted ewer and an object, perhaps representing a certain weight of metal, in the form of an ox's head, recur—together with the ingots with incurving sides among the gold offerings in the hands of the tributary Aegean princes—on Egyptian monuments of Thothmes III's time. These tributary chieftains, described as Kefs and People of the Isles of the Sea, who have been already recognised as the representatives of the Mycenaean culture, recall in their dress and other particulars the Cretan youths, such as the Cupbearer above described, who take part in the professional scenes on the palace frescoes. The appearance in the records of the royal treasury at Knossos of vessels of the same form as those offered by them to Pharaoh is itself a valuable indication that some of these clay archives approximately go back to the same period—in other words, to the beginning of the fifteenth century B.C.

Other documents, in which neither ciphers nor pictorial illustrations are to be found, may appeal even more deeply to the imagination. The analogy of the more or less contemporary tablets, written in cuneiform script, found in the palace of Tell-el-Amarna, might lead us to expect among them the letters from distant governors or diplomatic correspondence. It is probable that some are contracts or public acts, which may give some actual formulas of Minoan legislation. There is, indeed, an atmosphere of legal nicety, worthy of the House of Minos, in the way in which these clay records were secured. The knots of string which, according to the ancient fashion, stood in the place of locks for the coffers containing the tablets, were rendered inviolable by the attachment of clay seals, impressed with the finely engraved signets, the types of which represent a great variety of subjects, such as ships, chariots, religious scenes, lions, bulls, and other animals. But—as if this precaution was not in itself considered sufficient—while the clay was still wet the face of the seal was countermarked by a controlling official, and the back countersigned and endorsed by an inscription in the same Mycenaean script as that inscribed on the tablets themselves.

Much study and comparison will be necessary for the elucidation of these materials, which it may be hoped will be largely supplemented by the continued exploration of the Palace. If, as may well be the case, the language in which they were written was some primitive form of Greek we need not despair of the final decipherment of these Knossian archives, and the bounds of history may eventually be so enlarged as to take in the "heroic age" of Greece. In any case the weighty question, which years before I had set myself to solve on Cretan soil, has found, so far at least, an answer. That great early civilisation was not dumb, and the written records of the Hellenic world are carried back some seven centuries beyond the date of the first known historic writings. But what, perhaps, is even more remarkable than this is that, when we examine in detail the linear script of these Mycenaean documents, it is impossible not to recognise that we have here a system of writing, syllabic and perhaps partly alphabetic, which stands on a distinctly higher level of development than the hieroglyphs of Egypt or the cuneiform script of contemporary Syria and Babylonia. It is not till some five centuries later that we find the first dated examples of Phœnician writing.

The signs already mentioned as engraved on the great gypsum blocks of the Palace must be regarded as distinct from the script proper. These blocks go back to the earliest period of the building, and the symbols on them, which are of very limited selection but of constant recurrence, seem to have had a religious significance. The most constantly recurring of these, indeed, is the *labrys,* or double axe, already referred to—the special symbol of the Cretan Zeus, votive deposits of which, in bronze, have been found in the cave sanctuaries of the God on Mount Ida and Mount Dicta. The double-axe is engraved on the principal blocks, such as the corner stones and door-jambs throughout the building, and recurs as a sign of dedication on every side of every block of a sacred pillar that forms the centre of what seems to have been the inmost shrine of an aniconic cult connected with this indigenous divinity.

The "House of Minos" thus turns out to be also the House of the Double Axe—the *labrys* and its Lord—in other words, it is the true *Labyrinthos.* The divine inspirer of Minos was not less the Lord of the Bull, and it is certainly no accidental coincidence

that huge figures of bulls in painting and plaster occupied conspicuous positions within it. Nay, more, on a small steatite relief,
a couchant bull is seen above the doorway of a building probably intended to represent the Palace, and this would connect it
in the most direct way with the sacred animal of the Cretan
Zeus.

There can be little remaining doubt that this vast edifice, which
in a broad historic sense we are justified in calling the "Palace
of Minos," is one and the same as the traditional "Labyrinth." A
great part of the ground plan itself, with its long corridors and
repeated succession of blind galleries, its tortuous passages and
spacious underground conduit, its bewildering system of small
chambers, does in fact present many of the characteristics of a
maze.

Let us place ourselves for a moment in the position of the first
Dorian colonists of Knossos after the great overthrow, when
features now laboriously uncovered by the spade were still perceptible amid the mass of ruins. The name was still preserved,
though the exact meaning, as supplied by the native Cretan
dialect, had been probably lost. Hard by the western gate in
her royal robes, to-day but partially visible, stood Queen Ariadne
herself—and might not the comely youth in front of her be the
hero Theseus, about to receive the coil of thread for his errand
of liberation down the mazy galleries beyond? Within, fresh and
beautiful on the walls of the inmost chambers, were the captive
boys and maidens locked up here by the tyrant of old. At more
than one turn rose a mighty bull, in some cases, no doubt, according to the favourite Mycenaean motive, grappled with by a
half-naked man. The type of Minotaur itself as a man-bull was
not wanting on the soil of prehistoric Knossos, and more than
one gem found on this site represents a monster with the lower
body of a man and forepart of a bull.

One may feel assured that the effect of these artistic creations
on the rude Greek settler of those days was not less than that of
the disinterested fresco on the Cretan workman of today. Everything around—the dark passages, the lifelike figures surviving
from an older world—would conspire to produce a sense of the
supernatural. It was haunted ground, and then, as now, "phan-

tasms" were about. The later stories of the grisly king and his man-eating bull sprang, as it were, from the soil, and the whole site called forth a superstitious awe. It was left severely alone by the newcomers. Another Knossos grew up on the lower slopes of the hill to the north, and the old Palace site became a "desolation and hissing." Gradually earth's mantle covered the ruined heap, and by the time of the Romans the Labyrinth had become nothing more than a tradition and a name.

21. MICHAEL VENTRIS

The existence of Minoan script was brought to the attention of the world by Sir Arthur Evans, who tracked down mysteriously inscribed seal stones to the island of Crete. From time to time, a few strange symbole on excavated Mycenaean vessels were also observed, but it was left to Evans to identify the earliest script of Greece, which was in use six hundred years before Homer. In his attempt to establish and decipher this preclassical system of writing, Evans found the Minoan civilization. Yet, the mystery of the ancient script, of which he unearthed more extensive evidence in the clay tablets of the Palace of Minos and on fragments in the Diktaean cave, the legendary birthplace of Zeus on Crete, haunted him throughout his life. The meaning of the three Minoan scripts—the ancient pictographs (the best-known example is the Phaestos Disc) as well as Linear A and Linear B—eluded him to the end. A hoped-for Minoan Rosetta Stone never appeared. To the detriment of other scholars, Evans withheld from publication a major portion of the material, particularly of Linear B. On the other hand, not only did he notice the basic difference of the three scripts, but he deciphered the numerical (decimal) notation, drew attention to pictographic signs that probably corresponded to names in the Linear texts, and rightly concluded that the tablets represented, in the main, lists of articles, accounts, or business records. Even more important perhaps, he inferred from the occurrence of some seventy signs that the form of writing was syllabic, not alphabetic or ideogrammatic.

Besides Evans, many leading scholars tried their hands for five decades at deciphering the scripts. Attempts and hypotheses were legion. One thing practically all scholars were agreed upon—though Evans had not ruled out the possibility entirely—was that the language of the scripts could not be Greek. The first Greeks had entered the Mediterranean world as Indo-European barbarians at a time when the Minoan civilization in Crete had already been flourishing for about a thousand years. Since the script had clearly been originated by the Minoans and evidence of its use on the mainland during Mycenaean times was slight, the likelihood that the Minoan script was Greek seemed slim indeed. Some epigraphers and archaeologists were certain the scripts were in Hittite, or Basque, or Cypriot; others proposed Etruscan, a still not fully known language that Michael Ventris, the decipherer of Linear B, up to a few days of the final solution was convinced would offer the key. In 1940, when he was eighteen years old, he had published an article defending this thesis in the *American Journal of Archaeology*.

The person who probably made the greatest contribution before Ventris was Dr. Alice E. Kober of Brooklyn College, New York. She studied the nature of the language used in Linear B, established it as being inflected, and recognized distinctions in plural endings and gender. Had she not died in 1950, at the point when more samples of Linear B were forthcoming, she might very well have been the first to reveal the secret. John Chadwick, Michael Ventris' co-worker, writes: "I do not think that there can be any doubt that Miss Kober would have taken a leading part in events of later years, had she been spared; she alone of the earlier investigators was pursuing the track which led Ventris to the solution of the problem."

The breakthrough came as a great surprise. In 1939, the American archaeologist Carl W. Blegen and Constantine Kourouniotis had unearthed a late Mycenaean palace, believed to be that of King Nestor of Pylos, in the southwestern Peloponnesus. There they found 600 clay tablets in Linear B, baked by the fire that had consumed the palace. Work was interrupted by the war, and the tablets were not published until 1951; other texts which Blegen had found when he resumed excavations in 1952 were released subsequently. Other important finds of Linear B tablets were made by the English archaeologist Alan Wace in Mycenae in the houses of wealthy private citizens and merchants, thus proving clearly the widespread use of writing for ordinary purposes in Mycenaean Greece. Epigraphers working over Linear B scripts now had, for the first time, ample material. And soon there came the inspiration, tentatively announced by Ventris in 1952, that Linear B was written in no other language than archaic Greek, the language of the Homeric heroes and their Mycenaean ancestors, who were also full-blooded Greeks. The announcement left many scholars incredulous, but once Ventris elaborated his deciphering with the aid of John Chadwick, approval was almost unanimous.

Michael Ventris was not a classical scholar, philologist, epigrapher, or archaeologist by profession, and a great deal has been made of the fact that he was an amateur in a highly complex and abstruse field in which experts feared to tread. It is true that he was an architect, and that he had not attended Oxford or Cambridge. But the study of languages and scripts had absorbed him since boyhood. He was already a student of ancient writings when at the age of fourteen he visited Burlington House in London to view an exhibition celebrating the fiftieth anniversary of the British School of Archaeology in Athens. On hearing the aged Sir Arthur Evans lecture there on Minoan Crete and its mysterious writing, Ventris resolved that he would decipher the script, and sixteen years later he did so. His feat, though it benefited from the work of other scholars, is one of the towering contributions to twentieth-century archaeology and epigraphy. Because of the relative scarcity of records and the lack of a bilingual, it required a perhaps even greater effort of reasoning power, ingenuity and philological skill than the work of Champollion or Rawlinson. Appropriately, it has been hailed by R. I. Barnett of the British Museum "the Everest of Greek Archaeology."

Even though the deciphered writings were little more than inventories, as Evans had anticipated, the social and economic information which they impart about the late Minoan and Mycenaean ages (about 1400 to 1100 B.C.) is of the most vital kind. Basic concepts concerning the Mycenaean civilization had to be revised, for the Linear B writings from the Minoan palace at Knossos were in early Greek and not in a native Minoan language. Alan Wace and others had long insisted—in spite of Sir Arthur Evans—that Knossos in its last phases reveals strong Mycenaean influences from the mainland. For instance, features like the famous "beehive" tombs, which are also conspicuous at Ras Shamra and other parts of the Mediterranean area, indicate that cultural relations between Crete and Greece were not entirely a one-way traffic. And though Mycenaean Greece owes its awakening to Crete, it developed a civilization that was not just a Cretan carbon copy, but assimilated Minoan art and achievements to its own spirit and environment and in time contributed innovations of its own. It is very likely that Achaeans were in control of Knossos (though not of the entire island) when the city was destroyed in 1400 B.C., so they can no longer be blamed for its ruin. The Cretan records found by Evans were written in early Greek for the benefit of the Achaean masters of Knossos. In this light, Linear B represents an adaptation of the older Linear A to the Indo-European idiom. Whether this adaptation took place first in Crete or on the mainland is not known.

The success in reading Linear B helped to revive more intense study of Cretan hieroglyphs, Linear A, and the apparently related Cypro-Minoan script of Cyprus. Work on Linear A still suffers from the limited material so far available. In 1957, the year after Ventris' tragic death in an automobile accident, the American Orientalist Cyrus H. Gordon of Brandeis University—using Ventris' syllabic identifications—claimed that certain words in Linear A texts can be established as Akkadian, a Semitic language used widely in the second millennium all over the Near East. However, this assertion still awaits systematic verification.

Deciphering Europe's Oldest Script

MICHAEL VENTRIS

IT WAS JUST 150 years ago that Champollion, at the age of eleven, embarked on the studies which were to lead to the first classic decipherment, that of the Egyptian hieroglyphic writing. In 1802, the oldest known languages were Greek, Latin, and Hebrew; and no records which had been written down earlier than about 600 B.C. could be read or understood. All that was known of the earlier civilisations of the Near East was limited to those parts of the Old Testament which seemed historical, and to the garbled accounts of Greek and Roman writers.

But with the success of Champollion's system of decipherment, this situation was to change very rapidly, and during the course of the nineteenth century more and more early scripts came to be read, and their languages understood: Old Persian, Elamite, Assyrian, Sumerian, Mitannian, many of them completely unsuspected by earlier generations of scholars. The most recent success, in 1932, has been the reading of the Hittite hieroglyphs of Asia Minor; and as the result of many ingenious decipherments, we can now read nearly all the ancient languages of the Near East, and the frontier of literate history has been pushed back about 2,000 years over a large part of this area. But Europe herself has unfortunately been left out of this progress, though many of these languages were spoken on her own doorstep. Her own pre-classical civilisations have remained dumb, and the earliest inscription written by a European which can be clearly understood is still today, as it was in Champollion's time, one written in the Greek

From Ventris' BBC Third Programme talk, printed in *The Listener*, July 10, 1952. Copyright © 1955 by Michael Ventris. Reprinted by permission of Lois Ventris.

alphabet. But I shall try to show that this situation is likely to be transformed in the near future.

When Schliemann excavated the great site of Mycenae in 1876, he was unable to find any trace of writing. It was perhaps rather surprising that such a powerful and civilised city should have been completely illiterate. But Homer himself had made no explicit reference to writing at Agamemnon's court, and most people were content to believe that the Greeks had got their first knowledge of writing from the Phoenicians, some 400 years after the time of the Trojan War. Then, one day in 1889, Sir Arthur Evans, keeper of the Ashmolean Museum, was sent a peculiar-looking sealstone from Greece. On its four sides it was engraved with pictographic signs—animals' heads, a human arm, arrows—rather like the hieroglyphs which the Hittites had used. Evans searched Greece and the Islands for more examples of these early sealstones: many of them he found being worn as lucky charms by the Greek peasant women. He determined that they could all, in fact, be traced to the sites of ancient cities in Crete. And before long Evans came to the site of Knossos, the great palace of the legendary Minos, who had ruled Crete before the Trojan War, when she was a prosperous island of ninety cities.

Evans began to dig there in 1899, and it took him the rest of his life to catalogue, describe, and preserve all that he found. Among the brilliant remains of this 'Minoan' civilisation, beside which even Mycenae began to look decadent and provincial, he found ample evidence for not one, but at least four, different systems of writing. For the pictographs which he had collected on the sealstones, dating from about 2000 B.C., were only the crude beginnings of Minoan writing, and had before long given rise to various simplified scripts in local use throughout Crete. In the last great half-century of Knossos' prosperity, before she was destroyed about 1400 B.C., the royal scribes had reduced these systems to a highly standardised official script, which Evans called Linear Script B. The earlier pictographs may have been a kind of picture-writing, but this new script was so regular that it is clearly phonetic, the signs representing, not whole words or ideas, but sounds. Evans found about 1,800 clay tablets written in Linear Script B, stored in various parts of the palace. The writing on these tablets consists partly of groups of from two to six phonetic signs, each group representing some name or word in the Minoan language, and partly of isolated symbols in picture-writing followed by numbers. From these symbols, many of which are recognisable objects, it is evident that the tablets are inventories of cattle, food-stuffs, and equipment, and nominal rolls of men, women and children. They had, Evans supposed, been jotted down during the last months before Knossos was destroyed, and would in the normal way have been checked at the end of the year and then thrown away.

For half a century, these Knossos tablets have represented our main evidence for Minoan writing, and many people—classical scholars and archaeologists as well as dilettanti of all kinds—have been fascinated by the problem of deciphering them. Until now they have all been uniformly unsuccessful, largely for the reason that disgracefully few of the inscriptions were made generally available for study. When Evans died in 1941, he had still not published all the Knossos material which he had dug up at the turn of the century. He left behind him a mass of unfinished notes, together with his old drawings of the tablets; the originals having meanwhile been stored away, in some disorder, in the museum at Iraklion in Crete, where they fortunately survived the war.

For the last ten years Sir John Myres has been engaged in the difficult task of completing Evans' work for publication; and in the second volume of *Scripta Minoa,* published this spring, the whole Knossos material is at last made available. Myres has added a short commentary of his own, but has made no attempt to decipher the tablets. In fact he has remained sceptical of all the recent attempts to do so, and has rightly confined himself to presenting the tablets, as excavated, in as objective a way as possible. But it is one thing to edit inscriptions on the spot, as they are dug up, quite another to have to reconstruct them, as Myres did, from an old man's forty-year-old notes and from a poor and incomplete set of photographs. The drawings of the tablets given in *Scripta Minoa* are not, unfortunately, a hundred per cent reliable, and we shall have to check them against a new transcription of the originals which has recently been made in Iraklion.

To have incorporated these corrections in *Scripta Minoa* would have meant further delaying a book which has, as it is, appeared forty-two years after its first volume.

A further stimulus to Minoan research was given last year, when Dr. Bennett, of Yale University, published drawings of about 600 similar tablets which had been dug up on the mainland of Greece in 1939. They come from the ruins of the Mycenaean palace at Ano Englianos in Messenia, which some take to be the Homeric Pylos of King Nestor. Although they appear to date from about 1200 B.C., 200 years later than the Knossos tablets, they are written in an almost identical form of Linear Script B, and in the same language. Since it is generally believed that the people of Knossos were of some indigenous race and language, but that the Mycenaeans of the mainland were already Greeks, this involves us in some historical problems, to which I will return later.

With the almost simultaneous publication of the Knossos and Pylos tablets, all the existing Minoan Linear Script material is now available for study, and the race to decipher it has begun in earnest. It may be interesting to discuss just how one sets about a job like this. It is often alleged to be impossible to decipher a set of inscriptions where both the writing and the language are unknown quantities, and where there is no bilingual to help us. But provided there is enough material to work on, the situation is not hopeless at all. It simply means that, instead of a mechanical piece of decoding, a rather more subtle process of deduction has to be undertaken. It is rather like doing a crossword puzzle on which the positions of the black squares have not been printed for you.

There are four main lines of attack: First, we must look carefully at the picture-writing symbols on the tablets, and try to determine what the objects are which are being listed. To help us, we have our knowledge of what the staple items of the Minoan economy are likely to have been, and the analogy of other accounts from Egypt, Syria, and Mesopotamia. Secondly, we must do a detailed statistical analysis of the way in which each of the ordinary phonetic signs is used, in the hope of finding some indication of the kind of sound which it represents. If we find that a particular sign, or group of signs, is very common as an initial, let us say, then we may find some clue in the behaviour of initial sounds in some of the other languages of the period. Provided the language is known, a code can often be broken entirely by statistics of this kind (by knowing, for example, that in any given passage of English the letter E will always turn out to be the most frequent). Thirdly, we have to analyse all those cases where the same word seems to occur in different places with a change in the spelling of its last one or two signs. Many of these must be grammatical-endings; and if we can show that a particular ending generally occurs in a particular context, we may be able to determine what its function is—if it is, say, a genitive, or a locative, or a nominative plural, or some tense of a verb. Finally, we have to analyse the context in which each separate word occurs, and try to determine from this whether it is a personal name, or a place name, or an ordinary vocabulary word. If we can make a guess at what one of these words means, the next step is to try to fit its signs to words of the same meaning which we know from neighbouring languages. It may then turn out that Minoan is sufficiently closely related to some language that we already know for us to be able to work out the meaning of other Minoan words which are not clear from the context.

We have always faced the risk, of course, that no language related to Minoan has survived at all, which would make the prospect of a full decipherment very remote. But even those who are most pessimistic have reckoned on getting some help from the several hundred words, mostly describing unfamiliar institutions or wild life, which the Greeks had borrowed from earlier inhabitants of the Aegean. A few of these might well occur on the tablets, whatever language they are written in; and we might also expect to find on them some of the towns in Crete and on the mainland whose names we know from classical times.

The fully developed Minoan system of writing has about eighty letters. As few alphabets have more than thirty, we think it must be a syllabary; instead of one letter *t*, it probably has five or more signs from the syllables *ta, te, ti, to, tu* and so on. A syllabary of this type, common in the Bronze Age, was still being used by the Cypriot Greeks in classical times. In this system a Greek word like κασίγνητος, "brother," had to be broken into syllables and spelt *ka-si-ki-ne-to-se*. There is good reason to think that the Cypriot syllabary is descended from the Minoan script; and if we could simply apply the Cypriot values, which we know, to the Minoan words, the problem would be solved. But in 1,000 years of development the forms of Cypriot signs have evidently changed very radically and we cannot agree which signs ought to correspond.

The usual way of putting the signs of a syllabary into some standard order, when we know how they are pronounced, is to arrange them on a syllabic grid. This is a chequerboard, divided, in our case, into about eighty squares, with the five vowels lettered across the top, and the sixteen or so consonants down the side. The sign for *to*, for instance, is then put in the square where *t* and *o* intersect. The most important job in trying to decipher a syllabary from scratch, is to try to arrange the signs provisionally on a grid of this sort, even before we can work out the actual pronunciation of the different vowels and consonants. If we find evidence that two signs share the same vowel, like *ta* and *ra*, we line them up in the same vertical column; and if we suspect that they share the same consonant, like *ta* and *ti*, we fit them on the same horizontal line. Once we can determine, later on, how only one or two signs were actually pronounced, we can immediately tell a good deal about many other signs which lie on the same columns of the grid.

A great help in finding out which signs belong together is the fact of inflection. If Latin had been written in a syllabary, then a declension like *dominus, domine, dominum, domini, domino* would show the third syllable spelt in four different ways, all containing the consonant *n: nu, ne, ni, no*. We could confidently put all four of the syllables on the same line of our grid, even if we did not know what the common consonant actually was. And we could also assume that the same final vowel which we find in the genitive *domini* will also occur again in a number of other genitives, spelt with quite different signs, as it does in *amici, pueri, belli, novi,* and so on. Minoan was not Latin, but its inflections have the same effect. By following indications of this kind, we can gradually fill in all the terms of this simultaneous equation, and it can only be a matter of time before we hit on the formula which solves it.

A lot of information about the grammar of the language can be deduced from the way in which recurrent words are used on the tablets, without necessarily making any assumptions as to how they were pronounced. And one might think it would be quite easy to go on from there to identify the language itself which these forms represent. But opinions have up to now been very divided. Hrozny, Bossert and Sundwall think that Minoan was closely related to one of the Hittite dialects of Asia Minor. For Evans and Myres, the Knossos tablets are in some primitive Anatolian language, probably too unfamiliar to be decipherable. Sittig, of Tübingen University, recently claimed to have deciphered the Minoan tablets, and to have proved that they are in a "Pelasgian" language related to Etruscan. For a long time I, too, thought that Etruscan might afford the clue we were looking for. But during the last few weeks, I have come to the conclusion that the Knossos and Pylos tablets must, after all, be written in Greek—a difficult and archaic Greek, seeing that it is 500 years older than Homer and written in a rather abbreviated form, but Greek nevertheless.

Once I made this assumption, most of the peculiarities of the language and spelling which had puzzled me seemed to find a logical explanation; and although many of the tablets remain as incomprehensible as before, many others are suddenly beginning to make sense. As we expected, they seem to contain nothing of any literary value, but merely record the prosaic and often trivial details of the palace administration. We have lists of men and women, for instance, where each name has the person's trade next to it, and we rediscover familiar Greek words like Ποιμήν "shepherd," Κεραμεύς "potter," Χαλκεύς "bronzesmith," ΧρυσοϜοργός "goldsmith." Some of the persons have longer descriptions like "So-and-so, a goatherd watching over the quadrupeds belonging to So-and-so"; or "Three waitresses, whose mother was a slave and whose father was a smith"; or "Stonemasons for building operations." Other tablets are lists of commodities, such as wheels: "So many of elm; so many of metal; so many with metal bindings; so

many of willow." Most of the phrases are quite short. The longest
sentence I can find has eleven words and occurs on a tablet from
Pylos which seems to be an assessment for tithes, somewhat as
follows: "The priestess holds the following acres of productive
land on a lease from the property-owners, and undertakes to
maintain them in the future."

The Pylos tablets look like Greek throughout, which is only
what one would expect from their date and location. But
even if it turns out that only the main phrasing of the Knossos
tablets is in Greek, and that this is interspersed with names and
words of some indigenous language, we shall still be forced to
revise our conception of the history of this period. The last palace
of Knossos has all the appearance of being part of the native
island culture; but, if my suggestion is right, the Greeks must in
fact have arrived in Crete at its building and not merely been its
destroyers; and it must have been they who devised the new
Linear Script B for their own purposes. If this is so, there is a
case for calling the tablets, which Myres and Bennett have published, Mycenaean, and not Minoan in a strict sense at all.

I have suggested that there is now a better chance of reading
these earliest European inscriptions than ever before, but there
is evidently a great deal more work to do before we are all
agreed on the solution to the problem.

INDEX

313

ABOUT THE AUTHOR

Leo Deuel, who has been a member of the History Department of New York's City College since 1958, holds a Master's Degree from Columbia University and a Ph.D. from Zurich University in Switzerland. From 1948 to 1954 he served on the editorial staff of the Columbia University Press and of the *Encyclopedia Americana*. In 1955 he was a technical assistant for the World Health Organization in Geneva.

Dr. Deuel's first writings appeared in the Swiss publications *Neue Zürcher Zeitung* and *Weltwoche*. At the request of a Swiss publisher he wrote the introductions to German language editions of Whitehead's *Science and the Modern World* and John Dewey's *How We Think*. His anthology, *Teacher's Treasure Chest*, was published in 1956.

THIS BOOK WAS SET IN

CALEDONIA AND ALBERTUS TYPES BY

HARRY SWEETMAN TYPESETTING CORPORATION.

IT WAS PRINTED AND BOUND BY

THE HADDON CRAFTSMEN.

DESIGN IS BY LARRY KAMP

BLACK SEA

Istanbul

SEA OF MARMARA

GREECE

Athens

Mycenae
PELOPONNESUS

Pylos

SEA

ASIA MINOR

Ephesus

Boghazköy

HALYS R.

Knossos

RHODES

CRETE

CYPRUS

SYRIA

Ras Shamra

MEDITERRANEAN

SEA

Cyrene

Tyre

PHOENICIA

Damascus

ISRAEL

JORDAN R.

JORDAN

PALESTINE

Jerusalem

Khirbet Qumran

JUDAH

DEAD SEA

Alexandria

NILE DELTA

NEGEV

WADI ARABA

Memphis
Saqqara

Cairo

Medum

FAYUM

SINAI

Ezion-Geber

GULF OF AQABA

Oxyrhynchus

EGYPT

GULF OF SUEZ

N

W E

S

Tell el-Amarna

NILE R.

RED SEA

Scale of miles

0   50   100   200

map by palacios

Deir el-Bahri
VALLEY OF THE KINGS Thebes